Loan Modification FOR DUMMIES®

by Ralph R. Roberts, Lois Maljak, and Paul Doroh, with Joe Kraynak

WILEY

Wiley Publishing, Inc.

WILEY

About the Authors

Ralph R. Roberts, GRI, CRS, is an award-winning REALTOR® and author and a tireless defender of the American dream of home-ownership. Ralph experienced the loss of real estate to foreclosure and added a foreclosure division to his nationally recognized real estate business. Since then, Ralph has led thousands of families through the foreclosure maze, informing them of their options, including loan modification, and steering them clear of the most common pitfalls while empowering them with the information required to save their homes and get on with their lives.

Ralph is a nationally recognized expert in the fields of loan modification, foreclosure self-defense, and real estate and mortgage fraud prevention. He's also an award-winning author who has penned several successful real estate books, including *Foreclosure Self-Defense For Dummies* (Wiley) and *Protect Yourself from Real Estate and Mortgage Fraud: Preserving the American Dream of Homeownership* (Kaplan). For the latest news, information, and insight on foreclosure alternatives, including loan modification, visit www.KeepMyHouse.com.

Lois "Lane" Maljak is Ralph's second in command and a foreclosure expert in her own right. Lois formerly ran Ralph's foreclosure department, HomeSavers, during which time she met with hundreds of distressed homeowners every year, assisting them in foreclosure and pre-foreclosure, counseling them on their available options, and helping them leave a difficult situation in their past. Lois has a combination of compassion and expertise that makes her uniquely qualified to counsel distressed homeowners. She's also coauthor of *Foreclosure Self-Defense For Dummies* (Wiley).

Paul Doroh is an attorney and residential real estate professional who would like to see all homeowners empowered with the information and guidance they need to keep their homes, understand and lower their mortgage payments, make educated and sound financial decisions, and get on with their lives. Paul also coauthored *Foreclosure Self-Defense For Dummies* (Wiley) and periodically contributes to numerous real estate-related publications.

Joe Kraynak is a freelance author who has written and coauthored numerous books including *Foreclosure Self-Defense For Dummies, Flipping Houses For Dummies, Financing Real Estate Investments For Dummies,* and *Foreclosure Myths* (Wiley); *Take the Mic* and *Stage a Poetry Slam* (Sourcebooks); and *Master Visually: Optimizing PC Performance* (Wiley). For more about Joe, visit his blog at JoeKraynak.com.

Dedication

To the homeowners on Main Street and those who assist them in keeping the American dream of homeownership alive and thriving.

Authors' Acknowledgements

Thanks to acquisitions editor Lindsay Lefevere, who chose us to author this book and guided us through the tough part of getting started; and to our agent, Neil Salkind (www.studiob.com/salkindagency), who ironed out all the preliminary details to make this book possible.

A special thanks to Barbara Jacobs, owner and manager of B&S Consulting Group LLC in Southfield, Michigan, who shared her extensive knowledge and experience through several of the case studies presented in this book. The knowledge and skills she acquired while working as a senior credit analyst, in loss mitigation, and in special investigations for companies like Fannie Mae, Lehman Bros., and Aurora Loan Services are now put to work educating and helping homeowners (with a special focus on seniors) discover their modification options and interpret their mortgage loans.

Sarah Faulkner, our project editor, deserves a loud cheer for acting as a very patient collaborator and gifted editor — shuffling chapters back and forth, shepherding the text and graphics through production, making sure any technical issues were properly resolved, and serving as the unofficial quality control manager. Elizabeth Rea, our copy editor, earns an editor of the year award for ferreting out our typos, misspellings, grammatical errors, and other language faux pas, in addition to assisting Sarah as reader advocate — asking the questions we should have asked ourselves. We also tip our hats to the Composition crew for doing such an outstanding job of transforming a loose collection of text and illustrations into such an attractive bound book.

We owe special thanks to our technical editor, Craig D. Doyle, Esq., for flagging technical errors in the manuscript, helping guide its content, and offering his own insight and advice from the world of foreclosure self-defense and loan modification.

Publisher's Acknowledgments

We're proud of this book; please send us your comments through our Dummies online registration form located at http://dummies.custhelp.com. For other comments, please contact our Customer Care Department within the U.S. at 877-762-2974, outside the U.S. at 317-572-3993, or fax 317-572-4002.

Some of the people who helped bring this book to market include the following:

Acquisitions, Editorial, and Media Development

Project Editor: Sarah Faulkner

Senior Acquisitions Editor: Lindsay Sandman Lefevere

Senior Copy Editor: Elizabeth Rea

Assistant Editor: Erin Calligan Mooney

Editorial Program Coordinator: Joe Niesen

Technical Editor: Craig D. Doyle, Esq.

Editorial Manager: Christine Meloy Beck

Editorial Assistants: Jennette ElNaggar, David Lutton

Cover Photos: iStock

Cartoons: Rich Tennant (www.the5thwave.com)

Composition Services

Project Coordinator: Sheree Montgomery

Layout and Graphics: Reuben W. Davis, Melissa K. Jester, Christin Swinford

Proofreaders: ConText Editorial Services, Inc., Caitie Copple

Indexer: Valerie Haynes Perry

Publishing and Editorial for Consumer Dummies

Diane Graves Steele, Vice President and Publisher, Consumer Dummies

Kristin Ferguson-Wagstaffe, Product Development Director, Consumer Dummies

Ensley Eikenburg, Associate Publisher, Travel

Kelly Regan, Editorial Director, Travel

Publishing for Technology Dummies

Andy Cummings, Vice President and Publisher, Dummies Technology/General User

Composition Services

Debbie Stailey, Director of Composition Services

Contents at a Glance

Table of Contents

Introduction

The *Titanic* was unsinkable. That's what the experts thought, at least. Likewise, most experts believed that property values in the United States would continue to rise for as far as their foresight could see. Unfortunately, the short-sighted experts were tragically wrong. The housing bubble burst, as all bubbles eventually do, leaving many homeowners stranded at sea and drowning in debt.

If you're like most homeowners in default or facing foreclosure, you probably never imagined yourself in such a dire situation. Maybe your loan officer sold you a time-bomb loan, like a particularly high-risk adjustable-rate mortgage (ARM), and convinced you that if the interest rate rose too high, you could always refinance and get a lower rate. Maybe you purchased your house thinking your job was secure . . . and then the economy tanked. Perhaps you're one of the many people without medical insurance who got sick and was quickly buried under a mountain of medical bills.

Whatever hardship you've experienced, your American dream of homeownership turned into a nightmare. You now own a home you can't afford. You're way behind in your payments with little hope of catching up, or your monthly income is insufficient to cover the payments, or both. You probably can't qualify for refinancing. Due to falling property values or negative amortization (more about that later), you may even owe more on your home than you can sell it for. You want to do the right thing without filing for bankruptcy or simply jumping ship, but you really can't afford your current mortgage. Now what?

Welcome to *Loan Modification For Dummies* — a guide that can help you transform your leaky ship into your own personal lifeboat.

About This Book

Foreclosure is a lose-lose-lose-lose option. It hurts everyone. Homeowners lose their homes. Lenders lose performing assets and the costs of foreclosure ($50,000 to $80,000 by some estimates). Neighbors see their property values drop up to nine percent per foreclosure. Neighborhoods become less stable and more vulnerable to crime. The economy suffers. And foreclosure wipes out the property tax base, providing communities with less money for schools, police protection, fire departments, and other vital services.

On the other hand, an affordable loan modification is a win-win-win-win alternative. It keeps homeowners in their homes and makes their mortgage payments more affordable. Lenders avoid the full expense of foreclosure and are able to transform a non-performing asset into a performing asset. Neighborhoods remain stable. Property values stabilize. Homeowners have more money to pay bills and stimulate the economy, and tax revenues can begin to recover.

This book is designed to help you transform lose-lose-lose-lose situations into win-win-win-win situations through loan modification. Here, you discover field-proven strategies and techniques for negotiating an affordable loan modification with your lender to keep your home, lower your monthly mortgage payment, and catch up on any past due payments. In addition, you discover plenty of advice for developing long-term solutions to keep you on the right track.

Conventions Used in This Book

We use several conventions in this book to call your attention to certain items. For example:

- ✔ *Italics* highlight new, somewhat technical terms, such as *debt-to-income (DTI) ratio,* that we follow with straightforward, easy-to-understand explanations, of course.

- ✔ **Boldface** text indicates key words in bulleted and numbered lists.

- ✔ Monofont highlights Web and e-mail addresses. Note that some Web addresses may break across two lines of text. In such cases, no hyphens were inserted to indicate a break. So if you type exactly what you see — pretending that the line break doesn't exist — you can get to your Web destination.

- ✔ Throughout the book, we refer to third-party professionals whom you may choose to hire to represent you as *loan modification experts* rather than *professionals* or *specialists* because, during the writing of this book, nobody could really be certified or licensed in this field.

- ✔ You'll almost always be going through your *servicer* (the company that collects and processes your monthly mortgage payment) to get a loan modification, but for the sake of consistency and simplicity, we use the term *lender* whether referring to the servicer or the lender or investor from whom you borrowed the money.

In addition, even though a team of four authors wrote this book — Ralph, Lois, Paul, and Joe — the "we" are usually Ralph, Lois, and Paul talking. They're the foreclosure self-defense and loan modification experts. Joe's the wordsmith — the guy responsible for keeping you engaged and entertained and working with the editors to make sure *we* explain everything as clearly and thoroughly as possible.

What You're Not to Read

You can safely skip anything you see in a gray shaded box. We stuck this material in a box (actually called a *sidebar*) for the same reason that most people stick stuff in boxes — to get it out of the way so no one trips over it. However, you may find the case studies and brief asides in the sidebars engaging, entertaining, and perhaps even mildly informative.

Foolish Assumptions

When explaining the loan modification process, we assumed nothing. We're committed to providing detailed advice so that you can navigate the process with confidence. However, we did make a few foolish assumptions — the same assumptions that your lender is going to make when reviewing your loan modification application.

- ✔ You have or soon will have sufficient income to cover a reasonable, though lower, monthly payment. (If you have no job and no prospects of landing a job in the near future, loan modification is not an option.)

- ✔ You're committed to doing what's necessary to keep your home. (If you don't care about losing the house, a different option may be more suitable. We offer several alternatives in Chapter 3.)

How This Book Is Organized

Although we encourage you to read this book from cover to cover to maximize the return on your investment, *Loan Modification For Dummies* presents the information in easily digestible chunks, so you can skip to the chapter or section that grabs your attention or meets your current needs, master it, and then skip to another section or simply set the book aside for later reference.

To help you navigate, we took the 17 chapters and two appendixes that make up the book and divvied them up into six parts. This section provides a quick overview of what we cover in each part.

Part 1: Getting Up to Speed on Loan Modification

When facing the real possibility of losing your home, shifting into panic mode is far too easy and destructive. In a state of panic, you're vulnerable to making the wrong decisions, saying the wrong things, or falling victim to con artists who prey on people who aren't thinking clearly.

In this part, we encourage you to slow down and take a deep breath as you venture into the territory of loan modifications. We introduce you to the loan modification concept, show you how to take stock of your situation (it may not be as bad as you think it is), reveal several options for avoiding foreclosure (after all, loan modification is just one of the options out there), and provide you with the information you need to decide whether you want to work with a loan modification specialist or go it alone.

Part 11: Kick-Starting the Process: Applying for a Loan Modification

Obtaining a loan modification is like getting a job — you have to apply for it first, and if your application is lousy, you don't even get an interview. In this part, we show you how to prepare an impeccable loan modification application that meets or, even better, exceeds your lender's expectations and then submit it so it lands on the right person's desk.

We show you how to contact your lender; gather the facts, figures, and documentation needed to prepare your application; figure out the types of modifications you want to request from your lender; prepare and submit your application; and follow up to ensure that your application doesn't get lost in the shuffle.

Part 111: Hammering Out the Details with Your Lender

After most lenders receive and approve a request for a loan modification, they pitch an offer. Many homeowners see this as the end of a long process, but it's actually just the beginning of the end. You can now negotiate with the lender for a more attractive deal.

In this part, we show you how to explore different loan modification adjustments with your lender, how to evaluate your lender's initial offer and spot common red flags, and how to negotiate a better, more affordable loan modification.

Part IV: Dealing with an Uncooperative Lender

Lenders are beginning to "get it." They're beginning to grasp the magnitude of the problem they helped create and the magnitude of their potential losses if they choose not to modify troubled mortgages. However, every crisis has a few holdouts reluctant to make concessions.

If you lock horns with your lender, you may be able to apply some legal pressure to prod your lender into action. In this part, we reveal lending laws designed to protect consumers, show you how to audit your loan to uncover possible violations, and provide tips on how to use proof of violations to convince your lender to modify your mortgage loan.

Part V: The Part of Tens

Every *For Dummies* title comes with a Part of Tens, which contains chapters of ten strategies, tips, tricks, or other important items. In *Loan Modification For Dummies,* the Part of Tens offers ten tips for long-term success to help you avoid falling into the foreclosure trap again and ten common myths about loan modification that we bust wide open.

Part VI: Appendixes

As an added bonus, at no additional cost, we include two appendixes which, by their very nature, appear at the end of this book.

> ✔ **Appendix A:** A list of resources including Web site and contact information for the major lenders, a list of federal agencies and consumer advocacy groups you can contact for assistance, and contact information for the attorney general in each of the 50 states, the District of Columbia, and various U.S. territories. (We've done our best to provide accurate and timely information, but if you find that a contact phone number or Web site address isn't correct at the time you're reading this book, use your favorite Internet search tool to search for key phrases included in our descriptions.)

> ✔ **Appendix B:** A glossary of typically unfamiliar terminology and acronyms you're likely to hear bandied about, such as *loan-to-value (LTV) ratio* and *deficiency judgment.*

Icons Used in This Book

Throughout this book, you'll spot icons in the margins that call your attention to different types of information. Here are the icons you'll see and a brief description of each:

We want you to remember everything you read in this book, but if you can't quite do that, then remember the important points flagged with this icon.

Tips provide insider insight from behind the scenes. When you're looking for a better, faster, and/or cheaper way to do something, check out these tips.

This icon appears when you need to be extra vigilant or seek professional help before moving forward.

You're not alone. Plenty of homeowners have faced foreclosure and avoided it with a loan modification. To prove it to you, we've included several case studies that are composites created from real-world experiences.

Where to Go from Here

Loan Modification For Dummies is sort of like an information kiosk. You can start with the chapters in Part I to master the basics and then skip to Part II to prepare and submit your loan modification application, or you can skip around to any chapters that interest you most.

To get a handle on your situation and determine just how bad it is, check out Chapter 2. To get up to speed on your foreclosure options, including loan modification, skip to Chapter 3. You can also skip the preliminaries by jumping straight to Chapter 5 and getting your loan modification application underway. If some armchair expert on loan modification fed you some misinformation that's making you question some aspect of it, skip to Chapter 17, where we take on the most common myths.

If you're looking for information on a very specific topic, flip to the back of the book where you'll find a comprehensive index.

Part I
Getting Up to Speed on Loan Modification

"According to the information you put on your application, we were able to modify your mortgage into this. See? It's a crane."

In this part . . .

*W*hen you're in the midst of a personal financial
crisis, you don't have a whole lot of time to be
studying up on your options or trying to figure out what
this loan modification business is all about. You have a
day job to think about, or you're in hot pursuit of finding
one. You have bills to pay, errands to run, and perhaps a
family to take care of.

Fortunately, this part brings you up to speed in a hurry.
Here, you do a financial self-assessment to size up your
current financial situation, check out various foreclosure
alternatives to make sure loan modification is best for you,
and weigh the pros and cons of trying to do this yourself
or hiring an expert to represent you.

Chapter 1

Keeping Your Home by Modifying Your Loan

*1*f you're in the market for a quick primer on loan modification, you've come to the right place. This chapter introduces the concept of loan modification, explains the various ways a lender can modify a mortgage loan, assists in determining whether you're likely to qualify, and reveals what's involved, so you know what to expect.

Loan modification isn't the right foreclosure avoidance maneuver for everyone, so we list other common alternatives in this chapter and cover them in greater detail in Chapter 3. We encourage you to explore all your options before pursuing a loan modification.

Grasping the Loan Modification Concept

By definition, a *loan modification* is any change to the original agreement between borrower and lender. Assuming you qualify, a loan modification enables you to keep your home, lower your monthly mortgage payment, and catch up on any late or missed payments. In addition, your lender avoids the high cost of foreclosure, transforms a nonperforming asset into a performing asset, and removes a bad loan from its books.

Affordability is the key term in loan modification. If the loan modification results in an affordable monthly payment for the homeowner and is less costly for the lender than a foreclosure, it's a win-win solution for both parties. In the following sections, we discuss the various ways a lender can modify a loan to affordability. For additional details, check out Chapter 7.

Reducing and fixing the interest rate

During the run-up to the mortgage meltdown, many homeowners were suckered into *adjustable-rate mortgages* (ARMs) with low teaser rates. When interest rates rose, so did the house payments; in some cases, they jumped 50 percent or more. As rates were rising, property values were dropping, so many of these homeowners couldn't qualify for refinancing to get them out of trouble.

As a result, lenders are often willing to lower the interest rate, either temporarily or permanently. Loan modification rate adjustments are likely to come in one or more of the following forms:

- Reduced interest rate, sometimes below the going rate

- Converting an adjustable-rate mortgage into a fixed-rate loan

- Interest-only period to give borrowers time to recover their financial footing

- Step-rate adjustments, with a low rate for several months or years that increases gradually to avoid rate-adjustment shock

An interest rate reduction can result in considerable monthly savings. For example, dropping the rate from 7 to 5 percent on a $200,000 30-year amortized mortgage reduces the monthly payment from $1,330.60 to $1,073.64, a monthly savings of $256.96, or $92,505.60 over the life of the loan.

During the writing of this book, ARMs were going the way of the dinosaur as lenders tried to stabilize the market and avoid a future mortgage meltdown. This shift away from ARMs may prevent future problems, but if you're stuck in an ARM now, you need to get out of it soon, and loan modification may help you do just that.

Extending the term

You probably have a 30-year mortgage with at least a few years or perhaps a decade or two of payments to look forward to. Although most homeowners want to pay off their mortgages as quickly as possible, stretching out the *term* (the number of years you have to pay back the loan) can provide some relief for your monthly budget. Your lender may be willing to extend the term from whatever you have remaining on your mortgage to 30 or even 40 years.

Just because you have a 40-year mortgage doesn't necessarily mean you'll be making payments for 40 years. You can make additional payments to pay down the principal earlier. Extending the term gives you the flexibility to make larger payments voluntarily while obligating you to smaller monthly payments. This strategy can allow you to deal with fluctuations in your monthly income and expenses.

If your mortgage or loan modification agreement includes an early payment penalty clause, usually referred to as a *prepayment penalty,* make sure the penalty is phased out over a relatively short period — three years max. You don't want to get penalized for acting responsibly and trying to save some money.

Reducing the principal balance

If your lender can't achieve affordability by adjusting your loan's interest rate and term, it may agree to reduce the *unpaid principal balance* (the amount you owe on the loan) in one of these ways:

- **By forgiving a portion of the debt:** Under President Obama's Making Home Affordable (MHA) plan, this has become a more viable option for lenders who can recover a portion of their losses from the U.S. Treasury.

- **By deferring payment of a portion of the debt through principal forbearance:** For example, if you owe $150,000 on a home that's currently worth only $125,000, the lender may recalculate your payments using the $125,000 amount and let you pay the remaining $25,000 when you sell or refinance years later, hopefully after real estate values have recovered.

Dealing with delinquencies

When you miss a few house payments, your lender/servicer really starts to ladle it on with additional penalties and late-payment fees. Your lender has several options (all of which are usually negotiable) for collecting on missed payments and any associated costs:

- **Capitalizing delinquencies and other costs:** *Capitalization* consists of rolling any penalties and fees into the balance so that you pay them off over the life of the loan. Unfortunately, you also end up paying interest on those penalties and fees.

✔ **Waiving delinquencies and fees:** Your lender can choose to forgive the penalties and fees and then either capitalize the delinquent payments or negotiate a payment plan.

✔ **Negotiating payment plans:** Your lender may agree to an installment plan that enables you to pay the delinquencies, penalties, and fees over several months rather than as a lump sum. You may end up paying extra in interest, but you get to keep your house and buy some time.

If your lender/servicer is participating in the government's Making Home Affordable program, it's required to waive any penalties and fees. If your lender isn't a participant, push hard to have it waive any penalties and fees. Your lender shouldn't earn even more money from your misfortune.

Re-amortizing the loan

Amortization is a way of calculating monthly loan payments that keeps the payment the same every month and accounts for the fact that each payment reduces the principal. The end result is that the borrower pays way more interest with early payments and way less with later payments.

An average, everyday loan modification

Sherry Smith had been working two jobs to make ends meet, but when retail sales dried up, so did her part-time job at one of the nation's largest retail outlets. She could no longer afford the mortgage payment she'd been paying since June 2004 — $752.03 on a $96,467 30-year mortgage at 8.65 percent. Facing almost certain default, Sherry chose to do the right thing: She called her lender, described her situation, and requested a loan modification. The lender agreed and several weeks later offered to reduce her interest rate to 6.40 percent, lowering Sherry's monthly payment to less than $600.

For most homeowners, this would have been the end of the story. Saving more than $150 per month would have been enough, but again, Sherry did the smart thing: She requested a better offer because the payment still wasn't affordable for her. The lender took a second look at the numbers, dropped the interest rate to 5.60 percent, and extended the term, lowering Sherry's monthly payment to $447.40. Now *that* was affordable!

Sherry is one of many homeowners who have negotiated affordable loan modifications with their lenders. With a little cooperation from your lender and perhaps some haggling at the negotiating table, you can keep your home, save hundreds of dollars per month, and save thousands over the life of your loan.

When you receive a loan modification, the lender re-amortizes (recalculates) your monthly payment based on the other modifications — the interest rate reduction, term extension, any principal reduction, and the capitalization of missed payments and any penalties or fees.

One way a lender can modify your mortgage is to re-amortize the loan over a longer period of time but retain the maturity date. If you go with this option, watch out for the last payment you make! For example, if you took out a 30-year mortgage in the year 2000 and paid 10 years on it, the lender could re-amortize over 30 years and still require you to repay the loan in 2030. In this example, you'd have lower monthly payments, but you'd also have a significant lump sum (balloon) payment due in 2030.

Considering Other Foreclosure Alternatives

Facing foreclosure, homeowners often assume they have only two options — pay up or move out. The fact is they usually have several options, including one or all of the following:

- ✔ **Forbearance:** Delays any collection activities, including a foreclosure sale, so homeowners have time to explore their options or obtain gainful employment.

- ✔ **Bankruptcy:** Is often an ideal solution for homeowners drowning in unsecured debt, such as credit card debt.

- ✔ **Loan modification:** Helps to make the monthly payment more affordable and allows homeowners to catch up on missed payments.

- ✔ **Reinstatement:** Allows homeowners to bring their payments current, as if nothing happened. This option is only for homeowners who have recovered from a temporary setback.

- ✔ **Refinancing:** Puts homeowners in a lower-interest, fixed-rate loan.

- ✔ **Short refinancing:** Puts homeowners in a lower-interest, fixed-rate loan for an amount less than is currently owed on the home.

- ✔ **Government loan programs:** Includes HomeSaver Advance (HSA) for catching up on late or missed payments. (For more about the HomeSaver Advance program, check out Chapter 10.)

- ✔ **Selling the home:** Allows homeowners to get out from under an unaffordable home and cash out any equity in it.

- ✔ **Short sale:** Involves selling a home for less than the unpaid balance without owing the lender anything after the sale.

- ✔ **Selling to an investor:** May be appropriate when time to explore other options is close to running out and the investor has the resources to save the home (and the integrity to help). This option often requires a substantial amount of equity that the homeowners are unable to tap into because of credit or employment issues.

- ✔ **Redemption:** Involves buying back the home after the foreclosure sale. This option isn't available in all states.

- ✔ **Deed in lieu of foreclosure:** Gives the property to the bank, and the homeowners walk away without owing anything on it.

We provide this grocery list of options only to make you aware of some viable foreclosure alternatives. For additional details about each option, turn to Chapter 3.

Finally, you can consider the following two options. But be aware that they aren't bona fide foreclosure alternatives because you still end up losing your home in foreclosure.

- ✔ **Abandoning the home:** This is only an option after you've exhausted all other options and can't deal with the lender.

- ✔ **Doing nothing:** This is one of the worst options, second only to falling victim to a foreclosure rescue scam.

If you're considering either of these last two options, beware of the possibility of a deficiency judgment. In states that allow deficiency judgments, your lender may try to force you to pay the difference between what you owed the lender and what the lender recouped through the sale of your home.

Do You Qualify?

The only sure-fire way to determine whether you qualify for a loan modification is to apply for one and see what happens, and that's really not all that sure-fire either. You could meet all the eligibility requirements and have your request denied due to a technicality or a mistake made by you or your lender.

If your house payment is unaffordable, apply for a loan modification, even if something you heard or read leads you to believe that you're ineligible. Keeping this in mind, the following list can help you determine whether you're *likely* to qualify; if these statements apply to your situation, your chances look pretty good:

✔ The house is your primary residence, not a second home or vacation property.

✔ You're committed to doing what's necessary to keep your house.

✔ You have sufficient income to afford a reasonable house payment.

✔ You experienced a qualifying financial hardship that has made your current house payment unaffordable. (Chapter 8 describes qualifying hardships.)

Eligibility requirements may vary among lenders and can change over time. Contact your lender (see Chapter 5) or consult a loan modification expert (see Chapter 4) to determine whether you're likely to qualify for a loan modification or other workout solution.

Assessing Your Needs

We recommend pursuing several foreclosure alternatives at the same time. List your property for sale, consult a bankruptcy attorney, research the loan modification option, talk to a mortgage broker about refinancing, and so on. Eventually, however, you need to make a decision about what you really want and what's best for you and any significant others living in the home with you.

At some point in the process, earlier rather than later, gather the family's decision makers, discuss your exit strategies, and determine which options are viable for you. Chapter 2 shows you how to crunch the numbers and perform a realistic assessment of your situation, Chapter 3 describes the available foreclosure alternatives to consider, and Chapter 7 helps you decide what to ask for.

Opting to Work with a Pro or Go It Alone

Loan modification is a team sport. You have to work with your lender or through a third-party representative to get 'er done. So which option is best? Read on to find out why we recommend hiring a pro and what you should do if you opt to do it yourself.

Hiring a pro

We recommend hiring an expert to represent you for several reasons, including the following:

✔ Your lender usually has an attorney representing its interests, so you should have your own representative defending your interests.

✔ You may have only one shot at submitting your application correctly. Having an experienced expert prepare your application is like having a headhunter craft your resume.

✔ A loan modification expert knows the system and how to work it for your benefit.

✔ An expert can quickly prescreen you, so if you probably aren't eligible for a loan modification, you won't end up wasting time, energy, and money trying to get one.

✔ An expert can take all the hassles off your plate, freeing up your time and energy to get a better handle on your finances.

✔ An expert is free from the emotional baggage that can undermine negotiations. Being emotionally involved, you're more likely to engage in arguments and make poor decisions.

✔ A seasoned pro knows immediately whether the offer a lender pitches is fair and square.

✔ You'll probably more than recoup the cost of hiring an expert from the amount of money he or she saves you by getting a better deal than you could on your own.

Lenders often try to dissuade distressed borrowers from hiring their own representation. After all, lenders often claim, "We'll modify your mortgage for free." Sure, they'll modify it, but are they going to modify it to true affordability? Chapter 4 has details on finding, selecting, and teaming up with a loan modification expert.

Dealing directly with your lender

Although we strongly encourage distressed homeowners to seek expert representation, we're aware that many homeowners are do-it-yourselfers. They fix their own plumbing, install their own light fixtures, hang their own wallpaper . . . nobody's going to convince *them* to pay an expert for doing what they can do on their own!

If you're an avid do-it-yourselfer, we applaud you. With the right training (provided in this book), you can get up to speed on the process, avoid common pitfalls, and negotiate an affordable loan modification. Just be sure to read Chapter 5 prior to contacting your lender and Chapters 11 and 12 to avoid the most common traps.

Getting Your Ducks in a Row

Successful preparation can optimize the outcome of your loan modification, so spend some time upfront getting organized, setting realistic expectations, and keeping track of *everything*. In the following sections, we reveal what you should be doing to prepare for and stay on top of the process.

Gathering essential documents

A loan modification application may be a short form that appears deceptively easy to complete. The complicated part is gathering all the documents and information you need to fill in the blanks and to submit as supporting documentation. In Chapter 6, we provide a list of commonly required documentation, but you can get a jump on the process by tracking down or preparing the following items:

✔ Existing mortgage document and note

✔ Most recent mortgage statement

✔ Monthly budget showing income and expenses

✔ Proof of income, including federal income tax returns, W-2s, and recent paycheck stubs

✔ Home valuation showing your property's current market value

If you live in a jurisdiction that allows real estate agents to provide home valuations, you may be able to obtain this document for free or a minimal fee. Don't pay for an appraisal unless your lender requires it. If your lender requires an appraisal, it will usually order the appraisal and bill you.

✔ Proof of financial hardship (if available), such as divorce papers, hospital bills, or notice of a rate adjustment on an adjustable-rate mortgage

If you hire professional representation, gather authorization letters giving your lenders permission to share information with your representative (Chapter 6 provides a sample letter).

Plotting the timeline

Few things are more nerve-wracking than having to wait while someone else determines your destiny, and loan modification has plenty of waiting associated with it. You may submit your application and hear nothing for several weeks. To keep the stress of the waiting game at a dull roar, obtain some key dates and other information by asking the following questions:

✔ If you're hiring someone to represent you, how long is it likely to take to prepare your application?

✔ Does your application stop the foreclosure process? If not, will you be able to resolve this before the foreclosure sale?

✔ After submitting your application, when can you expect to hear something? If you don't hear something, whom should you call?

✔ When can you expect to have this all wrapped up? (A typical loan modification takes 30 to 90 days to complete.)

 Your lender probably has a timeline for every stage in the process. It should have no problem sharing this information with you. Some lenders receive so many modification requests that it takes them three to seven days just to retrieve information faxed to them.

Logging all correspondence

Only really neurotic people keep detailed records of correspondence and phone conversations, but when you're fighting to keep your home, being neurotic isn't necessarily a bad thing. In fact, it can pay dividends later, particularly if a dispute arises between you and your lender about something that was said or not said, done or not done.

In Chapter 9, we provide a contact log sheet and details on how to keep accurate records. If you contact the lender before reading Chapter 9, make sure you do the following:

✔ Keep copies of all written correspondence and include the date and time you sent or received it.

✔ Jot down the name, employee ID number (if available), phone number, and extension of anyone you speak to; an overview of what the conversation was about; anything that was promised or resolved; and the date and time of the conversation.

Following the Process from Point A to Point B

Earlier in this chapter, in the section "Plotting the timeline," we encourage you to ask your lender several questions about the timing of the process so you know what to expect. Having a bird's-eye view of the loan modification process can also put everything into perspective, enable you to develop realistic expectations, and provide a context for understanding each stage of the experience.

The following sections provide tips on optimizing the outcome and negotiating the most affordable deal your lender is willing to offer.

Preparing and submitting your application

The kick-off to loan modification is the application process. In most cases, you can obtain the application form and instructions by doing one of the following:

- ✔ Visit the lender's Web site, and then complete and submit the application online, assuming your lender offers a secure online form (a few do).
- ✔ Download printable forms from the lender's Web site and mail them to the lender.
- ✔ Call and ask your lender or servicer to send you a loan modification application packet.

The *servicer* is the company that collects and processes your mortgage payments. It can be (but rarely is) the lender or investor that owns your mortgage. You'll probably be dealing with your servicer, even if we tell you to talk to your lender.

Whether you apply online or via snail mail, your lender probably requires that you submit supporting documentation: copies of your federal income tax return and W-2s to verify employment and income; a signed Form 4506, which allows your lender to pull your tax returns; recent bank statements; and perhaps even proof of financial hardship. Follow your lender's instructions to submit everything required. See Chapter 8 for details.

Playing the waiting game

Lenders typically require two to three weeks to process a loan modification application, which means you get to wait and wring your hands for two weeks. To add to your aggravation, your lender will probably continue its collection activities, so don't expect the collection letters and phone calls to stop while you wait.

Remain active during this processing period. Explore other options described in Chapter 3, including bankruptcy, refinancing, and listing your home for sale. You should have a plan B, C, and D to fall back on if your loan modification falls through. In addition, keep an eye on the timeline and check in with your lender if you don't hear something when you were supposed to.

Making your case during the homeowner interview

At some point in the process, you're likely to be required to speak with someone about your situation — your representative (prior to applying) or your lender (after you apply). The person conducting the interview tries to determine whether

- ✔ You're credible and are pursuing a loan modification because you really *need* one, not just because you *want* one.
- ✔ You're committed to doing what's necessary to keep your home.
- ✔ You experienced an eligible financial hardship.
- ✔ You have or will have the resources required to deliver on your end of the new agreement.

In Chapter 10, we show you how to prepare for a homeowner interview and communicate effectively with your lender.

Be careful when speaking directly to your lender. Anything you say can and will be used against you. This is another reason we recommend working through your own representative, who can filter what you say.

Structuring a workout plan

A loan modification is actually an addendum to your original mortgage, laying out only what has changed from the original agreement, so it's typically shorter. In most cases, the loan modification is structured to make one or more of the following changes to the mortgage:

- ✔ Reduce the interest rate
- ✔ Convert an ARM into a fixed-interest rate mortgage
- ✔ Extend the term
- ✔ Reduce the unpaid principal balance
- ✔ Institute a lower, more affordable monthly payment
- ✔ State the plan for catching up on any late or missed payments

You may or may not have input on how the lender chooses to modify your mortgage to arrive at the lower monthly payment, but you should have input during the negotiating phase. The Making Home Affordable (MHA) plan recommends that lenders take the following waterfall approach to arrive at an affordable payment:

1. Reduce the interest rate.

2. Extend the term if an interest rate reduction alone is insufficient in achieving affordability.

3. Forgive or forbear a portion of the unpaid principal balance if an interest rate reduction and term extension are insufficient.

Reviewing the lender's initial offer

A loan modification can adjust anything stated in the original mortgage, so you need to read it carefully (and have your attorney review and approve it) before you sign on the dotted line.

Lenders often present their plans as take-it-or-leave it offers and give borrowers little time to respond. Don't cave in to the pressure by making a rushed decision. Review the lender's initial offer carefully, keeping in mind that the terms of the agreement are likely negotiable. In Chapter 11, we show you how to pick through the lender's initial offer without nit-picking your way out of a solution.

The most important part of any loan modification agreement is the monthly payment. Make sure it's affordable. If the agreement calls for *step-rate adjustments* (regular increases in the interest rate over time), find out what your payment will be with each adjustment. Make sure the worst-case scenario is still affordable.

Pitching your counteroffer

Unless your lender pitched you a golden egg of an offer, you probably want to negotiate one or more of the terms stated in the new agreement. You should always pitch your counteroffer in writing, and it should always include the following details about each clause you want changed:

✔ The clause itself, which you may be able to refer to by number

✔ The desired change using your preferred rewording, unless you simply want the clause removed

Chapter 12 can help you negotiate a better deal.

In real estate, everything needs to be in writing to be legally binding. Don't let anyone convince you that some understanding you reach outside the parameters of the contract is good enough. Get everything in writing.

Closing the deal: Now what?

After you sign and submit the loan modification agreement, your lender should provide you with copies of the executed agreement, signed and dated by all authorized parties. If you don't receive copies, or if the copies provided aren't signed and dated, request them from your lender. Your lender may also officially record the modification with the county register of deeds or the county clerk.

At this point, you've successfully completed the loan modification process and should have an affordable monthly mortgage payment. Your job now is to hold up your end of the deal by continuing to earn income and keep your discretionary spending in check. You don't want to go through something like this again. In Chapter 16, we provide ten tips for long-term success.

Taking Legal Action — Only If Necessary

As a borrower, you have rights. Your lender has the responsibility to honor those rights through full disclosure. Your lender isn't allowed to play a bait-and-switch, dangling an attractive offer in front of your nose and then sticking you with a high-cost mortgage. Several pieces of government legislation are designed to protect borrowers from unfair lending practices, including the following:

- ✔ **TILA (Truth in Lending Act)** promotes the informed use of consumer credit by requiring disclosures about terms and costs.

- ✔ **HOEPA (Home Ownership and Equity Protection Act)** is designed to curtail predatory lending practices, particularly the practice of placing homeowners in high-interest loans.

- ✔ **RESPA (Real Estate Settlement Procedures Act)** standardizes closing procedures and paperwork to keep transactions above-board and make the process less confusing for borrowers.

In Chapter 13, we cover these important pieces of legislation in greater detail. In Chapters 14 and 15, we show you how to use them to your advantage in negotiating a better deal with your lender.

Although these acts do allow victims to take legal action against violators, we usually recommend using these statutes to push for a settlement outside the courtroom. Litigation can be expensive, time-consuming, and aggravating.

Chapter 2

Taking Stock of Your Situation

*W*hen considering a loan modification, it helps to draw a map leading from where you are now to where you envision yourself being after you negotiate your loan modification. Start with a point labeled "You Are Here" that defines your current position and how you arrived at this point.

By determining the event or series of events that have led to the current financial crisis and by having a sense of where you stand at this point in time, you get a much clearer idea of what it will take to dig yourself out of this hole and which options are available to you.

Understanding How You Ended Up in This Mess

One of the best ways to solve any problem is to investigate its cause, formulate an immediate plan of action, and then develop a long-term solution. For example, if you can't pay your mortgage, you may trace the cause back to when your adjustable-rate mortgage adjusted up. Your immediate plan of action may be to cut spending so you can afford the higher payments. Your long-term solution may be to work out a solution with your lender to lower the payments.

When you're facing the possibility of being unable to afford your monthly house payments, the causes generally fall into either of two categories: something that happened to you, or something you did. In the following sections, we help you identify possible causes of your situation, starting with the mortgage meltdown that began in 2008. We then move on to other causes beyond your control before addressing some avoidable triggers.

Knowing how you ended up with house payments you can't afford is also important when the time comes to apply for a loan modification. Most lenders require a hardship letter explaining what happened, as we discuss in Chapter 8. Figuring out what happened can make writing the hardship letter much easier.

The mortgage meltdown: From Wall Street to Main Street

One of the top news stories in 2008 centered on the mortgage meltdown and the ensuing foreclosure epidemic — the worst foreclosure epidemic since the Great Depression.

Although homeowners/borrowers played a role in triggering the meltdown, many other factors contributed to it. When you have a general understanding of what happened, you benefit in two ways:

- ✔ You're less likely to feel guilty or embarrassed knowing that the current situation isn't entirely your fault.

- ✔ Knowing that others may have played a role may motivate you to seek relief through a loan modification.

In the following sections, we describe many of the factors that contributed to the mortgage meltdown and subsequent rise in defaults and foreclosures.

Historically low interest rates

To stimulate the economy after the dot-com crash in the 1990s, the Federal Reserve System lowered interest rates, enabling more people to borrow more money. Although having low interest rates is generally a good thing, this easy money contributed to the creation of a *housing bubble,* a condition in which home values and equity are artificially inflated.

Homeowners cashed out this artificially inflated value through refinancing and home equity lines of credit. When the bubble burst and the economy took a nose dive, they were left with little or no equity or negative equity, large mortgage payments, and insufficient income to afford those payments. Even worse, they couldn't refinance their way out of trouble because the equity they thought they had in their homes had disappeared.

Government policies and legislation — and lack thereof

Economists have identified several possible factors contributing to the mortgage meltdown related to policies and legislation. The first factor is the passage of the Financial Services Modernization Act in 1999, which essentially repealed the Glass-Steagall Act of 1933 that was in place to protect against the irresponsible lending practices that contributed to the Great Depression. The Financial Services Modernization Act enabled banks to diversify in ways that allowed them to operate in a less-regulated environment.

The second contributing factor is the U.S. Congress's failure to pass legislation to address warnings from Fed Chairman Alan Greenspan and others that government-sponsored enterprises (also known as GSEs) Fannie Mae and Freddie Mac needed to be more closely monitored and regulated. These two GSEs are responsible for making investor money available to the mortgage lending industry. The legislation may not have prevented the financial meltdown, but it would have significantly reduced its magnitude.

The third policy-related contributing factor is that, under pressure from Congress to make homeownership more affordable, Fannie Mae and Freddie Mac jumped headfirst into buying and guaranteeing subprime and Alt-A mortgage loans. This action flooded the subprime market with cash, and subprime originations boomed to over 20 percent of all mortgages originated in 2006, up more than 13 percent from just three years earlier. Congress bought it, and Fannie and Freddie retained their unrestrained preferred-status.

Lack of state and federal regulatory oversight

Even without the passage of the legislation discussed in the previous section, state and federal regulators had plenty of tools in place to keep lenders in check. The question of why regulators didn't crack down on both lenders and borrowers remains unanswered. The only possible explanation is that the regulators failed to do their job.

Soaring Wall Street demand for mortgage-backed securities

Over the years, Wall Street developed a voracious appetite for *mortgage-backed securities* (MBSs) made available through *securitization,* a process of bundling loans and selling them as securities to investors. Refer to the nearby sidebar for a blow-by-blow description of how this works.

The 123s of the securitization process

To understand securitization, it helps to know where banks get the money to lend to homeowners. The process includes investors, Fannie Mae and Freddie Mac, banks and other lending institutions, and you, the homeowner. Here's basically how it works:

1. You borrow money to purchase your home from a bank or other mortgage lender.

2. The lender sells the mortgage and loan to Fannie Mae or Freddie Mac so it (the lender) then has more money to loan to other borrowers.

3. Fannie or Freddie packages your loan with others to create *mortgage-backed securities* (MBSs), which it then sells to investors on Wall Street. Fannie and Freddie guarantee the principal and interest payments, so these are pretty safe investments for investors. By selling these securities, Fannie and Freddie replenish their supply of cash to provide to lenders.

Securitization in itself isn't bad, but what happened is that the demand for MBSs on Wall Street became so high that lenders began doing everything possible to feed the demand. One solution was to bundle high- and low-risk loans together, convince a credit rating company to assign a high rating to the packages, and sell them on Wall Street as triple-A-rated securities. In other words, investors were duped into paying top dollar for risky loans.

All was fine until the loans stopped performing. Then, investors lost confidence in the system and pulled out their money. Without money from investors, Fannie and Freddie began running out of money to provide to banks, which ran out of money to provide to borrowers. End result: a credit crunch of epic proportions.

The subprime boom

To make it easier for more applicants to qualify for mortgage loans, many loan originators (loan officers and mortgage brokers) placed borrowers into *subprime loans,* typically adjustable-rate mortgages (ARMs) that had low teaser rates and fewer restrictions than other loans.

Unfortunately, when rates adjusted up and property values dropped at the same time, lenders began tightening restrictions on even the subprime loans, which meant that subprime borrowers with no money and poor credit scores were really stuck, unable to qualify for refinancing under the new rules.

Big profits for brokering loans

During the mortgage boom in the late 1990s, mortgage brokers and loan officers were raking in the dough. Unfortunately, their commissions were usually based on their ability to manipulate the loan product and the number of loans closed rather than the number of *stable* loans approved.

Driven by a strong profit motive and often encouraged by lenders trying to feed Wall Street's appetite for mortgage-backed securities, brokers and loan officers pushed through as many loans as they could. As a result, they expedited the approval of many loan applications that should never have been considered.

Relaxed underwriting practices

Lenders and any of their representatives who originate loans (including loan officers and mortgage brokers) profit by lending money. Low interest rates and increasing property values fueled demand for loans, and almost all the players in the mortgage lending industry were making big bucks. At the same time, competition among lenders was heating up.

To thrive in this competitive marketplace, many lenders relaxed their underwriting practices — that is, they scrutinized loan applications and the applicants' finances much less closely. This made it easier for people to qualify for loans they never would have qualified for before. As a result, lenders often fostered a highly irresponsible corporate culture that led to the following:

- **Close-at-all-cost attitude:** The attitude among many mortgage brokers, loan officers, and lenders was that everyone should work together to do whatever required to have a loan approved.

- **Stated and no doc loan products:** Borrowers could qualify for mortgage loans without having to provide verification of employment or income.

- **Swift approval — lock, close, fund:** Instead of taking the time to properly review an application and its supporting documentation, mortgage brokers, loan officers, and lenders subscribed to a "lock, close, fund" attitude to push loans through as quickly as possible.

Clueless consumers

As long as most people can pay the monthly bills, they see no problem with cashing out the equity in their homes or carrying large balances on their credit cards. In addition, many borrowers are under-informed about the various types of mortgage loans available (over 400 by last count) and therefore are unable to imagine the worst-case scenarios that could occur with some types of loans.

Many borrowers, for example, assumed that taking out an adjustable-rate mortgage was a negligible risk or even a wise decision. Advertisements encouraged homeowners to refinance and take money out of their homes; presumably, the interest would be tax-deductible, thereby making it "good debt." They were told they could easily refinance into lower fixed-rate loans later.

New home developers also fed consumer greed by using teaser loans to sell more add-ons, such as decks, bigger garages, and upscale kitchens. (A *teaser loan* has a low introductory interest rate and lower initial payments to make the loan seem more appealing.)

Irresponsible borrowing

In addition to a lack of insight and foresight, many consumers simply bit off more credit than they could chew. This is nothing new; consumers in the U.S. have a well-earned reputation for being over their heads in debt, but irresponsible borrowing along with a bursting housing bubble and a collapsing economy created ideal conditions for the perfect storm. This storm broke in 2008.

Other events beyond your control

As the saying goes, "Stuff happens." Well, that's not exactly how it goes, but you catch our drift. Bad things happen to good people, and certain bad things can often drive people into foreclosure or at least make it very difficult for them to afford that roof over their heads. In the following sections, we explore some of the most common bad things that put homeowners in a financial bind.

Job losses and pay cuts

Over the course of several years, the U.S. economy has lost a lot of good-paying jobs. You can blame it on the global economy, union-busting, the American consumer's appetite for cheap foreign goods, the healthcare crisis, or whatever other factors you like, but the truth of the matter is that a good chunk of the population began to see incomes that weren't keeping up with inflation. As a result, many people cashed out equity in their homes and got buried in debt because they couldn't keep up with the increasing cost of living.

The mortgage meltdown only worsened already bad conditions, driving down demand for goods and services and wiping out even more jobs, which led to more defaults and foreclosures. As you can see, these events create a cycle in which bad news simply leads to more bad news.

Medical bills and burials

In good times and bad, people experience tragedies that can be costly — both emotionally and financially. Death and illness are the worst and often lead to defaults and foreclosures. This is especially true when families, especially those without health insurance, are hit with huge medical bills or when one or more breadwinners pass away or suffer an illness that prevents them from working.

In many cases, families lose their homes as a result of the financial straits accompanying illness or death, but if you can make a house payment, even a payment significantly less than you're currently paying, a loan modification can keep you out of trouble and keep you in your home.

Common triggers you may have some control over

Many homeowners suffer financial fallout as a result of certain decisions or behaviors — something they or someone in their family has done or is doing. The most common events that fall into this category are the following:

- ✔ **Divorce or separation:** This sort of change reduces the family income while increasing expenses because it typically results in the need to support two households on the same income.

- ✔ **Overspending:** Living beyond one's means leads to financial fiasco, plain and simple. Overspending is usually a problem family-wide, although one person may become the scapegoat.

- ✔ **Gambling:** Gambling addiction has become very common in the U.S., and unless the gambler is earning enough money to support the addiction, financial woe usually results.

- ✔ **Alcohol and substance abuse:** Alcohol and substance abuse are two expensive habits that also compromise a person's earning potential.

Other than not getting divorced or separated, you can't do much to address the root cause of your inability to pay your mortgage due to divorce or separation. For the other three items on the list, however, you need to deal with those issues (overspending, gambling, or substance abuse) in tandem with pursuing a loan modification. Otherwise, no loan modification is going to keep you out of default or foreclosure. To have a successful loan modification you may also need a life modification.

Don't play the blame game. Regardless of what decisions, behaviors, or events have led to your current financial problems, blaming your partner or others who may be responsible is counterproductive. If you're in this situation with others, you need to team up with them to address any and all related problems.

Sizing Up Your Financial Situation

Until you figure out how much money is flowing in and flowing out, where all that money's flowing, and how deep you are in debt, you can't even begin to develop a strategy for taking control of your finances. Taking a close, honest look at the numbers can help you reveal income and expense categories that are sinking your monthly budget, figure out just how deep in debt you are, and sort out the essential expenses from your discretionary spending.

Tallying your monthly income

Taking stock of your financial position begins by tallying your monthly income. To get started, list all your sources of income. The following list can tickle your memory into recalling where all the money's coming from:

- **Day job income:** This consists of all steady income from your main job. If you have a partner with a steady income, count that, too.

- **Moonlighting income:** If you have another job that produces steady income, such as a regular babysitting gig on weekends, include it as part of your household income.

- **Rental income:** If you collect rent from boarders, it's part of your household income.

- **Investment income:** If you have any stocks, bonds, real estate, or other investments that generate a steady monthly return, include those amounts in your calculations.

- **Other income:** Can you think of any other income, such as payments from a trust fund, 401(k) distributions, or retirement plan payments? If so, include it as part of your monthly income.

When calculating your monthly income, take a conservative approach. Earning some extra money on the side is always good in a pinch, but if you can't rely on getting that money each and every month, don't include it in your monthly income. You can use that extra money to catch up on your bills faster than your plan calls for, but extra dough isn't part of your plan.

Computing your payments on debt

Debt is relative both in terms of amount and how you feel about it. Some people are up to their gills in debt and seem not to have a worry in the world, whereas others constantly fret over owing $100,000 or more on their homes. Others flat-out refuse to use a credit card to pay for *anything*.

Although debt is relative, you need to quantify it somehow to figure out for yourself just how deeply you're in debt and how deep is too deep. In the following sections, you calculate your total debt and the total amount of your monthly payments on all your debt — including your mortgage and credit cards. Later in this chapter, in the section "Calculating your debt-to-income ratios," you see how to gauge your debt by comparing it to how much you earn each month.

Adding up your total debt

If you're like most people, you have other debts in addition to your mortgage loan. Use the following list to total the balances you're currently carrying on all your loans and other accounts:

- ✔ First mortgage
- ✔ Second mortgage
- ✔ Home equity loan or line of credit
- ✔ Construction loans, such as those for new windows or siding
- ✔ Car loans
- ✔ Student loans or parent-of-student loans
- ✔ Credit card accounts (don't include this item if you *always* pay off the full balance due when you receive your statement and don't carry a residual balance)
- ✔ Any credit card balances or loans that your partner has taken out only in his or her name
- ✔ Private loans, such as money you borrowed from your parents or sister-in-law

Your long-term goal may be to pay down this total debt over time, starting with the debt you're paying the highest interest on. In the short term, however, you simply want to be able to cover your monthly bills without going any deeper in debt, as explained in the following section. Your first priority should be your home loan.

Distinguishing good debt from bad

Investors can tell you that not all debt is bad. For example, if you can borrow money at 15 percent interest to fuel an investment that earns you a 25 percent profit, taking on that debt can be a very good idea. Paying 18 percent interest on a credit card used to charge grocery bills, on the other hand, doesn't constitute good debt. It only leads to way over-paying for your groceries.

Good debt consists of money you borrow to acquire items that increase in value at a rate that exceeds the interest you pay on that debt. You also can take on good debt by purchasing something on credit that enables you to generate income; for example, you may purchase a car to drive to work or buy a computer that enables you to earn significantly more money than the cost of that computer.

One of the best strategies for improving your financial position is to reduce the amount of bad debt you carry. One of the best strategies for building long-term wealth is to wisely manage the amount of good debt you carry.

Figuring out your monthly debt payments

Later in this chapter, in the section "Dissecting your current budget," you take a close look at your entire budget to determine whether your monthly take-home pay is sufficient to cover your monthly bills. For now, we want you to focus only on *debt payments* — monthly payments on all the loans and other balances you accounted for in the previous section.

List your minimum monthly payment for each of the loans and accounts you identified in the previous section. Now, add them up to determine your total monthly debt payments.

Calculating your debt-to-income ratios

One way to measure the financial well-being of your household is to look at your *debt ratio,* or *debt-to-income (DTI) ratio,* which is the percentage of your monthly income that you spend to service your debt. Lenders use the following two debt ratios to gauge the risk that a particular borrower represents:

- ✓ **Back-end ratio:** Accounts for all your debt payments, including your house payment, car payment, and credit card payments
- ✓ **Front-end ratio:** Accounts only for your house payment

Debt payments don't include what you spend on groceries, utilities, clothing, gas, and other such items. In addition, the calculation uses only the income of the person who's listed on the note. If you and your partner "own" the home together but only your name is on the note for the loan, only your monthly income is counted. If you're both listed as mortgagors (borrowers), your combined monthly income is used in computing your DTI ratios.

The house payment used in calculating the DTI ratio includes principal and interest along with any monthly escrow payments to cover homeowner's insurance, property taxes, and in some cases any homeowner association fees (HOAs). If you pay homeowner's insurance, property taxes, and HOAs separately rather than paying into escrow, total the costs and divide by 12 to determine the monthly amount for those items; then add that amount to your monthly house payment when calculating your debt ratio.

Back-end ratio

To determine your back-end ratio, use the following formula:

> Back-end Debt Ratio = Total Monthly Debt Payments ÷ Gross Monthly Income

Traditionally, the Federal Housing Authority (FHA) has recommended that a borrower's back-end ratio not exceed 41 percent. For conventional loans, many banks want to see a back-end ratio that's 36 percent or lower.

Front-end ratio

To determine your front-end ratio, use the following formula:

> Front-end Debt Ratio = House Payment ÷ Gross Monthly Income

Traditionally, the FHA has recommended that a borrower's front-end ratio not exceed 29 percent. For conventional loans, many banks require a front-end ratio that's 28 percent or lower. We recommend 30 percent as a ballpark figure. According to the Making Home Affordable (MHA) plan (often referred to as the Obama Plan), the front-end ratio target for modified loans is 31 percent.

A safer ratio

Although we present the standard formulas for calculating debt ratios, we recommend that you use different formulas in order to set safer goals.

Back-end Debt Ratio = Total Monthly Debt Payments ÷ Net Monthly Income

Front-end Debt Ratio = House Payment ÷ Net Monthly Income

These formulas use *net pay* instead of *gross pay;* in other words, they base the calculation on your take-home pay — the only money you really have to spend.

For example, suppose you have a monthly gross income of $3,000, but after deductions, your take-home pay is only $2,250. You have a monthly house payment of $800 (principal, interest, and escrow for homeowner's insurance and property taxes). Using the traditional DTI formula, your front-end ratio would be

$800 ÷ $3,000 = 26%

That's well below the 29 percent required by the FHA and even below what most lenders would approve for a conventional mortgage. But how affordable is that same $800 payment when the DTI is based on take-home pay? Do the math:

$800 ÷ $2,250 = 35%

That's way above the 29 percent required to qualify under FHA guidelines, and when you consider that 35 percent of everything you earn goes toward your house payment, you aren't left with a whole lot of spending money.

You probably won't see this approach gain nationwide support because it would further tighten lending restrictions and disqualify many would-be borrowers, but it's out there and something to be aware of. Debt ratio calculations based on net monthly income are also gaining some popularity among conservative financial minds. Consider using these alternative formulas, especially when looking at a major monthly payment like a mortgage.

In the section "Estimating an Affordable House Payment" later in this chapter, we show you how to rearrange these formulas to work backward and calculate an affordable house payment based on your net monthly income.

Dissecting your current budget

Except for people who majored in accounting and aced the math portion of their SATs, budgeting isn't exactly one of America's favorite pastimes. As long as they have enough money to pay the bills, most people can afford not to budget. When money is tight, however, you need to start tracking your income and expenses.

If you haven't yet accounted for your income, that's the first step. Skip back to the section "Tallying your monthly income" earlier in this chapter for details. When you're done there, you're ready to proceed to the following sections to begin itemizing your expenses.

Consider using an accounting program, such as Quicken, to track all your income and expenses. With an accounting program, you can assign every transaction to a category and then generate a report that displays all your expenses, itemized by category.

Totaling your monthly bills

When you're working on a budget, guessing doesn't work. Grab your check register or whatever you use to track deposits into and payments out of your checking account, and refer to those numbers to determine how much you're spending each month in various categories. If you don't use a check register or some other tracking device, now's the time to start.

Begin with the big-ticket items, such as the following:

- House payment
- Homeowner's insurance, unless it's paid out of escrow for you
- Property taxes, unless they're paid out of escrow for you
- Car payment(s)
- Credit card payments
- Other loan payments
- Childcare and/or tuition payments
- Auto insurance (if you don't pay it monthly, figure out how much you would pay if you were paying monthly)
- Health insurance, unless it's automatically deducted from your paycheck
- Life insurance, unless it's automatically deducted from your paycheck
- Utility bills, including gas, electric, phone, water, sewage, and trash bills
- Other bills that come every month, including your cable or satellite TV bill

Tracking other expenditures

Other expenditures essentially comprise your daily living expenses. These typically include the following:

- ✔ Groceries

- ✔ Personal care, including haircuts, toiletries, and the like

- ✔ Clothing

- ✔ Auto maintenance, including routine maintenance like oil changes and tune-ups

- ✔ Auto fuel

- ✔ Dining out

- ✔ Entertainment, including renting movies, going to movies and concerts, and so on

- ✔ Gifts

- ✔ Household repairs and supplies

- ✔ Gambling (yes, playing the lottery counts)

- ✔ Vacations, including holiday travel

- ✔ Scheduled savings (include an investment in your future and financial security as a monthly expense)

- ✔ Pet care, including food, toys, and vet bills

If you're unsure about how much you spend in each category, try to make as accurate an estimate as possible, and start tracking your spending in each of these categories and any others that you identify over the next several weeks.

Consider using a separate envelope to budget for each expense category. When you get paid, set aside a certain amount of cash in each envelope and use only that cash to purchase items and services in that category. If you're overspending in one category, you may find a surplus in other categories to make up the difference, or you may decide that you need to trim your spending in a particular category. Don't get discouraged if, after filling your envelopes, you're holding only a few bucks.

Identifying unaccounted-for expenses

Chances are pretty good that you can't account for every single penny you're spending, but minor expenses can add up to a good chunk of change over a month's time, so try to account for everything.

Consider one of the following techniques to keep better track of unaccounted-for expenses or to slash these types of expenditures:

✔ **Carry around a notebook and log all your purchases.** (This exercise lasts about six hours for most people.)

✔ **Pay yourself an allowance.** If you implemented the envelope budgeting technique from the previous section, create an envelope for yourself, too.

Estimating an Affordable House Payment

When you were looking at homes, somebody — your real estate agent or mortgage broker — probably told you how much house you could afford. To convince you to look at higher-priced homes and take out a larger mortgage, they probably used the FHA debt-to-income ratio guidelines to estimate affordability.

Unfortunately, they probably didn't take into consideration your lifestyle — how many children you have, what sorts of vacations you like to take, whether you smoke or drink, the kind of car you drive, and so on. In other words, they may have known your DTI ratio, but they probably didn't account for all that other stuff in your budget that had nothing to do with rent.

As a result, you may have ended up buying more home than you could really afford or buying a home that didn't accommodate your lifestyle or leave you with a sufficient buffer for any bad times. We recommend that you calculate a more realistic estimate yourself, using the methods described in the following sections. Use both methods, and then go with the lower of the two.

Basing your estimate on a conservative back-end ratio

Based on the formula used to calculate the back-end debt-to-income ratio, we developed the following formula for estimating an affordable house payment. This formula takes into account all your debt payments (mortgage, car loan, credit card payments, and so on) and projects a house payment based on a debt-to-income ratio of 36 percent and on net income (not gross income):

$(0.36 \times \text{Net Monthly Income}) - \text{Total Debt Payments, Excluding House Payment} = \text{Affordable House Payment}$

For example, suppose you're earning $3,500 per month take-home pay. You have a $250 car payment, $150 per month in student loans, and $200 per month in credit card payments; your total debt payments excluding your house payment equal $600. The formula would look like this:

$(0.36 \times \$3,500) - \$600 = \$660$ per month

 Get rid of the high-interest credit card payment of $200 a month, and you can afford a house payment of $860. The difference between an $860 and a $660 monthly house payment can mean an upgrade in neighborhood, more square footage, better schools for the children, safer streets, and so on. Slashing expenses can actually improve your quality of life. Make a commitment to yourself and your future to eliminate credit card debt. You'll notice a big difference.

Basing your estimate on your monthly budget

Assuming you've performed an honest accounting of all your income and expenses and you know within about $100 per month where you're spending your monthly take-home pay, you can start working backward to estimate an affordable monthly payment.

Begin by subtracting your total monthly expenses (excluding your house payment) from your total monthly income.

Monthly Income – Monthly Expenses, Excluding House Payment = Money Available for House Payment

Assuming you've been unable to make your house payment, that Money Available for House Payment number is going to be negative or closer to zero than any lender would consider. If it shows that you have plenty of money to make a house payment, you don't have an accurate estimate of expenses. Otherwise, you'd be able to make your payments and wouldn't be reading this book.

In cases where the Money Available for House Payment is too high, we usually observe a lot of small, unaccounted-for purchases (often paid for with cash). Even just $3 per day on a trivial item adds up to $90 per month, which is 14 percent of a $660 monthly house payment. When you're living within a budget (as we suggest you do), every little bit counts.

Suppose you have a negative amount or a very low amount for a house payment based on your current monthly income and expenses. What are your options? You basically have three:

✔ Increase your monthly income.

✔ Trim your monthly expenses.

✔ Increase your monthly income and trim your monthly expenses.

Short of getting another job in a hurry or convincing your partner to get another job, the solution requires trimming the fat from your budget, assuming you have some fat to trim. Review your budget closely, and identify categories in which you can realistically cut spending. Cut as much as you can, and then perform the calculation again to see how much of a house payment you can afford.

Chapter 3

Evaluating Your Options

*W*hen facing foreclosure, most homeowners think they have two options: pay up or move out. The fact is that you probably have about a dozen options — everything from refinancing to loan modification to selling your home or simply walking away and abandoning the property.

Although we recommend loan modification for most homeowners who qualify for it, we encourage you to consider all your options, so you can make a well-informed choice of what's best for you and your family. In this chapter, we describe the most common foreclosure alternatives available and present them in order from what experience tells us are generally the best options to the worst.

In this chapter, we merely introduce your options. This book focuses on loan modification solutions, so for more information about the other alternatives we mention in this chapter, check out *Foreclosure Self-Defense For Dummies* (Wiley).

Negotiating a Work-Out Solution with Your Lender

Contrary to what many homeowners believe, the bank probably doesn't want to kick you out of your home. Why would it? Over the life of your loan, you're probably going to at least double what you paid for the house in interest alone. In addition, if the bank forecloses, it stands to lose a lot of money — about $60,000 to $80,000 by some estimates. If property values have dropped since you purchased the home, your lender probably can't sell the home for enough to cover the balance on your mortgage.

As a result, lenders are typically motivated to work out a solution that enables you to stay in your home and keep making payments. In the midst of a foreclosure epidemic, they're even more eager to strike a deal, as described in the following sections.

If you've had nothing but trouble with your current lender, refinancing may be at the top of your list of options. See "Refinancing Out of Trouble" later in this chapter for details.

Modifying your existing loan

If you have a steady income but not quite enough for you to catch up on missed payments and continue making the payments you're paying now, a loan modification can be the perfect solution. You keep your home with a lower monthly payment. If you've missed several payments, the lender may add the payments to the end of the term or scratch them off the balance sheet (rare, but it happens).

Help your neighbors by helping yourself

Homeownership traditionally has been the foundation of the United States economy, so when foreclosure happens, everyone becomes a victim.

✔ Foreclosures reduce property values for everyone in the neighborhood.

✔ Lower property values lead to lower tax revenues for state, county, and local governments.

✔ Vacant homes attract vandals, vagrants, and other criminal types.

✔ Rising default rates convince lenders to tighten credit, making it more difficult and costly to borrow money.

✔ As families lose their homes, they have less money to spend on products and services, lowering demand and increasing unemployment.

✔ Foreclosures feed on foreclosures as the repercussions from one foreclosure ripple through the economy.

Don't feel guilty or ashamed to ask for help. By helping yourself stay in your home with a loan modification, you're helping your neighbors, too.

Throughout this book, we discuss loan modification in detail and show you what to do to pursue this option. To gain a general understanding of the concept and what it involves, see Chapter 1.

Reinstating the loan

As soon as your lender decides to move forward with foreclosure, it refuses to accept payments from you. This may seem a little odd, but if the lender were to accept payments, it could be setting a precedent that would compromise its ability to collect from you if you were to stop making payments again.

To get back on good terms with your lender, you may be able to *reinstate* the loan. This approach consists of paying the lender a lump sum that covers all missed and late payments along with any penalties and fees. You can then continue making your monthly payments as if nothing had ever happened.

Reinstating usually requires that you borrow the money from your rich uncle or some other well-to-do family member or friend (or have them gift it to you).

 Consider this option only if you've recovered from a temporary financial setback and can realistically afford your monthly payments plus any payments you would owe to the person who loaned you the money to reinstate. Never agree to a solution that places you back on the path to defaulting on your loan.

 Don't have a rich relative? Think again — you may have a rich Uncle Sam. At the height of the foreclosure epidemic, Fannie Mae announced a program called HomeSaver Advance (HSA) that allows lenders to loan up to $15,000 to homeowners who've recovered from a temporary financial setback but are having trouble catching up on missed payments. With this program, you sign a separate promissory note for the amount needed to cover delinquent PITI (principal, interest, taxes, insurance) and other advances and fees, along with funds to cover up to six months in unpaid homeowner association (HOA) fees — 12 months if the fees are paid once a year.

Negotiating forbearance

Forbearance is any delay the lender agrees to in moving forward with collection activities, including foreclosure. Forbearance may include a period of no required payments (special forbearance) or be accompanied by some sort of installment plan for catching up on missed or late payments. Instead of paying the whole amount you owe in missed payments and penalties in one lump sum, you spread your payments over several months. If you're $4,000 behind on payments, for example, the lender may let you pay about $667 extra per month for six months until you're all caught up.

Like the option of reinstating, forbearance is practical only for those who've recovered from a temporary financial setback and can now afford not only their original monthly payment but also a little (or sometimes a lot) extra each month.

Considering principal forbearance

Principal forbearance is sort of a "play now, pay later" option best suited to someone who's upside down in his mortgage, meaning he owes more on his home than it's worth. With principal forbearance, the lender modifies the mortgage by calculating payments based on the amount the home is worth rather than on the balance of your mortgage, which lowers your monthly payment.

Suppose you took out a 30-year mortgage for $420,000 at 7 percent, and you've been making payments of about $2,790 per month for five years. You owe a balance of about $395,000. Unfortunately, due to declining property values, your home's current market value is only about $300,000.

You and your lender work out a principal forbearance plan. The lender agrees to base your new payments on the market value of the home ($300,000 instead of the $395,000 you owe), drop your interest rate to 5 percent, and re-amortize the loan over 30 years (instead of the 25 years remaining on your current mortgage). This revision lowers your house payment to about $2,250 — a savings of over $500 per month.

What happened to that other $95,000? When you sell the home, hopefully at a higher price after the housing market recovers, you hand that money to your lender. Of course, if housing values fail to recover by the time you choose to sell your home, you're still on the hook for that $95,000, unless your lender agrees to a short sale, which isn't something you can count on.

For obvious reasons, the lender would prefer that you pay the money later rather than simply forgiving you a portion of the balance, as is sometimes done in loan modifications. If you can convince the lender to forgive a portion of the principal as part of your loan modification, a principal *reduction* would be a better deal than principal *forbearance*.

Refinancing Out of Trouble

Prior to the bursting of the housing bubble, when property values were soaring, refinancing was the option of choice for homeowners feeling the financial pinch. By refinancing, you use the equity in your home to bail yourself out.

When property values tanked, however, many homeowners found themselves with little, no, or even negative equity in their homes, which took the refinance option off the table. Lenders usually like to see a *loan-to-value ratio* (LTV) no higher than 95 percent. In other words, they don't want to lend you more than 95 percent of the property's true market value — $95,000 on a $100,000 home.

If you have a substantial amount of equity in your home, however, refinancing may be a realistic option for you, particularly if you can refinance into a fixed-rate mortgage with a lower interest rate than what you're paying now. We recommend fixed-rate loans because they allow you to plan your finances without the worry of having those plans shattered by an unexpected rate increase.

Make sure your current mortgage doesn't have a stiff prepayment penalty. If it does, try negotiating with your lender to have it removed before you refinance with another lender. Also, make sure your new loan has a reasonable prepayment penalty that's phased out over two to three years (or better yet, no prepayment penalty) and that the closing costs are reasonable. For more about shopping for mortgages, check out *Mortgages For Dummies,* 3rd Edition by Eric Tyson and Ray Brown, and *Mortgage Myths* by Ralph R. Roberts and Chip Cummings (both from Wiley).

In the following sections, we explore various ways to use the re-financing option to your benefit.

Consolidating your debts

If you have plenty of equity in your home but are buried in high-interest credit card debt, refinancing to consolidate debt is often the perfect solution. Consolidation consists of taking out one loan to pay off all or at least some of your outstanding balances, including your current mortgage, any auto loans, credit card balances, and so on. The goal is to have a monthly payment that's considerably lower than your current monthly debt payments combined.

Be careful when consolidating debt. This strategy can become a recipe for disaster if, after paying off high-interest credit cards, you don't stop using them and instead run the balances back up again.

To determine whether a consolidation can save you money, do the following:

1. **Add up all your monthly debt payments — house, car, credit card bills, and so on. Don't forget homeowners insurance and property taxes unless they're included in your monthly mortgage payment. (You may already have totaled your debt payments in Chapter 2.)**

2. **Add up all your loan and credit card account balances. (You may have already totaled your debt balances in Chapter 2.)**

3. **Access your handy-dandy loan calculator, and enter the total from Step 2 as the loan amount. This is the total amount you would borrow to pay off all your loans and credit card balances, including your current mortgage.**

   Loan calculators are available on the Web. (You can find several excellent ones at www.bankrate.com.) If you have a personal finance program, such as Quicken, it should have a loan calculator.

4. **Enter the going interest rate for a 30-year mortgage.**

   You can find the rates in most newspapers or online, such as at www.bankrate.com.

5. **Click the button, if necessary, to complete the calculations.**

If the monthly payment for the consolidation loan isn't significantly lower than the total you're currently paying on your loans (from Step 1) and what you would consider to be in an affordable range, refinancing alone probably isn't a viable alternative for you. A short re-fi, discussed in the later section "Doing a short re-fi," may still be a possibility, however.

Debt consolidation almost always transforms *unsecured debt* (including credit card debt) into *secured debt,* which is secured by some sort of collateral, such as a car or a home. If you have substantial unsecured debt, consult a bankruptcy attorney prior to considering debt consolidation, as explained later in this chapter in the section "Playing the Bankruptcy Card." Bankruptcy helps erase the unsecured debt more easily than the secured debt, so you don't want to transform unsecured debt into secured debt if there's even a remote possibility you may file for bankruptcy later.

Refinancing the old-fashioned way

A plain and simple refinance merely provides you with an opportunity to lower your interest rate, which usually results in lowering your monthly payment. For example, monthly principal and interest payments on a $200,000 30-year mortgage at 8 percent are $1,467.53. At 7 percent, they drop to $1,330.60. At 6 percent, they drop to $1,199.10.

To determine whether refinancing your current mortgage can make your monthly payments affordable, use any Web-based loan calculator to do the math. You can find several financial calculators, including a loan calculator, at www.bankrate.com.

If refinancing sounds appealing to you, meet with a reputable mortgage broker to discuss your options and crunch the numbers. A mortgage broker can quickly determine whether you're likely to qualify for a refinance loan. If you're not likely to qualify, knowing this early allows you to scratch the option off your list.

If refinancing into a lower rate requires you to pay huge amounts in closing costs and fees out-of-pocket, it may not be worth it. Sure you'll save thousands in interest over the life of the loan, but the re-fi should be designed to offer immediate payment relief, as well. Weigh the costs and comparison shop carefully.

Doing a short re-fi

A *short re-fi* is sort of a cross between a refinance and a short sale, discussed later in this chapter in the section "Selling to break even with a short sale." Your lender agrees to accept as payment in full less than is required to pay off the balance due on the mortgage, and you take out a refinance loan to make that payment in full.

The end result is that you have a new mortgage with a lower balance and lower monthly payments, while your original lender cuts its losses and moves on. Some lenders may even be willing to short re-fi their own loans, knowing that over the life of the loans they'll recapture any amount they discounted upfront.

The short re-fi option is often a practical solution if you want to refinance but you can't qualify for a new loan because you currently owe more on your home than it's worth. By agreeing to forgive a portion of the principal due, your lender can bring the LTV into a range that enables you to qualify for a new loan.

When considering a short re-fi, make absolutely sure the agreement frees you from paying the *deficiency*, which is the difference between the original loan balance and the new balance. Have your family attorney review the paperwork before you close. If you don't consult an attorney, at least find out what the lender's intentions are regarding the deficiency and your liability. Also, ask your attorney or accountant about any tax ramifications from having the deficiency forgiven. The Mortgage Forgiveness Debt Relief Act of 2007 "generally allows taxpayers to exclude income from the discharge of debt on their principal residence" for the years 2007 to 2012, but certain exclusions may apply.

Playing the Bankruptcy Card

Declaring bankruptcy is like driving a tank onto a battlefield where everyone else is waging war with peashooters. It's the big gun you draw when you're buried so deep in debt that you can't possibly claw your way out. Bankruptcy gives you a second chance by allowing you to start over.

Although several types (or *chapters*) of bankruptcy are available, each with its own benefits and drawbacks, Chapter 7 and Chapter 13 are the most common for consumers.

- ✓ **Chapter 7, Liquidation:** You sell assets, pay back as much as you can afford to with the proceeds, and walk away debt-free. A little known fact is that in 90 percent of Chapter 7 bankruptcies, the debtors keep all their property because it's protected by exemptions.

- ✓ **Chapter 13, Restructuring debt:** You work out a payment plan with the bankruptcy judge that enables you to repay all or most of your debt to your creditors.

This isn't a book on bankruptcy, so we merely introduce it as an option to consider. For details, check out *Personal Bankruptcy Laws For Dummies,* 2nd Edition, by James P. Caher and John M. Caher (Wiley), and consult a reputable bankruptcy attorney in your area.

When you file for bankruptcy, your lender is likely to shut down communications with you out of fear of being found in violation of the *automatic stay* prohibiting the lender from pursuing any collection activities. You may need to first *reaffirm the debt* (agree to pay back the loan) before the lender will negotiate with you, but don't reaffirm without your attorney's approval. Legislators have considered a *cram-down provision* that would give bankruptcy judges in a Chapter 13 bankruptcy the power to order lenders to modify unpaid principal balances of the debtors' mortgage loans, but at the time of this writing, the legislation hasn't been passed.

Getting Out from Under It: Selling Your Home

When property values were on the rise, we often advised home-owners facing foreclosure to sell their homes. In fact, in about 90 percent of the foreclosure cases we handled, selling the home was the best option. Selling enabled the owners to get out from under homes they really couldn't afford, cash out any equity in their homes, and move to more affordable accommodations.

As property values decline, the sell-your-home solution becomes viable for fewer and fewer homeowners. They're usually facing the prospect of selling at a loss, and that's not something we recommend. In the following sections, we describe various strategies for selling your home quickly and at least breaking even.

If you're facing the prospect of selling at a loss, explore other options first or at least look into a short sale, as discussed in "Selling to break even with a short sale."

Selling for a profit: Do's and don'ts

Listing and selling your home in the face of foreclosure is a whole 'nother ball game compared to listing and selling your home under normal circumstances. Time is *not* on your side. Following are some tips for selling your home quickly for as much money as possible in a down market:

- ✔ **Mum's the word.** If word gets out that you don't have a choice but to sell, buyers can use this nugget of knowledge as leverage to negotiate a lower price.

- ✔ **Hire a Realtor.** Don't settle for a run-of-the-mill real estate agent. A Realtor, a member of the National Association of Realtors (NAR), has additional training and is required to uphold a strict code of ethics.

- ✔ **Hire the best.** The agent who has the most SOLD signs around the neighborhood is usually the best choice.

- ✔ **Tell your agent about your situation.** Being upfront enables your agent to employ strategies for selling your home quickly.

- ✔ **Price it right the first time.** Consult with your agent to set an attractive asking price, which is likely to be less than you think it should be. A lower asking price attracts more potential buyers, which may drive up offers or even initiate a bidding war, and can make the home sell much faster.

✔ **Choose an agent who markets on the Web.** Your home should be marketed on at least eight Web sites, including www.backpage.com and www.craigslist.com.

✔ **Stay put until it sells (if possible).** A vacant home is harder to sell than an occupied one. Most buyers have limited vision, so having rooms laid out and furnished helps potential buyers see your house as a home and often brings a higher sales price.

✔ **Stage your home.** Staging transforms a house into a showcase home that typically commands a higher price and sells faster. Check out *Home Staging For Dummies* by Christine Rae and Janice Saunders Maresh (Wiley).

✔ **Be prepared for potential buyers at all times.** Make sure your home is ready to show every day, and let your agent know that prospective buyers are welcome any time (without having to give 24-hour advance notice).

✔ **Let the light in.** Prior to the showing, open all the curtains and shades to let the light in, turn on all the lights, and vacate the premises.

✔ **Appeal to the senses.** Prior to a showing, bake some cookies, set out a couple of vases of fresh-cut flowers, open the windows (if the weather is nice), or brew a fresh pot of coffee, but avoid scented candles and heavy air fresheners. Play some soothing background music during the showing.

Selling to break even with a short sale

Selling at a loss as your first option is for chumps, and it's usually unnecessary. If none of the other options discussed in this chapter is any better, or if you simply want to sell or have to sell for other reasons, selling is okay, but do everything in your power *not* to sell at a loss.

One very popular option is to negotiate a *short sale* with your lender; it's a deal in which the lender accepts an amount, as payment in full, that's less than the balance currently due on your mortgage. For example, suppose you owe $200,000 on your mortgage but can sell the house only for $180,000. With a short sale, the lender would agree to accept that $180,000 as full payment and let you off the hook for the other $20,000.

When negotiating a short sale, be careful about two potential drawbacks:

- ✔ **Deficiency judgment:** Have your attorney review the paper-work before you sign it to make sure that the lender has no recourse to collect the cancelled debt, called the *deficiency*.

- ✔ **Taxes on cancelled debt:** The government has tradition-ally taxed cancelled debt. During the foreclosure epidemic, Congress passed legislation to temporarily lift taxes on can-celled debt for the sale of a primary residence, but this legisla-tion may expire by the time you read this or it may not apply to your situation. Check with a reliable accountant or tax attorney to be sure.

Selling quickly to an investor

Real estate investors often have money when other people don't, so they're in a better position to purchase properties. In addition, they usually either have cash or readily accessible financing, so they don't have to wait for a loan approval. As a result, you may be able to sell your home to an investor more quickly than through normal channels. (The next section offers some advice on finding real estate investors.)

Even reputable real estate investors are focused on maximizing their profits, so selling to an investor may not be your best option. You may be better off working out a solution with your lender that allows you to stay in your home until property values recover (if and when is anyone's guess) and then selling it. If you need to move in a hurry, however, selling to an investor is certainly an option.

Teaming Up with an Investor to Stay in Your Home

Real estate investors typically swoop in to purchase properties at a bargain with the expectation that the previous owners vacate the premises as soon as possible, but this isn't always the case. Sometimes, investors are willing to team up with homeowners to help them keep their homes — either permanently or temporarily. In the following sections, we discuss these two options.

You can usually find reputable investors through reputable real estate agents, attorneys (especially foreclosure and bankruptcy attorneys), and perhaps even local banks. If you're really in a bind, you can try calling one of those numbers on the We Buy Homes ads, but be sure to run the name of the person past your attorney or real estate agent first. Be extra careful about anyone who contacts you before you contact them, especially the nicest ones who want to "help" you; they're more likely to be con artists wanting to help themselves to your money.

Never deed your property away to a third party as part of a so-called foreclosure rescue. These are usually scams in which the third party claims to be able to save your home for you. They claim that all you have to do is deed the property to them, and they'll pay off the underlying mortgage. In most cases, they just collect some money from you and have no intention of paying off the mortgage. Have your attorney review any and all documents before you sign.

Selling your home and buying it back

Assuming you've been a good steward to your home, an investor may be willing to purchase it at the foreclosure auction and then sell it back to you on contract. You can buy back a home using either of the following contracts:

- ✔ **Contract for deed or other seller financing vehicles:** With a contract for deed, the seller (in this case, the investor who purchased your property and is selling it back to you) acts as the bank. Instead of using a mortgage to secure interest in the property, the seller/lender retains possession of the property until the buyer fulfills the terms of the contract.

- ✔ **Lease option agreement:** With a lease option, you rent the property for a time (usually no more than about two years), at the end of which you have the option but not the obligation to purchase the property. This arrangement usually gives you some time to improve your credit rating so you can afford a conventional mortgage to finance the purchase of the property.

Buying the property back on either type of contract is usually an option if you have some equity in the property and run out of other options; for example, your lender won't modify your loan, you don't have enough time to sell it, and you can't qualify for refinancing.

Work only with reputable investors in your area, and have your attorney review all the paperwork and explain it to you until you fully understand everything in the contract before signing it. Most land contracts and lease option agreements contain a *forfeiture clause* that could prevent you from purchasing the property unless you meet all the conditions specified. You want to make sure that those conditions are reasonable before you agree to them.

Another potential problem you need to be aware of is that under certain circumstances, any liens against the property at the time of foreclosure could reattach to it when you buy it back, making you again responsible for paying off the lien holders. To prevent this from occurring, the investor must negotiate with the junior lien holders to release their liens.

To make sure the junior liens are erased, have a title company handle the closing and insure the title at the time of purchase with the understanding that a foreclosure has taken place. Another option is to ask the investor to contact junior lien holders prior to expiration of the sheriff's deed or even before foreclosing and offer a nominal payment in return for a discharge of their liens. The recorded discharges should satisfy any concerns.

Selling your home and renting it back

Bad stuff always seems to happen at the worst times, and foreclosure is no different. Maybe your kids are still in school, or you found a new job in another state but it doesn't start for two months and you need a place to stay until then. In situations like these, selling to an investor and then renting the property for a short time can be a very attractive solution. Simply put, you sell your home now and move when it's convenient for you.

As long as you haven't trashed the premises, an investor may be willing to go along with a deal. After all, it prevents him from having to line up tenants right away.

Ditching the Property

If, as Shakespeare wrote, all the world's a stage, then maybe you can exit stage left and leave all your problems in your past, including that ball and chain you've called a home. Although this is certainly an option, some ways of vacating the premises are better than others, as we reveal in the following sections.

Exchanging a deed in lieu of foreclosure

For homeowners who are unable to make mortgage payments (even significantly lower payments) and can't sell the property and at least break even on the sale, the lender may accept the deed in lieu of foreclosure. You sign your property rights over to your lender, vacate by an agreed-upon date, and your lender cancels your debt.

If you choose this option, hire an attorney to review the paperwork before you sign anything. You want a deal that lets you walk away totally debt-free and prohibits the lender from pursuing a deficiency judgment.

In some cases, the lender may be willing to pay you a small amount in exchange for keys and leaving the property "broom clean," which means you can move to more affordable housing. A variation on this cash-for-keys deal is a time-for-keys deal, in which the lender allows you to remain on the premises for some additional time (rent-free or rent-lite) to have someone look after the place and make it look lived in, which usually helps the property sell faster and for more money.

Living rent-free through redemption

You considered all your options and resigned yourself to the fact that you can't save your home, or maybe you're just not willing to do what it would take to save it. That's okay, but don't be in such a big hurry to move out. A little procrastination may get you back on your feet, especially if you live in a state that has a lengthy redemption period.

Here's how this strategy works: Your lender can't have you evicted until after the foreclosure sale *and* after the redemption period. In states like Michigan, that period can be as long as 6 months in most cases and 12 months in others. This means you can live in the property rent-free until your redemption period expires. Save up all that money, and you'll be in a much better financial position to move on with your life later.

In states with redemption periods, particularly lengthy redemption periods, unethical or ill-informed investors often try to intimidate or trick homeowners into moving out before the law requires. Don't fall for it. Call your county register of deeds or a local foreclosure attorney and ask for an explanation of your redemption rights. If you move out voluntarily or abandon the house, even if you're tricked into doing so, you may compromise or relinquish your rights.

If you're facing a deficiency judgment, as discussed in the previous section, you may be able to trade your redemption rights for a discharge of the deficiency. Discuss this option with your attorney.

Jingle mail

In the months following the worst of the financial crisis, many frustrated homeowners simply mailed their house keys back to their lenders. The phenomena spawned a cute but unfunny abandonment term known as *jingle mail* because of the sound that keys made inside envelopes mailed to lenders.

In many cases homeowners had better options, but some didn't know where to turn and became so frustrated with their lenders that they just threw up their hands, dropped the keys in the mail, and walked away. Obviously, this isn't something we recommend.

You may need to move out earlier than planned, but you can move without that debt following you.

Abandoning the property

Some homeowners become so discouraged that they don't even consider working out a solution with their lenders. They simply cram as many valuables as will fit into the family van and drive off to greener pastures, leaving the debt, the house, and the problems to someone else to sort out.

 Although abandoning ship is certainly an option, it's not always a good option because it can leave legal strings untied. In some jurisdictions, for example, the lender can sell the house at auction and then pursue a deficiency judgment against you for the difference between what the house sold for and the balance of the mortgage. In addition, abandoning your home can leave a blemish on your credit history that follows you for many years, and it's certainly not a neighborly thing to do.

Redeeming the Property Post-Auction

Many states give homeowners one last chance to save their homes from foreclosure through *redemption*. With redemption, you have the right to buy back the property from the investor or the bank that purchased it at the auction sale. To redeem your property, you need to pay the investor or the bank the full amount paid for the property at auction, plus any qualifying expenses.

Don't redeem the property unless you truly can afford to make payments on any loan you can secure to redeem the property. Otherwise, you're likely to find yourself facing foreclosure again really soon.

The sheriff in charge of foreclosure sales in your area or the public land recorder (register of deeds) can tell you the amount you need to redeem the property and the person you need to pay, or they can direct you to the right person for more information. When you know the amount and who you owe, you can head down with a certified check to pay the amount in full.

State redemption rules vary. To make sure you comply with them, contact your county deeds office, the county courthouse, your state attorney general (see Appendix A for contact information), or a foreclosure attorney in your area. Don't leave this to the last minute. Look into the procedure early so you know your rights and responsibilities. Spending some time educating yourself on the foreclosure process in your state (that includes redemption requirements) can keep you from being taken advantage of later by unscrupulous individuals looking to con you out of your house.

Doing Nothing — A Terrible Choice

One of the worst options (second only to falling victim to a foreclosure rescue scam) is to do nothing, in which case you lose your home along with any equity you may have had in it and then suffer the humiliation of being evicted.

Unfortunately, this is the option that some homeowners choose. They try to sweep the problem under the rug. Even worse, they try to hide the bad news from their partners. Too often, they succeed for a time, but the partners always find out — usually when it's too late to do anything about it.

Don't be clueless. If you own your home with your significant other, set aside some time every week (or at least once a month) to review your finances and pay the bills together. We've witnessed several instances in which the partner who was supposed to be paying the bills wasn't and kept the other in the dark when the default notices arrived. Working together, you can hold one another accountable.

If you're single and have no dependants, you're free to go down the path of inaction, but if others, especially children, depend on you, doing nothing is truly not an option. We haven't seen any studies that measure the effect of a full-blown eviction on the mental health of a child, but one could guess that the memory of such an event would be slow to fade and maybe never entirely forgotten.

The sooner you take action, the more options you have and the more time you have to explore those options. Ignoring the problem won't make it go away. It will only make it worse.

Keeping an Eye Open for Brand-New Options

Although we made every effort in this chapter to cover all the alternatives to foreclosure, we've probably left a couple out — not through any fault of our own but simply because new options are constantly popping up as government agencies, consumer advocacy groups, and lenders search for ways to save homeowners from foreclosure.

To find out about new programs and options, follow these recommendations to do some additional research:

- ✔ **Contact your lender and ask about any special programs it's offering to help distressed homeowners.** You may be able to find this information online. Refer to Appendix A for a list of lender Web sites and phone numbers.

- ✔ **Visit the HUD Web site, www.hud.gov, to find announcements about government-sponsored programs.** HUD is the U.S. Department of Housing and Urban Development.

- ✔ **Visit the U.S. Department of the Treasury's Financial Stability Web site, www.financialstability.gov, where you can find additional information about homeowner relief programs sponsored by the federal government.** This site also contains a link to the Making Home Affordable Web site at www.makinghomeaffordable.gov.

- ✔ **Visit the Fannie Mae Web site, www.fanniemae.com, to see if Fannie Mae is offering any new homeowner relief programs, or ask your mortgage broker to look into it.**

- ✔ **Contact your state attorney general's office (see Appendix A for contact information).** The AG's office sometimes knows where struggling homeowners can turn for help. A recent example is when the attorney general of California sued a lender for predatory lending and fraudulent lending activity. As part of the nationwide settlement, the lender agreed to modify loans for homeowners.

> ✓ **Contact HOPE NOW by calling 1-888-995-HOPE (4673) or visiting www.hopenow.com.** HOPE NOW is an alliance between HUD-approved counseling agents, servicers, investors, and other mortgage market participants that provides free foreclosure prevention assistance.

Remaining open to alternatives

In the early days of the mortgage meltdown, lenders tended to be less receptive to requests for loan modifications and often led distressed homeowners to believe that they had only two options: pay up or move out. I (Ralph) met a couple who were on the receiving end of such misleading messages from their lender. All the phone conversations and correspondence they exchanged with their lender had the same underlying theme: pay up or move out.

When I met with the couple, I advised them to put a slightly different spin on the message. Perhaps what the lender was really saying was, "Start paying again with a lower, modified payment, or move." And this is exactly what we sought to accomplish through a loan modification.

This couple was a textbook case of a hardship-triggered default. The wife had contracted a serious medical condition resulting in huge medical bills, and the downturn in the economy had landed a second blow to their household income. Still, the couple was committed to keeping their home, if they could afford it.

Together, we waded through the lender's loan modification requirements and submitted an application. A couple of weeks later, the lender made its initial offer, reducing the couple's monthly mortgage payment, but not to a level the couple felt confident they could afford paying. They requested a better deal with a more affordable house payment, but the lender wouldn't budge.

After wrestling with the decision of whether to sign the agreement, the couple, overwhelmed with medical bills and other debt, rejected the lender's offer. Knowing rejection would result in an inevitable foreclosure, the couple braced for the worst, continued exploring other options, and eventually decided to declare bankruptcy.

Through bankruptcy, they were able to give themselves a fresh start. The bankruptcy erased their medical bills and other unsecured debt, freeing up hundreds of dollars a month. The couple did lose their home, but with the drop in property values, they were able to purchase a much more affordable home — a new home for their new life.

Keep in mind that loan modification isn't always the best option, and it's really not an option if you can't modify to true affordability. Explore all your options, even those you may not want to consider, such as bankruptcy.

Chapter 4

Deciding Whether to Team Up with a Pro or Fly Solo

In This Chapter

▶ Hiring an expert . . . or not

▶ Knowing whom you can turn to for help

▶ Selecting a qualified professional

▶ Collaborating to achieve optimum results

*Y*ou've probably heard the expression that a person who represents himself in court has a fool for a client. This often applies to loan modification, too. Although you may be able to achieve some level of success by dealing directly with a reputable and cooperative lender, you can save time, effort, and anguish by hiring a professional to protect your interests. Having professional representation is even more important when the lender is inaccessible or unwilling to work out a solution.

In this chapter, we examine the pros and cons of hiring a loan modification expert, show you what to expect from such an expert and how to choose the right company or individual, and suggest ways you can team up with the expert to secure the best deal possible from your lender.

Weighing the Pros and Cons of Hiring a Professional

If you type "loan modification" into a search engine, you're going to get conflicting advice. Loan modification companies tell you to hire a professional. People hawking do-it-yourself loan modification kits and books (like this one?!) encourage you to do it yourself. Lenders encourage homeowners to "call us," because they don't want to have to deal with an attorney who may gum up the works.

Hire a pro or give up?

Many times, the choice isn't whether to hire a pro or fly solo but rather whether to hire a pro or give up. We worked with a couple who chose to hire a professional rather than give up their quest for a loan modification. They'd struggled for months to convince their lender to work with them on a loan modification. The lender was habitually difficult to contact, and when the couple finally got through, the lender routed them through a complex maze of departments that ultimately left them at a dead end. Instead of giving up, this couple contacted us.

Initially, the lender forced us to jump through the same hoops, but fortunately, we had experience on our side. Having developed a few tricks of our own for moving past the gatekeepers, we knew which questions to ask, which answers to give, which department to request, and whom we needed to speak with to get something accomplished.

Quickly, we discovered exactly what the lender required. We assisted the borrowers in gathering the information and documentation needed to complete and submit the paperwork. We gave the couple a timeline, so they knew when the lender would be likely to present an offer, which greatly reduced their anxiety over having to wait. We also informed them that the lender's first offer usually isn't its best offer, so they should expect further negotiations.

When the lender finally presented its offer, we were able to sit down with the couple and decide whether the monthly payment was truly affordable based on their budget. We then negotiated on the couple's behalf to obtain a truly affordable monthly payment.

When the going gets tough, the tough persist . . . or hire professionals who are likely equipped with the experience and resources to succeed.

We think most homeowners are better off hiring professionals to represent their interests. Although I (Ralph) tell people they can do it themselves (with the assistance of this book, of course), I also advise them that their interests may be better protected by working through a qualified and experienced third-party representative. In the following sections, you begin to understand why.

Examining the pros

Most people don't hesitate to call a professional when they need to borrow money, buy a home, plan for their retirement, or even fix a leaky faucet. When considering a loan modification, however, they assume they can negotiate a good deal with their lender on their own. This is certainly understandable. After all, lenders are experts, and if they truly want a long-term solution, they should be willing to arrange a deal that works for both parties.

The trouble is that lenders tend to protect their own interests. They have to earn a profit, and they expect people who borrowed from them to honor the terms of their original agreement. As a result, lenders often reject loan modification applications because they believe the borrowers can afford their payments or could afford to make their payments if they would only budget more carefully.

Hiring a qualified professional ensures that you have someone looking out for your interests. Following are additional reasons you should at least consider hiring a loan expert to represent you.

Assistance in evaluating all your options

Although a loan modification is the best option for most home-owners facing foreclosure, it's not the best option in every case. Filing for bankruptcy, refinancing with another lender, or selling your home may be more advantageous, as explained in Chapter 3. An expert can help you analyze your situation and explore other options. If your lender doesn't approve your request for a loan modification, the expert can often refer you to an expert who can assist you in pursuing another option.

Increased chance of getting your application approved

You may have only one shot at submitting your loan modification application correctly. The high demand for loan modifications has made lenders very selective in which applications they accept and ultimately approve. An expert who's familiar with the ins and outs of the system can ensure that you submit a complete and correct loan application that puts your best foot forward.

An ethical loan modification expert won't falsify or alter documentation — and neither should you — but an expert can give you an advantage by presenting the facts in a way that puts your case in a more favorable light.

Experience working with lenders

An experienced professional who knows all the right things to say and the right programs to ask for has a distinct advantage. Lenders are swamped with callers seeking loan modifications who don't really know what they want or how to ask for it. When a lender's representative picks up the phone and realizes that she's dealing with a professional who knows the language, she can cut to the chase without having to educate the caller.

For every one of you, 5,000 more distressed homeowners are wait-ing on hold. An experienced expert can make the lender's job much easier, improving your chances of gaining a more favorable out-come. (If your lender is participating in a government-sponsored home retention program, it must adhere to the government's established guidelines, in which case a third party can offer you no advantage in this respect.)

Able to take the loan modification hassles off your plate

Unless you're out of work (in which case you're unlikely to qualify for a loan modification anyway) and have all day to spend on the phone with your lender, you probably won't have the time to get it done. Some lenders haven't adjusted their hours beyond the 8-to-5 workday. (Don't forget the time-zone issue, too.) If you're working and struggling to make your monthly payments, you probably can't afford a day off work to haggle with your lender. A professional who does this for a living makes the time.

Hiring a pro doesn't mean that your job is done. You still have to gather documents and complete some forms (see Chapter 6), explain the situation to your representative, assist in writing the hardship letter and your financial statement (see Chapter 8), and perhaps meet with the lender for a homeowner interview (see Chapter 10). After you've done all that, the loan modification expert handles the rest, but be prepared to pitch in when called upon to do so (see "Teaming Up with Your Representative" for details).

If the lender calls you directly to discuss material matters that could affect the success (or failure) of your modification, be careful what you say. Gather as much information as you can about what the lender is asking you to do and then politely explain that you will discuss all these matters with your representative. Of course, don't forget to make a notation in the phone-conversation log you're keeping (see Chapter 9).

Freedom from emotional baggage

Anyone who negotiates for a living can tell you that you need to leave your emotions at the door. However, most homeowners aren't equipped to remain calm, cool, and collected when facing the prospect of losing a home.

Emotions can undermine your efforts in two ways. They can cloud your judgment, leading to poor decisions, and they can make you angry, leading to arguments. Irrational homeowners tend to get "accidentally" disconnected when they call their lenders. A professional can address issues matter-of-factly, so the lender's representative is more likely to cooperate.

Analyzing the cons

Hiring a skilled professional almost always delivers better results than trying to get your loan modified yourself. Think back to the last do-it-yourself home-improvement project you tackled. You probably saved some money, but the project consumed more of your time and may not have turned out quite as well as if you had hired a skilled contractor. Yet, hiring a loan modification expert has some potential drawbacks, as discussed in the following sections.

Cost

The biggest drawback is cost: Professionals may charge thousands of dollars, especially some of the better attorney-based services that charge retainers. When you're already strapped for cash, coming up with a few thousand bucks is no small feat. (We offer some tips for pulling the money together in the later section "Scraping Together Money for Upfront Fees.")

A good loan modification service often pays for itself in the amount of money it saves you over the life of the loan. If the expert can negotiate a payment that's a modest $100 less per month than you could negotiate on your own, that represents $1,200 per year or $36,000 over the life of a 30-year mortgage. In addition, the representative can often steer you clear of other legal pitfalls that could really cause you headaches down the road.

No guarantee of a successful loan modification

A loan modification service can offer a money-back guarantee, but it can't promise to successfully negotiate a loan modification on your behalf. The ultimate decision to modify or not falls to the lender; if it's not willing to modify, you can do little to force its hand (unless proof of fraud or significant regulatory violations is evident in the loan origination or processing, as discussed in Chapters 13 and 14). Some companies will return a portion of your fee if they can't secure an affordable loan modification.

Personality test: Can you take the backseat?

A professional keeps you one step removed from the action, which can be good or bad depending on your situation and personality.

If you're the kind of person who needs to know exactly what's going on, who said what, how they said it, and so on, being removed from the action can cause a lot of anxiety. On the other hand, if you prefer having someone else handle all the details and navigate the bumps in the road, you'll appreciate having a pro attend to the details. (Even if you hire a professional to represent you, keep close contact to ensure progress is being made.)

A money-back guarantee doesn't automatically mean that the company is reputable. Con artists often prey on people who can least afford to be scammed. Although falling victim to a con artist is always possible, you can significantly decrease your odds of becoming a victim by choosing a reputable service (see "Choosing the Right Individual or Company" later in this chapter for details).

Identifying Professionals Who Can Assist You

The increasing demand for loan modifications has attracted the attention of skilled and knowledgeable professionals in various fields. Some of these professionals have seen their incomes drop as a result of the recession and are looking for other ways to put their skills to good use to make up for lost income. Others are genuinely committed to helping homeowners and earn a fair profit doing so.

Some of these professionals are more qualified than others to negotiate loan modifications. In the following sections, we describe professionals who are likely to have the knowledge and skills required, and we provide some guidance about which are likely to be the most qualified as a group.

Although we can provide some general guidelines that rate particular groups, we can't offer advice on choosing a particular individual. Every profession has its share of standouts and hacks, so you must judge each person on his or her own merits, experience, and reputation.

Loan modification attorney

Admittedly, "loan modification attorney" is a bit of a made-up title. Nobody goes to law school to become a loan modification attorney. This term merely describes attorneys currently focusing on getting loan modifications for their clients. Even if it's not what they do all day long, they have experience providing this service to their clients. A loan modification attorney is usually the best choice because she

✔ Carries more weight than a layperson in terms of credibility and legal clout. Lenders tend to listen more carefully and respond more quickly when contacted by an attorney.

✔ Knows the laws that the lender must adhere to and can use those laws as leverage to persuade the lender to negotiate and offer you a more attractive deal.

✔ Is answerable to the Bar Association in the state in which she operates. This provides you with consumer protection.

✔ Is well connected with lenders. Especially if all an attorney does all day is loan modifications, she quickly identifies the strategies that work with specific lenders.

Foreclosure attorney

A foreclosure attorney (the type that represents borrowers, not lenders) is a pretty good choice. These folks have plenty of experience working with lenders and should be well aware of all the foreclosure alternatives available to you (see Chapter 3).

A foreclosure attorney is also better equipped than most attorneys and other professionals listed in this section to identify incidents in which the lender failed to adhere to a foreclosure rule or regulation; for example, she knows that a lender is in violation when it has posted the foreclosure notice for only four weeks when your state law requires that it be posted for five weeks. This may seem like a small point, but a foreclosure attorney can use this kind of error to stop a foreclosure in its tracks, buy you several extra weeks or months to pursue other options, and perhaps even negotiate an attractive loan modification with your lender.

Bankruptcy attorney

If you're buried in unsecured debt, such as credit card debt, a bankruptcy attorney may be the absolute best choice for you. Bankruptcy can often discharge the unsecured debt. In addition, in bankruptcy, certain assets are shielded from your creditors through exemptions. State exemptions vary a great deal from state to state, so a bankruptcy attorney can explain which assets are exempt, whether bankruptcy would be better than a loan modification, and whether bankruptcy with a loan modification is an option.

One potential problem with choosing a bankruptcy attorney is that the person may be more likely to recommend bankruptcy than other solutions that may be better for you or that you would prefer if you knew all your options.

Real estate attorney

Real estate attorneys tend to be more general-purpose legal eagles than bankruptcy or foreclosure attorneys. They deal primarily with agreements between buyers and sellers and disagreements over property lines and other real estate-related issues. A good real estate attorney, however, should be well qualified to negotiate a loan modification with your lender.

Ask the attorney about her experience in negotiating loan modifications. If she's done only one or two, you may want to look for someone who's had more time behind the wheel. Consider looking for a referral to an attorney who has successfully helped someone you know through a similar situation.

Credit counselor

The primary job of a credit counselor is to assist consumers in getting their financial houses in order primarily by slashing discretionary spending. Early in the process, however, a good credit counselor examines all your outstanding debt and tries to figure out ways to make your payments on that debt more affordable. Frequently, credit counselors negotiate with creditors to work out payment plans. As a result, credit counselors usually have the experience necessary to negotiate loan modifications.

If you authorize your credit counselor to negotiate your loan modification, we recommend that you have your attorney review the agreement before you sign it. (In this case, a general-purpose attorney is usually sufficient in helping to protect your rights.)

Many credit counselors are on the payrolls of organizations supported by credit card companies and other lending institutions, so they're more answerable to your creditors than they are to you. When choosing a credit counselor, ask lots of questions:

- ✔ Are you a division of or do you have an affiliation with any credit card company?

- ✔ Do you have a parent company? If yes, what's the parent company's name?

- ✔ How do you get paid? (Is another company funding the service?)

- ✔ Do you need to be licensed to operate in my state? If yes, are you licensed to operate in my state? Is your headquarters out of state?

Research to verify the answers you get. You can contact your secretary of state's office to find out whether the company is licensed (or needs to be) and to obtain a copy of the company's license. In the later section "Choosing the Right Individual or Company," we provide some guidance on choosing a reputable loan modification expert. Many of these same techniques are effective in choosing a reputable credit counselor.

Real estate agent

Homeowners often assume that all real estate agents do is assist clients in selling or buying homes. What homeowners tend to overlook is the fact that real estate agents are, by trade, successful salespeople and tough negotiators. A seasoned agent also knows the market — property values and trends — and is well aware of what the lender stands to lose through foreclosure. An agent can use this knowledge to negotiate an attractive workout deal for you.

An agent can also list and sell the home for you, in the event that you need or want to sell your home. If you're looking at the possibility of selling the home at a loss, your agent may even be able to negotiate a short sale with your lender that allows you to break even on the sale or even earn a small profit. (For more about short sales, see Chapter 3.)

One potential drawback to negotiating through an agent is that agents don't have the legal designation that often carries so much weight in dealing with lenders. Some states have rules that govern an agent's eligibility for negotiating loan modifications, so make sure the agent you're considering has satisfied them all.

Don't choose just any old real estate agent. Make sure the agent is a licensed Realtor — a member of the National Association of Realtors (NAR). The NAR requires its members to complete additional training and testing and encourages members to follow a strict code of ethics. If you're looking for an agent to handle a short sale, limit your search to agents in multiperson offices of at least 25 agents, and ask whether someone there has an expertise in short sales. Many agents don't even know what a short sale is.

Mortgage broker or loan officer

Many people stung by the mortgage meltdown are adamant against letting mortgage brokers or loan officers negotiate loan modifications. They blame these mortgage professionals for contributing to the problem and can't accept the possibility that these same people could potentially profit from the fallout.

This is an ethical issue that we're not about to tackle in this book. The question right now is whether a mortgage broker or loan officer is qualified to negotiate a loan modification on your behalf, and the answer is yes. Whether you want to negotiate through a broker or loan officer is another question — actually two questions:

- ✔ Can you trust someone who possibly placed borrowers into risky mortgages to negotiate an affordable modification for you now? (In particular, avoid the broker turned loan modification expert who placed you with the bad loan in the first place.)

- ✔ Is a mortgage broker or loan officer going to represent the best interests of you or your lender? A conflict of interest can easily result if the person representing you has a buddy-buddy relationship with the lender. Make sure your engagement agreement spells out that the person is representing you.

Choosing the Right Individual or Company

Whether you're in the market for an attorney, a real estate agent, or some other professional to represent you in your quest for a loan modification, you need to locate some potentially qualified candidates, gather information about them, and then whittle down your list until you find the best individual or company for the job. It also helps to know the common warning signs that illegitimate outfits emit, so you can steer clear of the worst ones.

In the following sections, we provide guidance and insight that empower you to perform your due diligence and track down the top professionals in your area.

Although you shouldn't rush your decision, time is most certainly of the essence, so work quickly.

Locating qualified candidates

One of the best ways to find a reputable loan modification expert is to obtain referrals from people you already know and trust who've hired the expert to represent them. Unfortunately, that can leave you with a very shallow pool to draw from. Here are some other suggestions for tracking down reputable, qualified candidates:

- ✔ **Contact local real estate brokers.** They should know attorneys in the area who are experienced in negotiating with mortgage lenders, including foreclosure, bankruptcy, and loan modification attorneys (see the earlier sections in this chapter for more info on each of these pros).

- ✔ **Call the local branch of your state Bar Association.** Someone there can direct you to an attorney who deals with situations such as the one you're facing.

✔ **Ask at your bank if you feel comfortable doing so.** You may not want to reveal your current financial woes to your friendly neighborhood bank, but if you do, the bank's manager may be able to offer a valuable reference.

Obtain the names of at least three companies or individuals who look like the most promising candidates, and then start vetting them, as discussed in the following section.

Doing some detective work

Before giving any company or individual on your list serious consideration, perform your own background check. Here's how:

✔ **Search the Internet for the company or individual, and read any comments that people have posted.** Don't rule out a service just because it has one or two rip-off complaint reports. If it does a lot of loan modifications, it's likely to have at least a couple of disgruntled customers. Be sure to ask about them though, and evaluate the representative's response.

✔ **If the candidate has a Web site, visit it.** Cross any candidate off your list whose Web site looks unprofessional. If the Web site looks shoddy, the loan modification application the service prepares for you will be just as bad or worse.

✔ **Obtain the company's street address and phone number, and do a reverse phone number lookup on the Web to see if the phone number and address match.**

✔ **Check the candidate's Web site or call and ask for a brochure or any additional materials the company can send you, including testimonials from past clients.** If the company can't supply additional information, cross it off your list.

✔ **Find out the names of the people who own or manage the operation, and run those names through your favorite online search engine.** If the owners/managers have professional designations, certifications, or affiliations, check with the certifying authority to verify the information and make sure no complaints that have merit have been filed against the person. For example, if the person is an attorney, check with the Bar Association in the state in which the person practices. If the person claims to be a Realtor, check with the National Association of Realtors (NAR).

Asking the right questions

Call the company or individual, explain that you need assistance negotiating a loan modification with your lender, and ask what the company or individual can do for you. Talk with a representative to see if you would feel comfortable working with him.

Don't give any sensitive information over the phone, such as your mortgage identification number, Social Security or driver's license number, or credit card information, until you're comfortable working with the service.

When you contact a company or service, ask the person you're speaking with the following questions:

- **Who will be negotiating my loan modification?** What are the person's credentials? Preferably the person is an attorney who specializes in loan modifications.

- **How successful is the service?** How many loan modification cases has the service taken on? Of those, how many clients have received affordable loan modifications? A service that has done hundreds of loan modifications and has a 75 percent or better average is pretty good. Having one satisfied customer creates a 100 percent average, but that's not saying much.

- **How many prospective clients have you turned away?** You want a service that's selective and doesn't just sign up everyone who calls.

- **How much do you charge?** The service should be able to quote you a price. A few thousand dollars may be reasonable. Ten thousand dollars is way too high.

- **Do I have to pay upfront?** Although many experts advise against paying upfront for services, charging upfront fees is standard business for attorneys. Just make sure the service is legitimate.

- **What is your refund policy?** This is good to know, but we can recommend no right answer. When you hire a professional to represent you, it's sort of like hiring a doctor to treat an illness — if he doesn't cure you, you still have to pay the bill. In addition, a 100 percent money-back guarantee doesn't replace skill, experience, or dedication. The best answer is probably that clients must pay for the service regardless of success and receive a refund for any unearned fees if the service can't negotiate an affordable loan modification. But even a refund policy like this can be corrupted, as explained in the nearby sidebar "Playing the arbitrage."

- **How many hours does an attorney spend on my file?** Having a licensed attorney doing most of the work is usually best. With some services, paralegals, legal assistants, file clerks, or customer service reps do most of the work, which is okay as long as a qualified attorney remains in charge and steps in when required.

✔ **If I reject the lender's offer, do I get a refund?** Anyone can negotiate a lousy loan modification and then justify the fee by claiming success. You want to make sure the service is dedicated to negotiating an *affordable* loan modification.

✔ **Will I meet with an attorney? Can I come to your office?** Meeting with an attorney face to face helps you avoid getting scammed by a company that just has a pretty face on the Internet or in an advertisement.

✔ **I'm also considering Company XYZ. Are you familiar with them?** Watch out for companies that are willing to immediately disparage the competition. You want to hear something like, "No, I'm not familiar with them," or "They're a good company. You'll have to decide for yourself who will best represent you, but let me tell you a little about our company/firm to help you make that decision."

✔ **How long has the company been around? How long have you been with the company? What's your background? What's the employee turnover like?** A well-established company with a low turnover rate that's staffed by highly qualified professionals is usually better than a company that just opened for business last week.

 Some states have restrictions on who's legally allowed to charge upfront fees for loan modifications. In California, for example, attorneys can collect an upfront fee from clients they represent, but other real estate broker services that want to charge fees upfront must first register with and have their services contract on file with the California Department of Real Estate. Your state attorney general can explain any laws — related to upfront fees and more — designed to regulate loan modification in your state. See Appendix A for a directory of state attorneys general.

Making an informed choice

In many cases, the process of gathering information about various service providers reveals a clear winner. If you're still not sure which candidate on your list is best, see how each one stacks up in terms of the following:

✔ **Does the individual/company seem legitimate?** If you can verify the individual's or company's existence, address, and phone number; determine that it's providing satisfactory service to most clients; and know it's in good standing with its professional associations, it's probably legitimate.

✔ **Did the person you speak with seem competent?** If the person you spoke with sounded as though he knew less about loan modification than you do, you can safely scratch this candidate off your list.

✔ **Did the person you speak with ask *you* the right questions?** Before asking for your money, the rep should ask questions to determine whether you're likely to qualify for a loan modification. The questions should cover facts such as whether you have a job; how much you owe; how many payments you've missed; what hardship you experienced; whether you've contacted your lender; and if you contacted your lender, what your lender said.

Congratulations! You made it through a grueling selection process. Hopefully, you've chosen a service that you're comfortable hiring to represent you. If you managed to scratch everyone off your list, go back to "Choosing the Right Individual or Company" and start over. Don't choose a service unless you feel comfortable with it.

Avoiding clever schemes and scams

Assuming you followed our advice and selected a reputable loan modification service, you don't need to worry about loan modification scams and schemes. However, we'd be remiss if we failed to mention some of the clever con games that have emerged to take advantage of distressed homeowners:

✔ **Take the money and run:** An individual or phony company charges an upfront fee and does nothing for you.

✔ **Foreclosure rescue on legal technicalities:** The con artist tries to convince you that your mortgage is invalid, usually because the big bad government just fires up its printing press to print the money for the big bad banks. For a few thousand dollars, the con artist promises to take the matter to court and prove that you don't owe the money. Unfortunately, you do owe it.

✔ **Foreclosure rescue buy-rent-redeem:** The con artist offers to buy your home and let you lease it until an investor purchases the home at the foreclosure sale, at which time, the con artist promises to redeem the property and sell it back to you. Trouble is, the con artist has no intention of redeeming the property. He just collects the rent payments for a time and disappears.

Playing the arbitrage

Disreputable services have been known to "play the arbitrage." They offer a partial refund and sign up customers but have no intention of helping those customers. They may collect $2,000 upfront, knowing they'll be refunding $1,500 in 90 days.

Prospective customers see the refund policy and think the service is legit, but the company does little or nothing to pursue a loan modification on their behalf. Ninety days later, the service refunds the $1,500, keeping $500 for doing nothing. The customer doesn't complain because the service provided the partial refund as promised. Do your homework, as outlined in the "Choosing the Right Individual or Company" section in this chapter, to avoid finding yourself in this situation.

Be particularly suspicious of anyone who shows up at your door offering to help you, especially if the person asks you to sign over a deed to your property. This is one of the most common red flags of a foreclosure scam. As soon as the person has a deed to your property, he can record the deed with the county register to become the new owner. The fraudster may then try to evict you; take out another loan against the property; or collect rent or fees from you, let the property go through foreclosure, and then disappear with the cash.

Scraping Together Money for Upfront Fees

When you're up to your gills in debt, how do you go about drumming up several thousand dollars for a loan modification, especially to a company that charges its fees upfront? Well, you have a few options:

- ✔ Seek a loan from relatives or friends — people currently in a position to assist you financially.

- ✔ Divert financial resources toward solving the problem rather than putting out fires. We're not advising you to stop making payments, but if you can't afford a full payment, your lender is unlikely to accept a partial payment, so using that partial payment to hire someone who can fix the problem may be a good investment.

- ✔ Work out a payment plan to cover the cost of the company's service. You should expect to have to pay something upfront, but the company may accept an installment plan.

You may be able to keep your attorney costs down by doing much of the heavy lifting on your own — placing phone calls, filing your application, and submitting supporting documentation. You can then call on the attorney to look over the paperwork. However, keep your attorney in the loop from the very beginning.

Teaming Up with Your Representative

In the best of all possible worlds, you could tell your loan modification expert your lender's name and your mortgage identification number, and the person could hammer out the details with your lender. Although that's pretty close to how it goes in the real world, you need to do some work upfront and team up with your representative for optimum results. Following are some suggestions:

- **Come clean.** Whatever the reason you ended up in this situation, come clean about it. Concealing information that's embarrassing or that you fear may hurt your chances of getting a loan modification can backfire. First, anything you hold back may be exactly what the expert needs to prove you qualify. Second, if the lender discovers something you failed to disclose, you could ruin your chances of getting a loan modification.

- **Deliver the goods.** Obtain all the documents your representative asks for and deliver them on time or ahead of schedule. See Chapter 6 for a list of documents typically required.

- **Let your rep do her job.** Don't micromanage the process or call every day for updates. The more time your representative spends on the phone assuring you that everything is being taken care of, the less time she has to take care of things.

- **Stay in the loop.** You don't want to badger your representative, but you should check in once a week if you haven't heard anything.

Ask your representative to provide you with a timeline, including a schedule of when she's going to contact you with updates so you know what to expect.

After you hire a professional to represent you, stop contacting the lender directly and don't discuss the matter with any of the lender's representatives if they call you. Refer the matter to the person who's representing you. Otherwise, you may say something that could compromise your representative's ability to negotiate an attractive deal on your behalf.

Part II

Kick-Starting the Process: Applying for a Loan Modification

The 5th Wave   By Rich Tennant

"I'm well aware that we ask for a lot when people apply for a loan modification, Mr. Harvey. However, sarcasm is rarely required."

In this part . . .

Your first goal in obtaining an affordable loan modification is to get past the gatekeepers — the lender's frontline defense. Typically overworked, overwhelmed, and underpaid, these folks are often looking for the path of least resistance; in some cases that means rejecting your request for a loan modification. Next in line, please. And if you fail to deliver to the right person all the required items in the right format, at the right time, and signed in all the right places, you've just given the gatekeepers the excuse they've been looking for.

The good news is that we're watching your back. In this part, we tell you how to contact your lender (online or off) to determine exactly what your loan modification application must include. We lead you through the process of gathering the facts, figures, and documentation required for your application. We reveal the various ways your lender can modify your mortgage so you have a better idea of what to ask for. Finally, we show you how to prepare and submit your application and then follow up to make sure it lands on the desk of someone who can and will assist you.

Chapter 5

First Things First: Contacting Your Lender

*A*pplying for a loan modification is like applying for a job. When applying for a job, you can significantly improve your chances of success by researching the company and the position you want and tailoring your application and résumé to the company and any openings it has posted.

Likewise, you can improve your chances of having your loan modification application accepted and approved by researching your lender's loan modification guidelines, what it may or may not be willing to modify, and its documentation requirements. This chapter shows you how to gather information from your lender so you can present your application in the most favorable light.

Checking Out Your Lender's Web Site

Almost every business on the planet has a Web site, lenders included, so if you have access to a computer connected to the Internet, fire it up and head to your lender's Web site. Appendix A includes a list of Web site addresses for numerous mortgage lenders. If your lender's not listed there, you have a couple of options:

▶ Check your most recent mortgage statement. It may contain a Web site address, phone number, and e-mail address.

✔ Visit the HOPE NOW Web site at www.hopenow.com, and see if your lender or servicer is included in the list under Find Your Mortgage Company's Website.

✔ Type the name of your lender or servicer into your favorite Internet search engine. A link to your lender's site should pop up at or near the top of the search results.

Clicking your way to something useful

The Web site address lands you on the home page that sort of acts like an information kiosk for everything the lender offers. Carefully inspect the home page, looking for links with words or phrases that apply to your current situation, such as "mortgages," "home mortgages," "avoiding foreclosure," "default," "trouble making payments," "financial hardship," "home retention," and so on; then click the link for more information on that topic.

You may need to poke (and click) around quite a bit to find what you're looking for. On one lender's site we visited, we had to click a link for home financing, another link for mortgages, and then a link for financial hardship programs.

 We spot-checked several Web sites listed in Appendix A and discovered that most (but not all) offer information for customers facing financial hardship. If you look really hard and don't find anything about loan modifications, use the Web site's search box to search the site for key words and phrases like those mentioned earlier in this section, or scroll to the bottom of the page and click the Contact or Contact Us link to find a phone number or e-mail address. Request to be directed to the area on the Web site where you'll find the information you need, or jump straight to the point and request the required information or an application packet to be sent to you via snail mail.

Knowing what to expect

Every lender Web site is different, but if the site offers assistance and information for distressed homeowners, it usually offers this information and assistance in one or more of the following forms:

✔ **A menu of options you can pursue to avoid foreclosure.** This menu may include special refinancing programs, fast-track loan modification, payment plans, or online payment plans. (See Chapter 3 for descriptions of more options.)

✔ **An online form requesting some general information about you and your situation, such as your name, address, phone number, loan number, and reason for financial hardship.** You complete the form, click a button, and a representative follows up with you later — usually by phone.

✔ **A list of documents and information you need to pull together in preparation for speaking with your lender.**

✔ **Printable forms to complete and sign or have someone else sign.** These forms may include an authorization letter giving your representative permission to contact your lender, a financial statement you need to complete, or a hardship letter form. See "Checking Application Requirements" later in this chapter for more on required paperwork.

✔ **Toll-free phone numbers and the lender's hours of operation.**

✔ **A toll-free phone number for contacting a HUD-approved credit counselor.** (HUD stands for the U.S. Department of Housing and Urban Development.)

✔ **Additional details and contact information for consumer assistance programs, such as those offered by HUD and HOPE NOW, which we describe in Appendix A.**

 Be careful when providing the lender with information online or off. The information should be accurate, not give too much away, and be consistent with anything you communicated to the lender in the past or will communicate in the future. Don't offer any deals or say what you're willing to pay. Let the lender make the first offer. It may be a better deal than what you're thinking of asking for. Keep in mind that the gatekeepers may be looking for any excuse to disqualify you, so be careful what you say.

Tracking Down a Representative Who Can Help

Contacting your lender is a snap. You pick up the phone and dial a number. The hard part is working your way to a living, breathing human being with the brain capacity and understanding to help you deal with your current situation. Like other large businesses, lenders can toss all sorts of obstacles in your way, including but certainly not limited to

✔ Automated phone systems that give you nine options to choose from, none of which applies to what you're calling about.

✔ Phone menus that lead to dead ends regardless of the option you choose.

✔ Hours of operation that require you to quit your day job to get anything resolved.

✔ Foreign call centers in countries that don't even have mortgages.

✔ Hold buttons that mysteriously disconnect you rather than placing you on hold.

✔ Representatives who can't locate you in their system even after you give your name, loan number, and your great-great-grandmother's maiden name.

We can't help you much when it comes to your lender's hours of operations. Maybe you can schedule phone calls during your lunch break or work out some flex hours with your supervisor so that you can spend part of your mornings or afternoons on the phone. Another option is to take vacation or personal days or negotiate some comp time so that you can work weekends to make up for time missed during the week.

Devote an hour or two solely to placing phone calls and speaking with representatives. Allowing sufficient time to complete your business can alleviate some of the stress.

In the following sections, we provide suggestions and tips for over-coming the other challenges we mention and moving as quickly as possible from your initial call to someone who can really help.

Making the initial call

The first call is usually the most difficult because you may not have a number that connects you directly with the lender's loss mitigation department. You have to start somewhere, though, so dig up the best phone number you can find by examining the following items:

✔ Any correspondence you received from your lender, including a late payment notice or notice of default

✔ Your most recent mortgage statement

✔ The lender's Web site, as discussed earlier in this chapter in the section "Checking Out Your Lender's Web Site"

✔ Any e-mail messages you received from your lender

As soon as someone picks up and asks how she may help you or direct your call, request the number for the loss mitigation department and jot it down for the next time you call. Don't just ask to speak with someone in the loss mitigation department. In most cases, the operator will give you the number and then offer to transfer you to that department.

Arghhhhh!

Contacting the lender and negotiating a loan modification certainly sounds easy enough, but as many homeowners have discovered, the process can be much more complicated, convoluted, and exasperating than it sounds. Here's a story that's not at all uncommon.

Due to economic hardships, a couple finds they can no longer afford their monthly house payment. Following the advice they've heard from personal finance experts and the federal government, they contact their servicer (the party that collects and processes their mortgage payments) for help.

After several days of frustrating telephone calls and transfers, the couple finally connects with someone who sounds as though she can help. The representative politely collects the couple's financial information and explains that they do indeed qualify for a modification. She'll send them the modification offer. All the couple needs to do is sign the agreement, have it notarized, and return it, and the deal is done. Hurray for the homeowners!

A week passes, and the couple receives nothing from the servicer, so they call to make sure everything is okay. The servicer assures the couple that the modification is pending and they can expect to receive the modification packet "any day now."

Another week passes, and the couple still hasn't received anything from the servicer. They call to check on the status of their application. This time, the representative informs them that they've failed to execute and return the modification package and the time for doing so has expired. After picking their jaws up off the floor, the couple explains that they never received any paperwork or they surely would have executed it and sent it back. They desperately want to save their home.

Again, the representative takes their financials over the phone, explains that they still qualify for a loan modification, and again gives them the terms of that modification. Relieved that they haven't missed the boat, they agree to send back the paperwork immediately after receiving it. Again, the package never arrives. When they call to check up on it, the representative informs them that the lender never received the package from them. Furthermore, due to the couple's repeated failure to respond and return the loan modification agreement, the lender is no longer willing to modify their loan. Fighting back tears, the borrowers are at a loss.

Unfortunately, this isn't an uncommon scenario. You can do everything right and still end up on the wrong side of a raw deal. At this point (and probably even earlier in the process), the couple would be wise to seek legal counsel. The lender obviously can't be trusted.

Bypassing automated systems

If you call and get stuck in one of those automated phone menu systems, try one of the following tricks:

✔ Press zero to bypass the system and get an operator who can transfer your call to the right department. (Many companies are disabling this option because so many people know about it, but it still works with some businesses.)

✔ Wait for the options to cycle through to the end. Sometimes, making no selection is enough to transfer you to an operator. In other cases, instructions at the end tell you what to do to connect to a representative, such as, "If dialing from a rotary phone, please stay on the line, and somebody will be with you shortly." In this case, just pretend you're using a rotary phone and wait it out.

✔ Call the number for new customers. Lenders are often more eager to speak with prospective customers than existing ones. After you get in the door, you can ask to be transferred.

✔ Try a different phone number if you have more than one.

✔ If you're calling from a cellphone, hang up and call back on a land line. Sometimes automated systems have a tough time detecting when buttons are pressed on a cellphone.

Communicating effectively with foreign call centers

When you're dealing with lenders who have outsourced their customer service to foreign lands, all we can recommend is to do your best to deal with the situation. Sometimes, the people manning the phones in a foreign land are actually more helpful than their domestic counterparts. Assuming you can adjust to a certain accent, you'll do just fine. If you can't understand the representative or he can't understand you, here are some suggestions:

✔ Let the person know that you're having trouble understanding him. The "It's not you, it's me" approach can come in very handy here.

✔ Ask to speak to a manager.

✔ Hang up and try again at a different time, during off-peak business hours, such as first thing in the morning. During peak business hours and after business hours, calls are more likely to be diverted to a foreign call center.

CASE STUDY

Talking to the right person makes all the difference

Maria was the family breadwinner and was gainfully employed at the time her family purchased their home. Over the course of four years, she never missed a payment ($1,500 per month). Then, through no fault of her own, she lost her job of 14 years and fell behind on her payments.

She received an Alternative to Foreclosure notice from her lender informing her of her options — loan modification, short sale, or deed in lieu of foreclosure. She called her lender and explained that she had lost her job and was collecting unemployment ($355 per week, $1,420 per month) and supplementing her income with savings.

The person she spoke to showed no compassion, informing Maria that she needed to bring her account current immediately or the lender would foreclose the following month. Afraid of losing her home, Maria agreed to make the $1,960 payment, which consisted of her current monthly payment plus penalties and interest. After making this first payment, she realized she was burning through her savings at an unsustainable rate, so she decided to seek help. She called Ralph.

What Maria failed to realize was that the person she spoke to was the gatekeeper, not anyone who could really help her. When Ralph called, he quickly moved past the gatekeeper to the loss mitigation manager. He had a couple of questions:

✔ How did you expect this homeowner to remain in her home and remain current by giving her a payment arrangement that's not possible to meet or maintain?

✔ What income figures did you use to qualify her for her current payment plan?

Ralph also pointed out that under fair debt collection laws, the lender can't instill fear in the borrower to collect payments. He reminded the loss mitigation manager that this default was foreseeable, that economic conditions were miserable, and that the borrower had an excellent payment history leading up to the default.

As a result, the loss mitigation manager offered Maria a special forbearance, giving her time to find a new job. Maria had to accept a position paying far less than her previous job, so the lender granted her loan modification request, lowering her monthly payment from $1,500.00 to $985.00 with an interest rate reduction from 9.75 to 5.25 percent and a term extension to 40 years.

By speaking to the right person and knowing your rights, you have a much better chance of obtaining a truly affordable loan modification.

TIP

Calling early in the morning has the added benefit of connecting you with someone who's not already exhausted from having to deal with irate customers for eight hours. (Make sure you're calling during off-peak hours in your lender's time zone; 8 a.m. for them could be 5 a.m. for you.)

Hanging up and starting over is also an effective strategy if you're dealing with someone who speaks your language just fine but is uncooperative or incompetent. Calling back usually gives you a second chance with a fresh voice, especially with large lenders. If the fresh voice mentions notes in your file that you just called, say you were disconnected and ask if this person can now assist you.

Taking names and extensions

When you finally reach someone who's helpful, jot down the person's name, identification number, and direct phone number with extension. Having the person's name and direct extension benefits you in several ways, enabling you to

- ✔ More easily contact the person later.

- ✔ Pick up where you left off.

- ✔ Keep a record of the person you spoke with and what that person said, which can come in handy if your case lands in court. In Chapter 9, we provide a log sheet for recording all discussions and correspondence you have with your lender.

 At some companies, the representatives just give their first or last names, which could even be fake. Be ready to write when asking for the person's ID number. Many representatives turn into the world's fastest talkers when asked for their ID numbers.

Describing Your Situation

When you first contact your lender, one of the first things the representative is likely to request is your version of what happened and where you stand — financially speaking.

Chapter 2 tells you how to take stock of your situation. If you haven't yet gone through that process, take some time to do it now — before you discuss your situation with your lender. You may even want to skip ahead to Chapter 8 and write your hardship letter and draft your financial statement before speaking with your lender. Don't read the letter or financial details over the phone — just use them to keep yourself on point. By having the information clear in your own head first, you're much better prepared to lay out the details in an understandable and succinct way.

 Just the facts, ma'am. When recounting your story and describing your finances, present the details as accurately as possible without placing judgment or turning this into a blame game. Treat your situation as a problem that needs to be resolved, not as an opportunity for a verbal boxing match.

Your story should have a beginning, middle, and future, as follows:

- ✔ **Beginning:** Describe the hardship (event or series of events) you experienced that has made it difficult or impossible to catch up on missed payments and/or continue to make your monthly payments.

- ✔ **Middle:** Describe your current financial situation in broad strokes, if possible, to explain just how unaffordable your monthly payments have become. In many cases, the lender wants to prequalify you over the phone by gathering specifics; this is another good reason why you may want to prepare your financial statement in advance (see Chapter 8).

- ✔ **Future:** Express your desire to stay in your home and work out a solution with your lender, but avoid getting knee-deep in details. Save the details for Chapter 8, when you prepare your application and have a clearer idea of the solution you want and changes you need to make to achieve that solution.

If you're unemployed and your lender's representative asks about it, let her know what you're doing to pursue a new job. Saying, "I lost my job, and it ain't coming back" or anything else along those lines is likely to get you tagged in the system as ineligible for a loan modification, which you may be, but at this point, you want to keep your options open as much as possible.

Finding Out What Your Lender Is Willing and Able to Do

Most companies have policies in place so their employees don't have to act rationally or explain anything to customers. For example, if you ask why a store's charging you a 15 percent restocking fee when the salesperson sold you the wrong part, the representative points to the sign behind the counter and says something like "We have a policy of charging a 15 percent restocking fee on all returns." When you ask why, you hear something like, "Because that's our policy."

Lenders have all sorts of policies for rejecting a loan modification request. Some of their restrictions are reasonable. If you're not gainfully employed, for example, you can't afford a house payment, regardless of how much a loan modification would lower your payment. Others vary depending on how aggressively the lender wants to offer relief. At the height of the mortgage crisis, for example, lenders became more motivated to assist homeowners and lifted some of their restrictions.

One of the first questions to ask your lender is "What is your loan modification policy?" or "What are your loan modification eligibility requirements?" If you're ineligible for whatever reason, you want to know early on, so you can

- ✔ Resolve any issues preventing you from qualifying. For example, you may be able to liquidate assets or shed obligations to make yourself eligible.
- ✔ Pursue other options, such as those presented in Chapter 3.
- ✔ Move up the chain of command to someone who may be willing to make an exception in your case.

You may need to clear several hurdles before reaching the ultimate decision maker. Begin with the servicer, but remember that the servicer is probably working within parameters set by the lender, investors, and any other parties that hold a stake in your mortgage. Assuming you qualify and ask for a modification that meets the prerequisites, the servicer can accommodate your request.

If your request falls outside the predetermined parameters, you may be able to get an exception from a loss mitigation supervisor.

What do you mean, you *can't?*

Many homeowners become disgruntled when they contact the company servicing their mortgage and the servicer claims to be unable to help. What homeowners often overlook is the fact that the lender's or servicer's hands may really be tied, as they're claiming.

This isn't the good ol' days when if you had trouble making your mortgage payments you could stroll down to your local bank, discuss your situation with the bank's president, and hammer out a deal. Nowadays, the person you're dealing with may not be the person to whom you owe the money. Several other parties (other than the lender and servicer) may be setting the eligibility rules and deciding which debt-relief programs to offer, including private investors who purchased your mortgage outright or as mortgage-backed securities; hedge funds (managers) that own pools of mortgage-backed securities; Fannie Mae or Freddie Mac (also investors); Federal Housing Administration (FHA) or Veterans Administration (VA) if they're insuring your loan; or the federal government, as it has done with its Making Home Affordable program.

The moral of the story is this: Don't beat up the messenger. You may need to negotiate with the servicer's or lender's representative, but that person may not make the rules. The person you're talking to may have little or no decision-making authority, but she does have the authority to hang up on you if you become belligerent. You'll never get to the decision maker if you offend the gatekeepers.

If the lender/servicer refuses to help you and you have private mortgage insurance (PMI), you may be able to enlist the assistance of your PMI company. Many if not all PMI companies have started operating home retention campaigns. They want to modify the loans so they don't have to pay out on the PMI claims after foreclosure.

Fannie, Freddie, FHA, and VA also can play a role in your modification by working through their approved lenders to offer streamlined loan modifications and other forms of relief to homeowners whose mortgages they own or insure. If your mortgage is owned or insured through any of these parties, visit the party's Web site to look for any relief programs — usually you gain access to such programs through your lender.

On March 4, 2009, the federal government became a major rule-setter when it rolled out its Making Home Affordable (MHA) program. Through this plan, participating lenders must refinance or modify qualifying loans to affordability in accordance with the program's guidelines. For more information about this program, including whether your lender is a participant and whether you qualify for refinancing or modification, visit `makinghomeaffordable.gov`.

Checking Application Requirements

When you first applied for the loan to buy your home, the loan officer or mortgage broker probably asked you a bunch of questions about your finances and required you to deliver a short stack of documents, including one or two federal income tax returns, W-2 forms, recent pay stubs, and so on.

When you apply for a loan modification, your lender's representative is probably going to request the same stuff plus a couple of extra items. If you're asking the investor for a special exception, the investor probably will want to see all your financials documented and verified. When you visit your lender's Web site or speak with a representative, find out

✔ Which forms and other documentation you need to submit.

✔ Where to mail or fax your application.

✔ How long the process is going to take. (Better yet, obtain a detailed timeline for all stages of the process.)

Listing the items required

When you visit your lender's Web site or speak with a representative on the phone, obtain a comprehensive list of required documents. The list is likely to contain the following items:

- ✔ Form for supplying general information
- ✔ Hardship letter describing the qualifying event or series of events that have compromised your ability to make your monthly payments (see Chapter 8)
- ✔ Proof of hardship, such as medical receipts, layoff notification, divorce documents, or copies of mortgage statements showing a sudden increase in your monthly payments
- ✔ Financial statement documenting all assets and liabilities (debts) and detailing your monthly income and expenses (see Chapter 8)
- ✔ Listing agreement for your home if it's for sale and listed with a real estate agent
- ✔ Past two years' federal income tax returns
- ✔ Past two years' W-2 statements
- ✔ Recent pay stubs or other income verification from each source of income (may include child support and alimony, Social Security disability payments, and so on)

Some lenders require that you use their loan modification application forms, so be sure to ask. If you're given a choice, you're better off using the lender's forms to present all the information the lender needs in an accessible format. In addition, if the lender allows or encourages applicants to apply online and you have access to the Internet, apply online to simplify the process for your lender.

If your lender has its own loan modification application packet and you can't download it from the Internet, request that it be mailed to you pronto — preferably overnight.

Getting a shipping address and fax number

Whether you apply online or via snail mail, you probably still need to send hard copies of your supporting documents to the lender, so ask for the following:

- ✔ Shipping address
- ✔ Phone number (most shipping labels have a space for the recipient's phone number, in case something gets mixed up en route to the recipient)
- ✔ Fax number

Why get a fax number *and* a shipping address? Because we recommend that you both fax and mail in your application to improve your chances that it arrives at its destination.

Asking about timelines

Find out about any deadlines and timelines. Specifically, ask the following questions:

- ✔ How long will it take you to process my application?
- ✔ How long does the entire loan modification process take?
- ✔ When can I expect to hear back from someone?
- ✔ What should I do if I continue to receive late payment notices?
- ✔ Does my applying for a loan modification stop any foreclosure proceedings?

  In most cases, the answer is no, unless you have a written agreement from your lender or servicer to halt all foreclosure activities.

- ✔ Whom do I call (name or employee ID number and phone number with extension) to get a status update on my modification?

Keeping the Debt Collectors at Bay

Chances are pretty good that your lender is going to try to contact you before you contact it. This is certainly understandable — the lender wants its money. In most cases, the best way to get it to stop calling you is to communicate.

When you're up to your gills in debt, however, and you're doing everything you can to catch your breath, dealing with harassing phone calls and letters can become counterproductive. You may need to tell debt collectors to back off, and if you do tell them, they're required by law to honor your request. Know your rights:

✔ Debt collectors are prohibited from calling before 8 a.m. and after 9 p.m. local time.

✔ Debt collectors aren't allowed to instill fear in you as a way to collect the debt, such as, "Pay up, or we're going to evict you."

✔ If you tell debt collectors to stop contacting you, they're required to stop calling you and sending you notices.

If a debt collector is harassing you, the Federal Trade Commission (FTC) recommends you do the following:

> Make a copy of your letter. Send the original by certified mail, and pay for a "return receipt" so you'll be able to document what the collector received. Once the collector receives your letter, they may not contact you again, with two exceptions: a collector can contact you to tell you there will be no further contact or to let you know that they or the creditor intend to take a specific action, like filing a lawsuit. Sending such a letter to a debt collector you owe money to does not get rid of the debt, but it should stop the contact.

If the harassing contact continues, you can sue the collector. You can also file a complaint with the FTC and your state attorney general (see Appendix A for contact information). For additional details, check out the FTC's Debt Collection FAQs: A Guide for Consumers online at www.ftc.gov/bcp/edu/pubs/consumer/credit/cre18.shtm.

Chapter 6

Gathering Facts, Figures, and Documentation

*N*obody exactly plans on falling behind on their house payments and ending up on the wrong side of a pending foreclosure. But when you look at all the hoops you have to jump through to get a loan modification, you begin to wonder whether your lender thinks you planned the whole thing. If you want help, you'll need to prove that you're not staging the scene just to get a lower house payment; that you really need the help; and that, if you get some help, you won't end up in the same predicament three to six months from now.

All that proving requires documentation — and lots of it. Just as knowledge is power, information is power when negotiating a loan modification. You need to gather all the facts, figures, and documentation the lender is likely to request along with other documents required to complete the application forms and make your case. This chapter shows you how to pull it all together.

Digging Up Documents

Lenders don't grant loan modifications just because borrowers ask for them and claim to be in financial distress. They need proof. Your lender wants to see that you're earning enough money to afford a *reasonable* house payment and some proof that you experienced a financial setback. It needs to look at your monthly income and expenses to make sure you're not squandering your earnings on bonbons and trinkets. And if you have something to document the current market value of your home, it wants to see that, too.

In Chapter 8, when you prepare your application and assemble the supporting documents your lender requires, we get into the specifics of which documents you need to submit with your application. At this stage, we recommend gathering *all* the documents you *may* need to prepare your application and support your claim.

Compiling all your documents may expose pieces of your financial puzzle that you didn't know about or that you can adjust to make your mortgage more affordable. Even if you don't have to actually send hard copies of the supporting documents into your lender, it's good to work off of them when filling out your financial statement.

In the following sections, we list the documents you need to dig up and explain how they're likely to come in handy when you're applying for or negotiating the terms of a loan modification.

Proof of income

Without income, you can't afford a house payment, regardless of how low the lender is willing to go, so the first thing the lender wants to see is proof that the major breadwinners of the household are winning a steady and sufficient supply of bread. Depending on your lender's requirements, you need to supply proof of income by way of one or more of the following documents:

- ✔ Pay stubs for the most recent two to four pay periods
- ✔ Federal tax returns for the last two years
- ✔ W-2s for the last two years
- ✔ Letter from a new employer stating your wage or salary and start date

Proof of hardship

Lenders consider requests for loan modifications only if the applicants have experienced financial hardship. They're not about to approve a loan modification because you had an off night at the blackjack tables. They want to see proof that you've experienced some real financial pain — preferably due to something you had no control over.

In Chapter 8, we show you how to pen an effective hardship letter, but having documented proof of the hardship, such as one (or more) of the following items, can also help you make your case:

✓ **Pink slip or notice showing a suspension or termination of employment or an income reduction (such as a notice of no overtime or temporary revolving lay-offs):** An approved or pending unemployment application from your state's unemployment office may work if you didn't get a formal release from your employer.

✓ **Birth certificate showing a new arrival:** This may support a claim that unexpected expenses derailed your budget or maternity leave temporarily reduced the household income. An employer's Family and Medical Leave Act (FMLA) letter acknowledging your qualified time off may be enough.

✓ **Death certificate:** This may support a claim that funeral expenses sank the family budget or lost income from one of the household's breadwinners caused a financial setback.

✓ **Medical bills:** These support a claim that increased medical expenses strained the family budget or an illness resulted in reduced income from the person who suffered the illness or a caregiver.

✓ **Legal papers showing a separation or divorce, either of which typically results in a reduction of household income.**

✓ **Mortgage statements:** These statements can show an interest rate increase on an adjustable-rate mortgage that made the monthly payment unaffordable.

Although your lender may not require documented proof of the hardship, it's likely to have you sign an affidavit of hardship that's subject to perjury penalties. Either way, having the proof available can help you pen your hardship letter and can back up your statement in the event that your lender questions your claims.

Your lender may be willing to entertain hardships such as alcohol or drug addictions if you're being treated. Some lenders even recognize incarceration as a qualifying hardship.

Mortgage statements and related documents

One of the most important figures you and your lender will toss around is your house payment, which breaks down into four amounts collectively referred to as PITI: principal, interest, taxes, and insurance. (Sometimes, a fifth amount comes into play — homeowner association, or HOA, fees.)

If your payment calls for principal to be paid, part of your monthly payment covers principal with the rest going toward interest. Depending on how your account is set up, a portion of your payment may also be set aside in an escrow account out of which the servicer (the party processing your payment) pays your property taxes, homeowner's insurance, and any HOA fees when they come due.

If your monthly payment covers everything, all you really need is a copy of your most recent mortgage statements. If you're not sure what your payment covers, call your servicer. If you pay your taxes, insurance, and any HOA fees separately, you need to obtain all of the following documents:

- **Mortgage statements:** Your mortgage statements show the current payment due and the loan balance along with a breakdown of how much of the payment is applied to principal, interest, taxes, insurance, and HOA fees.

- **Property tax statement:** Counties are usually charged with collecting property tax related to real estate, so if you don't have a copy of your property tax statement (bill), contact your county tax department.

  To be on the safe side, call your local taxing authority to find out if any outstanding taxes are due. Sometimes local assessments haven't yet been transferred to the county. You want to make sure you're accounting for *all* taxes due.

- **Homeowner's insurance statement:** This is typically a bill you pay once or twice a year, showing the total amount you pay to have your home insured. If you don't have a copy, contact your homeowner's insurance company.

- **Flood/wind/earthquake insurance statement:** If you have additional insurance to cover any damage from natural disasters, you can obtain a copy of the policy from your insurance provider.

At this point, you may also need to factor in the cost of private mortgage insurance (PMI) if you're paying it. Lenders don't typically calculate PMI into your front-end DTI, but it's an expense you pay each month (if your loan requires you to pay PMI).

Your lender may not require you to submit these documents with your loan modification application, but they're useful to refer to when preparing your financial statement. It's also a good idea to locate them beforehand just in case your lender asks for them.

Be sure that when your lender is estimating an affordable house payment, included in the calculations are monthly amounts for your home's property taxes, insurance, and HOA fees. Leading up

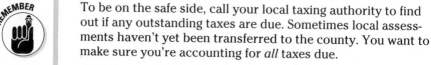

to the mortgage meltdown, some loan originators omitted these amounts from their calculations in order to "help" their clients qualify for loans based on lower house payments. In so doing, they simply helped approve risky loans and set up their clients to fail.

Other loan statements

At some point, your lender's going to want to know how bad it really is — how deeply you are in debt — so gather copies of your most current credit statements, including any of the following:

✔ Car loan statement

✔ Credit card statements

✔ Student loan statements

✔ Other loan/credit statements

Obtain your most recent statements, showing the most current balance on the account and the minimum monthly payment. All these statements will come in very handy when you sit down to prepare your financial statement in Chapter 8. Again, your lender may not require copies, but keep them on hand just in case.

Your lender will eventually total all your debts and use that number (along with your total monthly income) to calculate your debt-to-income (DTI) ratios, as explained in Chapter 2. The DTI ratios are key in determining whether you qualify for a loan modification or other debt-relief program and in formulating a viable workout solution.

 Obtain a fresh copy of your credit report. Your credit report shows all outstanding and revolving credit items being reported to the credit bureaus under your name. Lenders are now routinely pulling credit reports to verify the financials, so you should know what they're going to see. You're entitled to one free credit report per year, and you can obtain it in one of the following ways:

✔ Submit your request online at www.annualcredit report.com.

✔ Phone in your request by calling 877-322-8228.

✔ Download the Annual Credit Report Request Form from www. annualcreditreport.com/cra/requestformfinal. pdf, fill it out, and mail it to Annual Credit Report Request Service, P.O. Box 105281, Atlanta, GA 30348-5281.

Monthly bills and expenses

In Chapter 2, we encourage you to do some preliminary calculations to size up your financial situation for yourself. When you're preparing your financial statement, however, use actual amounts in your budget calculations rather than estimates. You can obtain accurate numbers from your most current bills, invoices, and your own written records; turn to the following documents:

- ✔ Car insurance statement showing how much you pay for car insurance annually, semi-annually, quarterly, or monthly

- ✔ Utility bills, including gas, electric, water/sewage, telephone, Internet, and trash removal

- ✔ Cellphone statement

- ✔ Other monthly bills, such as cable or satellite TV bills or sub-scriptions to other services

- ✔ Insurance statements, including medical, dental, disability, and life

- ✔ Medical expense statement for expenses not covered by insur-ance, including co-pays and prescriptions

- ✔ Proof of child care or tuition payments

- ✔ Savings and checking account statements for the last two to four periods

- ✔ Checking account register (where you record all your depos-its and withdrawals and the checks you write)

If you don't keep a record of deposits, withdrawals, and checks you write, start doing so. A bank representative can get you up to speed on the basics and even provide you with detailed printouts of recent transactions so you can get caught up.

All these documents can help you develop an accurate and detailed monthly budget or income and expense report. Such a document comes in handy both to empower you to take control of your finances and to develop a realistic workout plan with your lender.

Closing papers

Whenever you close on a mortgage loan, the mortgage or title com-pany usually presents you with a fancy folder containing all the closing documents. You can't miss the folder because it doesn't fit in a standard size filing cabinet without a little creative shoving.

Although the lender may not require the documents in the following list, we recommend that you gather them just in case the lender is uncooperative and you need to seek legal counsel. If your attorney decides to audit your mortgage or hire a third-party specialist to perform an audit (as explained in Chapter 14), or if you ultimately decide to file bankruptcy, you'll need copies of all these documents.

Closing papers include fully executed copies (signed by all parties) of the following documents:

- ✔ **Loan application:** This is the document you filled out requesting the loan. It's usually labeled Uniform Residential Loan Application (Form 1003) and is commonly referred to as a "ten oh three." It may contain signs of predatory lending or other red flags that may encourage your lender to give you a loan modification (see Chapter 14 for details).

  You probably have two copies of the 1003 for your loan — the initial 1003 and the final 1003. The initial 1003 (sometimes called the *handwritten 1003*) was filled out when you first met with and applied with the loan originator. The final is a neatly printed computer-generated copy. It may be different if something changed, so compare the two.

- ✔ **Good Faith Estimate (GFE):** Lenders are required by law to present you with a Good Faith Estimate prior to closing so that you can compare loan costs among lenders. By comparing the costs quoted on the GFE against the actual costs on the HUD-1 (described later in this list), you may be able to identify discrepancies that qualify you for a loan modification.

- ✔ **Promissory note:** The promissory note is sort of an IOU stating that you'll make timely payments in the agreed-upon amount until you've paid back the loan in full with interest.

- ✔ **Mortgage:** The mortgage names your house as collateral for securing the repayment of the loan.

- ✔ **HUD-1:** The HUD-1 is a statement of actual charges and adjustments associated with the closing. The Real Estate Settlement Procedures Act (RESPA) requires that both the seller and buyer receive a copy of the HUD-1 at least one day prior to closing. The HUD-1 may include signs of predatory lending or mortgage fraud that entitle you to a loan modification.

If you have a second mortgage or a home equity loan or line of credit, gather the closing papers for those loans, as well. However, focus on modifying your first mortgage first. You can then work on having any other loans modified.

If you can't find your closing packet, or if it contains unsigned copies of some or all documents, contact the title company that hosted your closing and request a copy. If you're not sure which closing company you used, call your lender or servicer to find out.

Documenting Your Property's Market Value

It's no surprise that lenders want to know about the value of a property before approving a loan to purchase it. They want to make sure that the collateral is sufficient to secure the repayment of the loan. When a lender wants to know your property value for a loan modification, however, the reason may not seem so clear.

Although we recommend obtaining a valuation at this point in the book, don't let it slow down the application process. You can apply for a loan modification prior to obtaining the valuation.

Actually, you and the lender should want to know the property's current market value for the following reasons:

✔ **To weigh the options:** If the home has plenty of equity in it (meaning it's worth a lot more than you owe on it), for example, refinancing or selling the property may be a better option.

✔ **To gauge the risk of any workout deal:** The lender wants to know how much of its investment it's likely to be able to recover if foreclosure is necessary.

✔ **To determine whether a short sale would be a viable option:** For more about short sales, see Chapter 3.

✔ **To calculate a principal reduction in the event that it becomes a part of the loan modification.**

We don't recommend paying for an appraisal at this point. If your lender requires an appraisal (usually for a short sale, refinance, or short re-fi, as discussed in Chapter 3), it will hire an appraiser and perhaps charge you for the appraisal, so save yourself the time and money of arranging one yourself. You may be able to obtain a pretty good estimate of your property's true market value, in writing, for free or for a very reasonable fee by consulting a local real estate agent. Many agents offer *broker's price opinions,* or BPOs, for free in the hopes of someday earning the homeowners' business and referrals to other potential clients. A BPO is also commonly referred to as a *comparative market analysis* (CMA) or *home valuation.* (In some areas, only appraisers are allowed to provide property valuations.)

Ask for a valuation that reflects what you could sell your house for within 30, 60, and 90 or more days of listing. This information gives you insight into what the agent would list the price for initially and reduce it to over time. The 90-day estimate is more conservative and probably more in line with the property's true market value.

Authorizing Your Representative to Speak with Your Lender

You've no doubt received copies of privacy policies from just about everyone you do business with — everyone from credit card and insurance companies to your doctor and dentist. If you're like most folks, you toss these in the trash as soon as you catch a glimpse of those two words, "Privacy Policy."

When you apply for a loan modification, however, especially if you decide to hire a third-party representative (see Chapter 4), you can no longer afford to ignore your lender's privacy policy. It probably contains a clause stating that the lender can speak only with you or your authorized representative and the lender cannot share any details of your account with any company or individual other than you without your written consent. In other words, if you want your representative to be able to deal with your lender, you need to authorize this in writing — usually with a letter of authorization.

Your lender should have a copy of a fill-in-the blank authorization letter you can use. Download a copy of the letter from your lender's Web site (if available), or contact your lender and request a faxed or mailed copy of the letter you need (see Chapter 5 for details on contacting your lender).

You simply insert the name and any other information requested by your lender, sign the letter, make a copy for your records, and then mail or fax the letter to your lender. If your lender doesn't have a standard letter of authorization, you can create your own by using the sample letter in Figure 6-1.

Some lenders accept only their own authorization letters or forms. If your lender has a form, use it. Also, make sure you give your third-party representative a copy of your signed and dated authorization. If your lender were to misplace the form (it has been known to happen), your representative can fax over a copy of the original as soon as possible to avoid delays.

Third Party Authorization Form

Today's Date: _____

Loan Number: _____

Borrower Name: _____

Co-Borrower Name: _____

Property Address: _____

City, State, & Zip Code: _____

Phone Number: _____

I/We authorize [Insert lender name] to (mark all that apply):

  □   Share copies of loan documents and any written communication related to my
      above-referenced loan with the Authorized Party.

  □   Discuss all information regarding my above-referenced loan with the Authorized
      Party.

  □   Allow the Authorized Party to change contact information (phone number and
      mailing address) on my above-referenced loan.

  □   Other (describe): _____

This authorization is valid for ninety (90) days unless a different expiration date is inserted
and initialed below.

  □   Authorization is valid until _____/_____/_____.

  □   Authorization is valid until revoked by the undersigned or until the loan is paid in
      full.

Name of Authorized Party(s) and Company Name (if applicable) — please print:

_____

Relationship of Authorized Party to Borrower: _____

Authorized Party Mailing Address: _____

Authorized Party Phone Number: _____

_____   _____
Borrower Signature   Co-Borrower Signature

Figure 6-1: Sample letter of authorization.

Chapter 7

Knowing What to Ask For

. . . .

. . . .

The ultimate goal of any loan modification is to make the monthly payments affordable, but a loan modification can do this in any number of ways. It can drop the interest rate, extend the term, reduce the principal (which is rare), and/or roll missed or late payments and other costs into the modified loan.

Prior to negotiating with your lender, you need to evaluate your needs and determine what you want out of the deal. This chapter shows you how to do this and how to anticipate the lender's evaluation of your situation by playing a little game of "What If?". We also help you assess some of the possible effects of a loan modification.

Recognizing Your Three Main Objectives

 This chapter assumes you've already considered all options described in Chapter 3 and you've concluded that you want to do all the following:

✔ Cure any default (catch up on missed or late payments)

✔ Lower your monthly payment

✔ Keep your home

Generally speaking, these are the three main objectives of any loan modification, and they carry the added benefit of helping you repair your credit. How you achieve these objectives, however, can vary significantly depending on your wants, needs, resources, and what the lender or investor is willing to accept.

In the following sections, we reveal the most common approaches to curing defaults, lowering monthly mortgage payments through a loan modification, and keeping your home. In the section "Playing 'What If?'" later in the chapter, we lead you through the process of assessing the benefits of each approach as it applies to your situation.

To a great extent, the ultimate outcome hinges on the lender or investor and the individual(s) handling your case. Some lenders are truly consumer-conscious, treating applicants courteously and teaming up with applicants to develop long-term solutions. A few even reach out and team up with mortgage insurance companies to develop solutions. Others are notorious for dragging their feet, offering terrible terms, or shifting policies midstream. If your lender is cooperative, move forward as quickly as possible; lenders have been known to change policies and procedures without warning.

Curing any default

Being in default is like trying to bail out a leaky boat in a thunderstorm. No matter how fast you bail water out of the hull, the level keeps rising. Unless you catch a break, the skies clear, and help arrives soon, you're sunk. Fortunately when you're in default, your lender may be able to cut you the break you need by

- ✔ **Forgiving any penalties and fees charged against your account due to late or missed payments.** Lenders are often willing to drop the charges, so to speak, and you really should push to have any penalties and fees removed from your account.

- ✔ **Adding the late or missed payments to your mortgage balance and then re-amortizing the balance, so you can cure the default over the life of the loan.** This option may be the most costly over the life of the loan, but it eases the strain on your current monthly budget. (See the sidebar "What's re-amortization all about?" for an explanation of this action.)

- ✔ **Instituting an installment plan that lets you cure the default over several months.** This option cures the default more quickly than other options but can place a heavy burden on your monthly budget. You need to be able to afford the regular monthly payment plus a percentage of the outstanding delinquency.

If you negotiate paying off the default amount over time with an installment plan, factor these separate payments into your budget and make sure you have enough money to cover them. This option is usually practical only if you've recovered from a temporary financial hardship and now have sufficient income to cover the extra payments *plus* your house payment. Most lenders let you bring any default current with a "six months same as cash" plan and won't rule out a future loan modification if you come up short.

✔ **Forgiving some or all default amounts.** Lenders are typically very reluctant to accept this option unless you're negotiating a short sale or deed in lieu of foreclosure, as discussed in Chapter 3.

Ask about Fannie Mae's HomeSaver Advance (HSA) loan for curing deficiencies. An HSA is a separate loan payable over 15 years at a fixed rate of 5 percent with no payments or interest accrual for the first six months. In this case, your lender isn't actually cutting you a break. You're taking out another loan to bring your payments current, and you have to pay it back eventually.

A lower monthly payment, as explained in the following section, can also help in curing your default by freeing up money in your budget you can use to catch up on your bills.

Lowering your monthly payment

Lenders have all sorts of tools at their disposal to lower your monthly payment, including the following:

✔ **Trim your interest rate, either temporarily or permanently.**

✔ **Extend the term by re-amortizing the loan over a longer period.**

✔ **Accept interest-only payments until your finances improve.**

✔ **Forgive a portion of the principal.** Lenders are typically very reluctant to accept this option.

✔ **Offer a *principal forbearance*, in which the loan is re-amortized based on the current market value of the property rather than what's owed on it.** You pay the difference (between what you owe on the mortgage and the balance on which your monthly payments are based) at the end of the term or whenever you sell the home. (Turn to Chapter 3 for more about principal forbearance.)

What's re-amortization all about?

Amortization is a process of retiring debt through regularly scheduled payments that remain constant over the life of the loan. The monthly payment remains constant (for a fixed-rate loan), but the amount applied toward paying down the principal balance increases and the amount put toward interest decreases with each payment.

Here's an example: On a $200,000 30-year fixed-rate mortgage at 7 percent interest, your monthly payment is $1,330.60. In the first month, $1,166.67 of that payment goes to pay interest, and $163.94 goes toward principal. You now owe $199,836.06. Because the principal balance is lower (slightly), you pay less interest next time and a slightly larger portion of your payment is applied toward the principal. So in the second month, $1,165.71 is paid in interest and $164.89 goes toward principal. (Lenders receive their interest first, and then you pay on the principal. This means that the first 15 years of the 30-year mortgage are mostly interest payments. Yep, it seems like a rip off, but that's the way it works.)

When your loan is re-amortized through a loan modification, your monthly payment is recalculated based on whatever terms you and your lender agree to. Suppose you've already paid ten years on that $200,000 mortgage, so you now owe $171,624.77. You have a total of about $5,000 in missed payments. The lender agrees to lower your interest rate to 5 percent, add the $5,000 to your balance, and re-amortize the loan from the 20 years left in your term to 30 years. This new mortgage is now a $176,624.77 30-year mortgage at 5 percent, which lowers your monthly payment by about $250 to $1,073.64.

We strongly encourage you to opt for a fixed interest rate instead of a variable- or adjustable-rate mortgage (ARM), even if the fixed interest rate is higher, which it almost always is. A fixed interest rate helps keep your financial plans on track. A *reset* that bumps up the monthly payment $100 or more can sink a budget faster than a spending spree at your local department store.

Keeping your home

Keeping your home is pretty straightforward. As long as you achieve the first two objectives of curing any default and lowering your monthly payments, you get to keep your home . . . and hopefully pay less for it. Achieving the first two objectives is a little more complex than simply keeping your home because, as we explain in the two previous sections, different paths lead to the same destination.

Establishing a Baseline with Your Current Mortgage

Before you start comparing various loan modification scenarios, you should have a clear picture in your mind of your current mortgage, including the interest rate, term, principal balance, and monthly payment. This information helps you set a *baseline,* or establish a context for arriving at meaningful comparisons.

To establish a baseline, jot down the following information about your current mortgage (get the information from your most recent mortgage statement or your closing documents, as explained in Chapter 6):

- ✔ **Initial balance:** The total amount you initially borrowed to finance the purchase of your home.

- ✔ **Interest rate:** The current interest rate you're paying. For a fixed-rate mortgage, figuring this is easy: Just jot down the interest rate. Adjustable-rate mortgages are more complex, and we discuss them a little later in this section.

- ✔ **Term in years/months:** The total number of years/months you're scheduled to pay off the mortgage. For example, if you have a 30-year mortgage and have paid 10 years already, the term is still 30 years/360 months.

- ✔ **Monthly payment:** The total amount you're currently paying in principal and interest on the loan. If you're also paying into escrow to cover property taxes, insurance, and homeowner association (HOA) fees, subtract the escrow amount from your monthly payment for comparison purposes.

- ✔ **Principal balance:** Also known as the *unpaid principal balance* (UPB), this is the amount you still owe on the mortgage.

Don't confuse the pay-off amount with the principal balance. The pay-off amount may be larger, accounting for the UPB, accrued interest, and other advances the mortgage company has made. You can obtain a current pay-off statement from your lender, which will include the UPB, other amounts, and a total pay-off balance.

- ✔ **Remaining term:** The number of years and months remaining on your mortgage. For example, if you have a 30-year mortgage and have paid 10 years already, the term is now 20 years/240 months.

- ✔ **Total to be paid:** The amount you will have paid your lender in interest and principal over the life of the loan. For a fixed-rate loan, multiply your house payment by 12 (months) and then by the term (number of years) to get the total. For an adjustable-rate mortgage, calculating the total paid in principal and interest over the life of the loan requires some guesswork. The best approach is to locate an adjustable-rate mortgage calculator and plug in the numbers to obtain an estimate. You can find an excellent collection of mortgage calculators, including one for adjustable-rate mortgages, at www.bankrate.com.

✔ **Total current delinquency:** The total amount of money you owe in back payments.

Here's a mini-form for jotting down all the numbers from this list:

Initial balance:	$ _____
Term in years/months:	_____/_____
Interest rate:	_____
Monthly payment (principal and interest):	$ _____
Current balance:	$ _____
Remaining term:	_____/_____
Total to be paid:	$ _____
Total current delinquency:	$ _____

If you have an adjustable-rate mortgage, jot down a few additional numbers:

✔ **Months before first rate reset:** The number of months before the initial rate is scheduled to change

✔ **Periodic rate cap:** The highest percentage the rate can adjust in a given period

✔ **Maximum rate:** The absolute highest interest rate you will ever have to pay

✔ **Months between rate adjustments:** The number of months that must pass before the interest rate can change

Here's a mini-form for jotting down the numbers from this list:

Months before first rate reset:	_____
Periodic rate cap:	_____
Maximum rate:	_____
Months between rate adjustments:	_____

Some experts recommend ignoring the total amount the loan modification costs over the life of the loan. They advise homeowners to focus, at least in the short term, on negotiating an affordable *monthly payment.* Although we somewhat agree, in our opinion, knowing the cost over the long haul can improve your ability to compare different offers and make a well-informed decision.

Playing "What If?"

When your lender receives your loan modification application, it engages in its own game of "What If?" Usually, the lender begins by examining your financials and estimating a monthly payment it believes you can afford to pay. It then works backward, playing with the three key numbers that determine your monthly payment: principal, term, and interest rate. In the following sections, we show you how to play "What If?" with different scenarios so that you're aware of the possibilities before the game begins.

Fortunately, given the accessibility of mortgage calculators, crunching the numbers is a snap. You can find excellent mortgage calculators on the Web, such as at www.bankrate.com. If you have a personal finance program, such as Quicken or Microsoft Money, it may also contain loan and refinance calculators.

Test-driving a lower interest rate

On a $200,000 30-year mortgage, a single percentage point change in interest can represent over $100 per month or $36,000 over the life of the loan. This is good to know when you're applying for a loan modification. Even better is knowing the effect that an interest rate cut can have on your mortgage.

One of the easiest ways to lower a house payment is to drop the interest rate. Using your handy dandy mortgage calculator, take a few lower interest rates for a test drive. Plug in the following numbers:

- ✔ **Principal balance:** The amount of money you'd need today to pay off your mortgage in full.

- ✔ **Interest rate:** The rate you want to test-drive. Consider reducing your current interest rate by one, two, or three percentage points to explore the possibilities.

- ✔ **Remaining term:** The number of years or months you have left to pay on your mortgage. (The calculator should indicate whether you need to enter months or years.)

Try several different interest rates, and jot down the results in the following table. To calculate the value for the Total Paid column (the total amount paid to the lender over the life of the loan), multiply the term by 12 months and then by the monthly payment. For example, if the term is 30 years and the monthly payment is $750, then the Total Paid would be $30 \times 12 \times \$750 = \$270,000$.

	Interest Rate	*Monthly Payment*	*Total Paid*
Scenario 1:	____	____	____
Scenario 2:	____	____	____
Scenario 3:	____	____	____

When playing "What If?" change only one variable at a time — principal, interest rate, or term. Later in this chapter, in the section "Mixing it up by adjusting several variables," you have the opportunity to adjust two or more variables at a time, such as extending the term and lowering the interest rate.

Many loan modifications include step-rate adjustments; for example, you may pay 5 percent interest for the first three years, after which the rate rises by a percentage point each year to a maximum of 8 percent. Be sure to account for these step increases — especially the worst-case scenario (8 percent in this example). (Step-rate adjustments don't make the loan an adjustable-rate mortgage because the steps are predictable and not tied to an index that's susceptible to market fluctuations.)

Spreading payments over a longer term

Not very long ago, paying off your mortgage early was all the rage. Homeowners were talking about refinancing into 15- or 20-year mortgages, paying a couple hundred dollars extra every month, and retiring early. Now, homeowners just want to hold onto their homes, and that involves a lower monthly payment. They're often willing to take the opposite approach of past homeowners — tacking on several years to the end of the loan term or extending a 30-year mortgage to 40 years, dropping the house payment by $100 or more. (For more about the benefits of an extended term, see Chapter 11.)

To see how an extended term would affect your monthly payment and the total you'd end up paying over the life of the mortgage, plug the following numbers into a mortgage calculator:

✔ **Principal balance:** The amount of money you'd need today to pay off your mortgage in full.

✔ **Interest rate:** Your current interest rate.

✔ **Extended term:** The number of years or months you're willing to consider paying on the mortgage until it's paid in full. We're talking the *entire* term here, not just the number of years or months added on. (The calculator should indicate whether you need to enter months or years.)

Try several different extended terms, and jot down the results in the following table. To calculate the value for the Total Paid column (the total amount you're going to pay the lender over the life of the loan), multiply the term by 12 months and then by the monthly payment.

	Extended Term	*Monthly Payment*	*Total Paid*
Scenario 1:	____	____	____
Scenario 2:	____	____	____
Scenario 3:	____	____	____

Adjusting the principal balance

Depending on the main objective of your loan modification, you may see your principal balance rise or fall. If your goal is to catch up on late and missed payments, one option is to add them to the principal so you can pay them back over the life of the loan. If an interest rate reduction and/or term extension isn't enough to make your house payment affordable, the lender may agree to some sort of principal reduction or forbearance.

In either case, you may want to play "What If?" to see how a principal increase or reduction may affect your monthly payment and the total amount you stand to pay over the life of the loan.

Rolling late and missed payments into the principal

If you owe $5,000 in late and missed payments, trying to play catch-up with a six-month or two-year installment plan can be tough. You're facing a monthly payment of more than $200 in addition to your normal house payment. However, spread the payments over 30 years (at 7-percent interest), and you're looking at about $35 a month. Yes, you'll end up paying more than double that $5,000 over the life of the loan, but the lower payment may enable you to keep your home.

To play "What If?" with rolling missed payments into the principal balance, add the total missed or late payments to your principal. Then plug the new principal into your mortgage calculator and jot down the result:

	Balance	*Monthly Payment*	*Total Paid*
Current:	____	____	____
New:	____	____	____

At this point, you're playing around with one variable at a time to see how that one variable can affect your monthly payment and the amount paid over the life of the loan. Admittedly, this is unrealistic because lenders usually change two or more variables. We get into this later in the section "Mixing it up by adjusting several variables."

Reducing the principal

When you borrow money to buy a home, your lender assumes you're going to pay that amount back in full. No one really cares whether your home's value fell 30 percent or your car dropped its transmission at the intersection of Main and Pain. You're expected to make good on the IOU you signed — the *promissory note* or *mortgage note*.

Lenders are often willing to consider tweaking the term and the interest rate because what they collect in interest is profit — the gravy ladled over their meat and potatoes. The meat and potatoes are the principal, and lenders really want that back in full. Every reduction in principal ends up in the loss column on their balance sheets.

Mortgages are often converted into mortgage-backed securities (MBSs) and sold to Wall Street investors, where they're held in MBS pools. Investors may let lenders or servicers adjust the interest rate and term on an MBS but are much more reluctant to adjust the unpaid balance on a loan.

If the lender can achieve the goals of curing the default and making the house payment affordable through rate and term adjustments, it's probably not going to consider reducing the principal balance due on the loan. If the lender adjusted the interest rate and term and is just shy of meeting the goals, it may consider reducing the principal, but don't hold your breath for a drastic reduction. If you compare the process to getting a haircut, don't expect a buzz cut when you're more likely to get a little off the sides.

Still, you should take some time to see how a principal reduction could affect your monthly payment, so plug the following numbers into your mortgage calculator:

- ✔ **Principal balance:** The amount of money you'd owe your lender after the principal reduction.

- ✔ **Interest rate:** Your current interest rate.

- ✔ **Remaining term:** The number of years or months you have left to pay on your mortgage. (The calculator should indicate whether you need to enter months or years.)

Play "What If?" with several different principal amounts, and jot down the results in the following table. To calculate the value for the Total Paid column (the total amount you're going to pay the lender over the life of the loan), multiply the term by 12 months and then by the monthly payment.

	Principal Balance	*Monthly Payment*	*Total Paid*
Scenario 1:	___	___	___
Scenario 2:	___	___	___
Scenario 3:	___	___	___

Your lender may be more willing to consider *principal forbearance* than an outright forgiveness of principal. With principal forbearance, the lender lets you pay back a portion of what you currently owe after you sell your home or refinance. Suppose you borrowed $160,000 to buy a home, its value has since dropped to $120,000, and you still owe $140,000 on it. With principal forbearance, the lender calculates payments based on the property value of $120,000, and then you pay the difference ($20,000) when you sell the home or refinance it. Portions of the unpaid principal balance (UPB) are rarely forgiven — they're almost always just postponed.

Mixing it up by adjusting several variables

In the preceding sections, we encourage you to play "What If?" with adjustments to your mortgage principal, term, and interest rate, changing only one value at a time. This gives you a pretty good feel for how each of those numbers affects the bottom lines — your monthly payment and the total you end up paying over the life of the loan.

Now, mix it up a bit. Change two or three numbers at a time to determine how various combinations can play out on paper. Try the following:

- ✔ **Adjust the interest rate and term.** Try dropping the interest rate a point *and* giving yourself 40 years to pay it off.

- ✔ **Adjust the interest rate and principal.** Reduce the interest rate by 2 percent and chop $10,000 off the principal balance.

- ✔ **Adjust the term and principal.** Extend the term from whatever's left on your mortgage now to 30 years, and reduce the principal to the estimated market value of your property.

- ✔ **Adjust the interest rate, term, and principal.** If you have missed or late payments, add them to the principal and then play with lowering the interest rate and term so you can cure the default *and* make the monthly payment affordable.

The Making Home Affordable (MHA) loan modification plan employs a waterfall approach to making the monthly payment more affordable. First, it calls for an interest rate reduction. If that doesn't do the trick (make the monthly payment affordable), lenders are encouraged to extend the term. If the rate reduction and term extension don't do the trick, then lenders can reduce the principal.

Trying on an interest-only loan

With traditional mortgages, a portion of each payment is in the form of interest paid to the lender, and another portion is applied to the principal. Make all your payments over the term of your loan, and eventually you pay the money back in full, with interest.

Negative equity with interest-only loans

Interest-only loans may be okay for investors who are focused more on a property's cash flow than on equity considerations. With a lower payment, the investor has more money to invest in other projects.

In the years leading up to the housing crisis, when the housing bubble was in inflation mode, home buyers also were attracted to interest-only loans because they could buy "more house" and have lower monthly house payments. As long as property values were on the rise, they were building equity in their homes without having to pay down the principal.

When the housing bubble burst, however, the inflated equity disappeared. Many homeowners found themselves in *negative-equity* territory, owing more on their homes than their homes were worth, even if they'd never missed a payment.

With an interest-only loan, the majority of the payment goes to the lender in the form of interest, with a portion going to the servicer (for services rendered). You could make payments for the next 1,000 years and never pay off the principal because no portion of the payment is applied to principal. Generally, we discourage homeowners from taking out interest-only loans because they never get a chance to pay down the debt and build equity in their homes by making payments (see the nearby sidebar for more on these types of loans).

With a loan modification, however, an interest-only arrangement can be a useful adjustment in helping you catch up on missed payments and penalties. It can lower your monthly payment considerably over the short term, freeing up some money in your budget to pay down deficiencies. Be careful with an interest-only arrangement, making sure it meets the following criteria:

- ✔ **It's temporary.** Paying only interest for two to three years so you can regain your financial footing is okay, but then the mortgage should revert to something more normal, in which a portion of each payment is applied to the principal.

- ✔ **It gives you sufficient time to plan and prepare for any balloon payments.** Most interest-only loans come with *balloon payments* — a big chunk of money that comes due when the term expires. Make sure you have plenty of time to secure the funds to cover your balloon payments when they're due.

 Because you're not reducing the principal on an interest-only loan, you don't really need a fancy calculator to calculate the monthly payment. Just multiply the principal by the interest rate, and divide by 12. For example, on a $150,000 mortgage at 7 percent, the interest-only monthly payment is

$$(\$150,000 \times 0.07) \div 12 = \$875$$

You're still playing "What If?" here, so compare this interest-only payment with what you would be paying with a more traditional mortgage. In this case, you'd pay about $998 with a traditional 30-year mortgage.

Considering the Potential Fallout

We obviously get pretty revved up about loan modification and think it's often the ideal solution for eligible homeowners. However, the loan modification option does have some potential drawbacks you should consider before seizing the opportunity.

Assessing the effect on the former loan

Other than changing the interest rate, term, and perhaps unpaid balance, a loan modification typically changes little or nothing stated in the original mortgage and promissory note. As a result, the loan modification document remains relatively short, around 2–5 pages as opposed to the 10–24 pages for a new mortgage plus 3–15 pages for a new note.

We've seen instances in which lenders attempt to grab one or two additional rights inside the loan modification agreement. They may try to slip in a clause, for example, saying that you agree to sign a new note if they can't produce the original. For this reason, have a knowledgeable attorney review the documents before you sign them and send them back to the lender. Provide your attorney the original documents for comparison.

Forecasting the effect on your credit rating

Whenever you have trouble making payments on a loan or credit card account, it shows up as a blemish on your credit report and negatively affects your credit rating. Any delinquencies leading up to the loan modification may have a negative effect on your credit rating. However, the loan modification itself can have a positive effect.

A loan modification allows the credit bureaus to update any non-payment issues as "settled" or some other favorable designation. This is far less detrimental than a deed in lieu (DIL) of foreclosure, a short sale (SS), or, heaven forbid, a full-blown foreclosure.

Gauging the effect on your ability to pursue future actions

Sometimes lenders try to insert waivers into loan modification agreements to protect them from any legal actions you may decide to pursue against them in the future, such as if you think you've been a victim of predatory lending practices. (Most loan modification agreements include *estoppel affidavits* requiring the borrower to agree to waive and release any past defenses in exchange for the mortgage company agreeing to modify the loan and waive any current default.)

We certainly can't advise you of what to do or whether you even have a case at all against your lender or loan originator. If you think you've been wronged, speak with an attorney who's well versed in the rules and regulations governing the mortgage lending industry *before* you pursue a loan modification.

 Prior to signing off on a loan modification agreement, have your attorney review it and point out any instances in which the lender is requesting that you sign a waiver relinquishing your rights.

Assessing the tax implications for discharged debt

When it comes to charging and collecting taxes, the government can be brutal. Suppose you can't afford your house payments and face the prospect of selling your home at a loss. Your lender agrees to a short sale (see Chapter 3), accepting $10,000 less than you owe, so you can sell and break even. According to the tax code, discharge of debt is a taxable event, so you owe taxes on that $10,000!

Fortunately, President Bush and Congress provided some respite from this apparently irrational practice with the Mortgage Forgiveness Debt Relief Act (MFDRA) of 2007. For qualifying homeowners, this legislation exempts discharged debt from federal income tax. (The MFDRA applies to debt forgiven in calendar years 2007 through 2012, but it may be extended, as President Obama extended it from 2009 to 2012.)

MFDRA isn't a blanket tax exemption; some restrictions apply, and you have to complete and submit the necessary paperwork, so consult a tax expert if any portion of your unpaid balance is discharged or reduced for whatever reason.

 Regardless of whether the MFDRA is still in force when you read this, be sure to discuss any tax implications of discharged debt with your attorney and accountant if you're considering pursuing a loan modification option in which a portion of the principal balance will be forgiven. Being blindsided by a tax bill for a profit you never even touched can be mighty painful.

Pushing back

Knowing your situation and your options often places you in a stronger position to negotiate. Such was the case with Paul and Carol in Michigan, who were expecting a new baby in the midst of an economic downturn. When we met the couple, they were three months behind on their payments of $1,377.78 per month and six months pregnant.

When we presented Paul and Carol's situation to their lender, it was quite receptive to their request for a loan modification. After the standard couple of weeks of processing, the lender presented its first offer: a monthly payment of $1,220.00, saving the couple $157.78 a month.

We thanked the lender for the offer but explained that the suggested payment still wasn't affordable for the couple. We pointed out that about one out of every two loan modifications fail because the payment isn't truly affordable. We also pointed out some key points the lender may have overlooked: Paul and Carol had a new baby on the way, the job market in Michigan was tough, property values had dropped significantly, and REOs (bank-owned repossessed properties) were lingering on the market.

A week later, the lender presented its second offer: a monthly payment of $918.00, saving the homeowners $459.78 per month. This represented a truly affordable house payment for the couple, and they signed on the dotted line.

The moral of this story is to know what you want prior to entering into negotiations and to identify all exits. The homeowners had a clear idea of what would be affordable for them. They wanted to keep their home and were committed to doing so, but they weren't willing to jeopardize everything else in their lives to do it. They knew that if they couldn't negotiate an affordable payment, they would need to move, and they were willing to do that, if necessary. Knowing what they wanted and having another option to fall back on allowed them to hold firm and push back when the lender presented its initial offer.

Chapter 8

Preparing and Submitting Your Application

• •

In This Chapter

▶ Demonstrating your need in a hardship letter

▶ Painting your financial portrait — current and projected

▶ Signing and copying your entire packet

▶ Ensuring proper delivery of your application

• •

*I*f you're lucky, either your lender supplies you with all the forms to complete and a checklist of supporting documentation to submit with your loan modification application or you can easily download and print everything from your lender's Web site. (See Chapter 5 for information on how to contact your lender and Chapter 6 for more about gathering the supporting documents you may need.) You simply follow the instructions, make copies for your own records, and mail your application to the lender. If you're not so lucky, you have a rough list of items you gathered from phone conversations with the lender's representative.

In either case, you need to prepare a hardship letter and financial reports. In this chapter, we show you how to pull everything together for these documents and then submit your entire application to your lender.

On February 17, 2009, President Obama signed into law H.R.1, commonly referred to as the *Stimulus Bill*, which contains a provision to standardize loan modification qualifications, paperwork, and procedures. This legislation is likely to cut down on the differences among lenders in evaluating and processing loan modification applications.

Penning Your Hardship Letter

A key component of any loan modification application is the *hardship letter,* the homeowners' description of the financial setbacks they've experienced that resulted in their inability to pay their monthly mortgage. An effective letter achieves the following:

- ✔ Describes the event or series of events that caused the financial hardship — what happened and when
- ✔ States whether the hardship is temporary or permanent
- ✔ Describes the current situation as you see it
- ✔ Expresses your sincere commitment to keep your house
- ✔ Explains what you have done, are doing, and plan to do to resolve the issues that have placed you in default and that are making your house payment unaffordable

In the following sections, we explain what qualifies as a hardship, ask you several questions about your situation that you need to answer in preparation for writing an effective hardship letter, and provide you with a couple of examples to inspire your inner muse.

Recognizing eligible hardships

Not everything qualifies as a bona fide financial hardship. If the reason you can't afford your house payment is because you just blew $50K on a really awesome speedboat, your lender isn't going to shed a single tear at the foreclosure sale. On the other hand, if your spouse fell off a ladder at work and is now on disability, you have an excellent case.

The word of the day is *verifiable.* You need to prove that you experienced a genuine hardship *and* that it compromised your ability to pay. Most lenders give consideration to the following hardships:

- ✔ Job loss or relocation, such as a layoff or reduction in force (RIF).
- ✔ Income reduction, such as a wage reduction or loss of overtime.
- ✔ A failed business or one that's suffering from an economic slowdown.
- ✔ Divorce or separation.

- Newborn child, namely maternity leave and the increased expense of having another dependent. Some lenders even consider adoption a hardship.

- Death in the family, especially if the person who passed away was helping to make the payments.

- Payment shock, as in a bump in the interest rate on an adjustable-rate mortgage.

- Property damage resulting in bills not covered by insurance.

- Theft resulting in losses not covered by insurance.

- Illness or injury that either reduces income or increases medical expenses or both.

- Too much debt accumulated over time.

- Military duty.

- Gambling by one of the household's wage earners who's currently seeking treatment.

- Alcohol or drug dependency of one of the household's wage earners who's currently seeking treatment.

- Incarceration of one of the household's wage earners.

Don't rule out a hardship just because it's not on our list, even if you did buy that $50K speedboat mentioned earlier just before receiving a pay cut. If you're willing to sell the boat and work out a deal with your lender that's good for both of you, your hardship may be a less critical part of your application.

Answering a few questions

Good writing anticipates the readers' questions or objections and responds to them. The same holds true for a hardship letter. The people reading the letter come to it with questions they want answered, so you'd better have the answers straight in your own mind first before you put them down on paper. Following are the questions your hardship letter needs to answer:

- What event or series of events caused the financial hardship that has made your monthly mortgage payments unaffordable?

- When did the hardship occur? Provide a specific date or range of dates.

✔ Is the hardship temporary or permanent? A temporary hardship could be medical bills not covered by insurance, an injury or short-term illness, or a job layoff. A permanent hardship is more like a death in the family or a divorce or separation.

✔ How badly do you want to keep your home? If you really don't care about keeping the home, the lender may not care enough to try to negotiate a loan modification. One of the other options described in Chapter 3 may be better for you.

✔ Are you behind on your house payments? If yes, how many months are you behind? What's the total dollar amount of your deficiency?

✔ Can you afford to make a house payment? If yes, how much can you afford to pay? (Chapter 2 helps you break down your current finances and estimate an affordable payment amount.)

✔ What are you doing to address the root cause(s) of the hardship (assuming you have any control over them) and recover your financial footing? This can be anything from budgeting more carefully to finding a new job or liquidating assets — selling your collection of baseball cards or Beanie Babies, for example.

The goal of your hardship letter is to convince your lender that you're worthy of a loan modification. It should show that you meet all the lender's eligibility requirements and convince the lender that you're committed to a long-term solution and able to follow through on your end of the deal.

Reviewing sample hardship letters

Imitation may not really be the sincerest form of flattery, but it's certainly a good way to start writing a hardship letter. Begin with a suitable model, add your own details, spice it up with a dash of sincerity, play on the reader's emotions, and you can end up with a prizewinner. Figures 8-1 and 8-2 provide the models you need to get started. (Looking at examples is a good way to start, but do your very best to make it your own.)

This is a letter, not a novel or even a short story, so keep it short — one page is plenty. Underline the most important points, including the terms of your current loan, the total deficiency amount (if any), the date on which the trouble began, anything you've done to resolve the problem, and so on. Refer to the section earlier in this chapter entitled "Answering a few questions" to determine what's most important.

Herman and Lilly Crane
Loan #: 131313

1313 Mockingbird Lane
Los Angeles, CA 90013
January 13, 2013

Madoff Savings & Loan
2008 Meltdown Drive
Lovelock, Nevada 89419

Dear Madoff:

We are writing this letter to request a loan modification and to inform you of recent financial hardships that have made our current monthly mortgage payments unaffordable:

- Due to health problems, <u>Lilly</u> has had to change jobs, resulting in a <u>pay reduction from $60,000</u> (teaching math) <u>to $16,000</u> (as a teacher's assistant) per year.

- <u>Herman</u> is a freelance writer who <u>was earning approximately $85,000</u> per year; due to the current recession, he is struggling to <u>now earn $50,000 to $60,000 per year</u>. He continues to look for other sources of income but has not been successful in this slow economy.

- Our daughter just started college at UCLA, which offered her <u>very little financial aid</u>. She is working and has taken out loans to cover her contribution to tuition and expenses, but <u>we are responsible for about $12,000</u> of the cost annually.

- During our transition to a more meager lifestyle, we have managed to accumulate <u>over $15,000 in credit card debt</u>. We have recently <u>stopped using our credit cards</u> and are living on a very tight budget.

- We are still <u>falling behind a couple hundred dollars per month</u> and have <u>no surplus for catching up on the $5,678.00 we owe in late mortgage payments</u>.

While we fully intend to pay what we owe, we need some relief. We are committed to keeping our home. We truly hope that you will agree to work with us to regain our financial footing.

Sincerely,

Herman & Lilly Crane

Figure 8-1: Sample hardship letter.

Ward and June Hatchet
Loan #: 256789-1

485 Mapleton Drive
Mayfield, CA 68824
May 12, 2012

Sundown Federal
100 West 24th Street
Cheyenne, WY 82002

Dear Sundown:

We are writing to explain the situation that has resulted in our need for a loan modification. We purchased our home 3 years ago on an adjustable rate mortgage with an interest rate of 3%. The interest rate has risen dramatically to 9.75%. The monthly payment has risen from approximately $843/month to over $1,700/month. This has made it impossible for us to afford the monthly payments. We have tried to refinance into a lower fixed-rate loan but have been rejected each time. We have exhausted all of our financial resources trying to remain current on our mortgage payment. Each month we fall further behind.

Staying in our home is our number one priority. We are committed to doing whatever it takes to save our home. My husband is looking for a second job, and I've already gone back to work to generate additional household income. Even with the additional income, we find ourselves short and unable to make the mortgage payment. We love our house, but unfortunately we will be unable to save it without help from you.

We are comforted to read on your Web site that your company has made such a strong commitment to home retention. We honestly feel that with a little help from you we will be successful once again. Attached to this letter are the financial statement and other documentation you need to consider us for one of your home retention programs.

Thank you for your consideration.

Sincerely,

Ward and June Hatchet

Figure 8-2: Sample hardship letter.

Creating Financial Statements

Transitioning from the emotions of financial hardship to the cold, calculating arena of number crunching can be quite chilling, but eventually the decision of whether your lender agrees to a loan modification and the terms you ultimately agree on come down to numbers. You and the lender need to take an honest look at your household income and expenses, and you do this by laying everything out in a *financial statement.*

In the following sections, we encourage you to complete two financial statements:

✔ One showing an accurate accounting of your finances at this very moment

✔ Another illustrating any cost-saving changes you're planning to implement, such as going with the basic plan on your satellite TV service

You may already have most of the information needed to complete your financial statement if you worked through Chapter 2 on taking stock of your situation or Chapter 6 on gathering all the forms and supporting documentation required for completing a loan modification application. If you haven't worked through Chapter 2 or 6, don't flip back (unless you really want to, of course) — the financial form is pretty straightforward.

If your lender has its own financial forms, use those instead of the samples we provide here. Using the correct forms may make the difference between having your application approved or rejected. Contact your lender as we advise in Chapter 5 or visit your lender's Web site to see whether it has downloadable financial forms. Appendix A is full of contact information for lenders, including their Web site addresses.

Painting a current financial portrait

Many lenders require only one financial statement: a detailed account of your current monthly income and expenses along with a list of anything valuable you own and how much it's worth. They want to see on paper whether you're really in financial straits or are blowing too much money on a lavish lifestyle.

Figure 8-3 provides a sample financial form you can use to supply the details that most lenders require. Some lenders want additional information, including your employer's name, your current job title, and how long you worked at your current job . . . assuming, of course, that you're currently employed. They may also want Social Security numbers, driver's license numbers, and to know whether you've filed for bankruptcy. Use the lender's forms to make sure you provide all the information required, but if the lender doesn't supply forms, you can use the sample in Figure 8-3 as a guide.

The only number that's likely to trip you up is the first one under Monthly Expenses: 1st Mortgage (PITI). *PITI* stands for principal, interest, taxes, and insurance. If part of your monthly payment goes into an escrow account to pay your property taxes and home-owner's insurance, the PITI amount is equal to your monthly payment. If you pay property taxes and insurance separately, total the amount you pay in taxes and insurance for the year, divide by 12 months, and add the result to your monthly house payment in order to fill in this item.

When you're working with a lender who requires only one financial statement, knowing which numbers to plug in can be a real challenge. If you know you're overspending on groceries and other stuff every month, for example, do you plug in the real numbers or the amounts you know you could get by on? If you plug in the real numbers, the lender may reject your application on the premise that you *could* afford your house payment by curbing your spending. If you plug in numbers that are too low, you may get rejected because your financial statement shows that you can easily afford your current monthly payment.

When making your estimates, don't overanalyze. Use realistic numbers so you don't end up committing to something you can't really afford.

Every lender has its own *affordability thresholds* to determine whether you have sufficient income to afford your house payment. The lender wants to be sure that you can't afford your payment due to financial hardship, not because you like to eat out every night at fancy restaurants. If you've hired expert representation, your representative is likely to know the lender's affordability threshold and be able to massage the numbers in your financial statement to qualify you while still providing an accurate representation of your budget.

If you're completing the financial statement on your own, you're usually better off using actual numbers from your budget and letting the lender suggest expense categories where you may need to cut back, assuming your lender thinks you need to tighten your belt.

Financial Statement

Loan Number:	Property Address:
Borrower Name:	Co-Borrower Name:
Home Phone:	Home Phone:
Work Phone:	Work Phone:
Mobile:	Mobile:

Monthly Net Income

Borrower Wages	$	Rental Income	$
Co-Borrower Wages	$	Other Income	$
Child Support	$	Other Income	$
Alimony	$	**Total Net Income**	**$**

Monthly Expenses

1st Mortgage (PITI)	$	Life/Other Insurance	$
2nd Mortgage	$	Travel (gas, bus fare)	$
Auto Loan	$	Groceries	$
Student Loans	$	Dining Out	$
Other Loans	$	Entertainment	$
Credit Cards	$	Home Phone	$
Child Care	$	Cellphone	$
Child Support/Alimony	$	Cable/Satellite	$
School/Tuition	$	Internet	$
Utilities	$	Gifts	$
Auto Insurance	$	Other	$
Health Insurance	$	**Total Expenses**	**$**

Assets

Savings Account	$	Other Real Estate	$
Checking Account	$	Car	$
Money Market Account	$	Other Vehicle	$
IRA/Keogh/401k	$	Boat	$
Stocks & Bonds	$	Other	$
Home (market value)	$	**Total Assets**	**$**

Borrower Name: _____ Signature: _____ Date: _____

Co-Borrower Name: _____ Signature: _____ Date: _____

Figure 8-3: A financial statement.

Projecting your post-modification finances

Lenders often want to see a projected financial statement illustrating the budget sacrifices you're willing and planning to make to regain your financial footing after the loan modification. For example, you may be planning to sell one of the family cars to eliminate a payment and save a little on auto insurance and maintenance, trim the grocery bill by a couple hundred bucks a month, cut back your dinner-and-a-movie dates from twice a week to twice a month, and so on.

Knowing what your lender needs to say "Yes"

Serena decided to go after a loan modification alone. She contacted her lender, who gathered her financial information over the phone. A couple of weeks later, she received the bad news: "At this time there are no workout options available to you based on your current financial information provided to us." In other words, "You can't afford the home, so move!" Serena called us instead.

We sat down with Serena and carefully examined her finances. Immediately we discovered $85 per week she was receiving in rent. When we asked whether she had reported this income to her lender, she said, "No." She hadn't realized that the rent was an acceptable source of income; she assumed the only income she could claim was job-related. This extra $85 per week meant Serena had an additional $340 per month to apply toward her monthly payment.

Serena's only mistake is that she didn't know what to ask the lender. But how would she have known? She doesn't do loan modifications for a living, and the lender never told her exactly what qualifies as an "acceptable source of income." As a result, Serena supplied incomplete information to the lender, and the lender based its bad decision on this bad information.

When completing your loan modification application or supplying information over the phone, be sure to ask what may seem like dumb questions to reveal the minor details that can make a huge difference. You may think you know what *income* means, but you really may not know what the lender considers income. (Many borrowers don't know that cash gifts can also qualify as acceptable sources of income, as long as the givers sign affidavits stating that they're giving the borrower a certain (specific) amount of money each month to help with the payments.)

In addition, if the lender denies your initial request for a loan modification, find out why, so you have a clearer idea of what the lender needs to know to say "Yes." Request a second review of your case in order to give your lender an opportunity to make a good decision based on accurate and complete information.

After you have a current financial statement, creating this projected statement should be much easier. Add income to the categories where you realistically think you'll be pulling in more income (if any), and trim back in the expense categories where you realistically think you can save money. And don't forget to account for that lower house payment resulting from the loan modification.

Remain very conscious of your debt ratios in your projected financial statement. We recommend a front-end ratio of 30 percent or lower. (The government's Making Home Affordable program sets the target at no higher than 31 percent.) Your back-end ratio should be in the 35–40 percent range. Turn to Chapter 2 for more about debt ratios and estimating an affordable house payment. You can calculate your debt ratios based on gross income, but it's safer to base your calculations on net income.

If your lender doesn't have a projected financial statement form for you to complete, use the form shown in Figure 8-3. This time, instead of filling in your current numbers, put your projected financials in the blanks.

Signing, Sealing, and Delivering

With hardship letter and financial statement(s) in hand (as explained earlier in this chapter) and all your supporting documents (see Chapter 6) stacked up and ready to go, you're ready to package everything and submit it to your lender . . . or are you?

In the following sections, we show you how to carefully assemble all the components of your loan application and submit it to make absolutely sure everything arrives safely and in the proper format.

Arranging your documents

If your lender provides an application packet or checklist of items to include in your packet, arrange your documents in the order they appear in the list. If your lender doesn't have such a list available, use the checklist provided here to arrange all items in your packet and make sure you're including everything:

❏ Copy of this checklist showing all items included in the packet

❏ Hardship letter

❏ Current financial statement

❏ Projected financial statement

❏ BPO (broker's price opinion), CMA (comparative market analysis), or appraisal if required.

❏ Proof of hardship (birth certificate, death certificate, medical bills, divorce papers, or bankruptcy papers, for example)

❏ Federal tax returns (for the last two years)

❏ W-2s (for the last two years)

❏ Pay stubs (for the last four pay periods)

❏ Bank statements (for the last four periods)

If you owe more on your property than you can sell it for, consider including a BPO, CMA, or appraisal from a local real estate broker. A BPO or CMA is an estimate of a property's market value. Proof that your home is worth tens of thousands of dollars less than the amount you owe your lender shows that the lender will probably lose more money in foreclosure than by lowering your monthly payment. (Some states prohibit anyone other than an appraiser from offering home valuations. Your real estate broker should know whether she's allowed to provide valuations and help you find a licensed appraiser, if you need one.)

Signing on the dotted lines

Flip through the papers you prepared for your application, particularly the hardship letter and financial statement(s), and make sure you and any co-borrowers on the loan have signed and dated the documents.

If you're submitting copies of tax returns that you prepared and submitted electronically, be sure your tax returns are signed and dated, too. You don't need to sign other supporting documents, like W-2 forms or bank statements.

Labeling every page

Lenders are often bombarded with loan modification applications and may have trouble keeping track of all the documentation. An overworked customer service representative can easily drop a stack of applications, shuffling Smith's paperwork with Smyth's and throwing the entire process into utter chaos. To minimize the risk of mix-ups, print your last name, loan number, page number, and number of pages in the upper right corner of each page, like this:

> Roberts, Loan #: 123456789, Page 1 of 27

Numbering the pages is a good idea because it helps the customer service rep keep all the pages in order and enables you to quickly reference items in the future. For example, if someone asks for income verification, you can tell him, "Look at page 14 of 27 to find a copy of my W-2s." Simple and efficient is the name of the game. (If you have two loans with the same lender, make two separate packages and submit them separately.)

Print a sheet of sticker labels with your last name and loan number on them, and apply the stickers to the upper right corner of each page in your application packet. Then you just fill in the page numbers by hand.

Copying the entire packet

After you've arranged all documents in the proper order, copy the entire packet, so you have a complete set of everything you're about to submit to your lender. If your application gets lost in transit or misplaced by the lender, you'll have a backup copy. In addition, if your lender references a particular document in the future, you can easily refer to your copy of the document.

Send the originals of your hardship letter, financial statement, and any other documents you prepared specifically for this application. For any other forms, such as your federal income tax return, W-2s, and bank statements, keep the originals and send copies.

Submitting your application

Finally! You've completed all the necessary forms, gathered all the supporting documentation, and copied everything. Now, you're ready to mail, fax, e-fax, or scan and e-mail the documents.

Ask the lender for its preferred method of receiving the application (usually fax or shipping, such as U.S. Postal Service, UPS, or FedEx). If, upon following up with the lender, you discover that the lender has lost or misplaced all or part of your application package, consider sending future submissions using multiple methods — fax, overnight shipping, and e-mail, for example. This approach may seem like overkill, and it probably is, but it also protects you. If one method of delivery fails, your lender receives the information another way. Some lenders even allow you to apply online by filling out a form, but you probably still need to ship or fax supporting documents. Print or save a copy of all electronically submitted forms for your records.

If possible, address the package (no matter what method you use) to the attention of a specific individual, preferably someone who knows the package is coming. Even if all applications wind up in the same department, your package is more likely to arrive on the desk of the intended recipient if it's addressed to an individual than if you send it generically.

When shipping your application the old-fashioned way, spend a little extra for premium shipping, such as Priority Mail or Next Day Delivery, and request delivery confirmation and any available tracking information. Keep a record of the date and time you sent the application and the address of where you sent it.

When you mail the package, ask when it should reach its destination. The day after the package is scheduled to arrive, follow up with your lender to verify receipt of the package, and keep a written record of when you called, the number you dialed, and the person you talked with. Continue to follow up until your package is either confirmed received or confirmed lost in transit. For more about keeping the process on track and keeping records of *everything,* see Chapter 9.

Chapter 9

Keeping the Process on Track and on Time

A typical loan application takes 30 to 90 days to process. That gives you a whole lot of time to worry and wonder: Maybe they didn't get my application. Did I remember to sign all the forms? Did my application get lost in the shuffle? What if they rejected it?

Regardless of whether you have an expert representing your interest, your head is on the block, so feeling anxious is normal. In this chapter, we offer some suggestions on how you can alleviate some of that anxiety and remain proactive without becoming too intrusive. Here, we show you what you should be doing during that 30- to 90-day waiting period.

 The 30- to 90-day period is the average time required to process a loan modification application and work out a deal. The more complex your situation and the more concessions the lender is required to make, the longer the process.

Knowing What to Expect

Automated phone systems often contain a message indicating the average hold time — something like, "Due to the volume of calls, all of our operators are busy at this time. The average wait time is three minutes." The people who design these systems have realized that people don't mind waiting so much as long as they have some idea of how long they'll have to wait.

The same is true when you apply for a loan modification. Knowing what to expect can significantly reduce your stress and alleviate any anxiety you may feel. Whether you're dealing directly with your lender or a loan modification expert, ask these questions upfront:

- ✔ **How long is the process likely to take?** Find out the best- and worst-case scenarios, and then count out the days and mark them on your calendar.

- ✔ **When can I expect to hear something about my case?** Mark this date on your calendar.

- ✔ **If I don't hear anything by the specified date, whom should I contact?** Get the person's name, employee identification number (if available), phone number, and any extension you need to dial to reach the person directly.

Your lender should have a timeline for just about every step in the process and can probably even tell you how many days it takes for items you fax to get to where they need to be. Some lenders, for example, have a four-day delivery schedule for faxed items. Ask how long each step in the process takes. If a key date passes and you haven't heard anything, follow up.

Documenting the Process for Your Records

When you're trying to negotiate a loan modification, you bump into a lot of people, send and receive a good share of written correspondence, and have plenty of conversations. Even people with photographic memories have a difficult time recalling and recounting everything that happened, the names of the people they spoke with, the dates of calls, who said what, what they sent, how they sent it, and so on.

To improve your memory, use the Contact Log shown in Figure 9-1 to log *everything,* including phone calls you placed, phone calls you answered, items you faxed, e-mail or snail mail correspondence, notices you received, items you shipped, payments you made, and any other attempts you've made to cure the default.

In the following sections, we provide some additional suggestions of how to keep a detailed record of your loan modification journey and verify everything you're told with a reliable source.

Contact Log					
Date	Time	Contact Name	Phone/Fax Number or Address	Ext.	Notes

Figure 9-1: Contact log.

Recording conversations

Audio-recording your telephone conversations may seem over the top, but if it's legal in your state and you don't find it too troublesome or creepy, capturing your conversations on tape provides you with the most detailed and accurate account of what each party agreed to. Your local bar association should be able to tell you whether recording your own telephone conversations is legal in your state (it usually is) and admissible in court.

If you can't (or don't want to) record your phone conversations, take detailed notes. Keep a notebook or legal pad along with a couple of pens or pencils next to your phone so you don't have to search for them when the phone rings. After you hang up, fill in the details of what you talked about while the conversation is still fresh.

If you hired professional representation, you shouldn't be talking details directly with your lender. Anything you say may generate confusion or compromise your representative's ability to negotiate the best arrangement on your behalf.

Keeping copies

You're likely to be sending and receiving plenty of letters and documents throughout the process, so keep a copy of *everything* you send and receive. That may seem obvious, but doing it right is more complex. Follow these recommendations:

- ✔ **Print the date on everything you send *and* receive.** Most people think of placing a date on outgoing correspondence, but it's equally important to record the date you receive correspondence. An office supply store may even have an inexpensive "Received" stamp for convenience.

- ✔ **Keep the envelopes you receive.** Staple the envelope to the document because the postage stamp is an accurate indication of when the document was mailed.

- ✔ **Photocopy the envelopes you use to send documents to prove that you sent them to the correct addresses.**

- ✔ **Send everything with a return receipt request, especially when you're sending something important like your loan modification application.**

- ✔ **If you send a fax, do so from a fax machine that prints a confirmation receipt to prove it went through and was received.**

- ✔ **Print copies of any e-mail correspondence sent or received.**

- ✔ **If you're required to send certified money, keep the check or money order stub.**

Create a separate file folder for all your records, and arrange documents by date — most recent first or most recent last doesn't matter as long as you file documents consistently. Scanning documents and storing them on your computer is fine and provides an easy way to submit documents via e-mail, but keep backup paper copies in case your computer crashes.

Cross-checking the "facts"

Over the years we've observed that homeowners are often fed misleading or even wrong information by sources that should know better. In one case, a bank informed the homeowners that they had six months to *redeem* their property (buy it back after the auction) when they really had an entire year. The six months were up, and the bank was ready to evict the homeowners, even though they had six more months to redeem their property or live in it rent-free!

The moral of this story is to verify everything your lender tells you to the greatest extent possible. For example, if your lender tells you the foreclosure sale that was scheduled has been adjourned, call your county sheriff's office (or whoever's in charge of foreclosure sales in your area) and confirm it. Or ask your lender to confirm the adjournment in writing (via e-mail or fax).

Following Up with Calls and Correspondence

A proactive approach is typically more effective than a reactive one, so keep the process moving forward and check in with your lender (or the person you hired to represent you) occasionally to make sure everything is on track. In the following sections, we provide some suggestions for staying in touch by phone, fax, and e-mail.

Keeping in touch by phone

Time is of the essence, so call your lender or representative at least once a week to make sure everything is on track and everyone has everything they need to keep your modification moving forward. If your lender is missing a document, or if anything else is holding up progress, you want to know about it sooner rather than later so you can provide whatever's needed.

Maintain a list of direct phone numbers and extensions so you don't have to weave your way through the automated system every time you call your lender. Don't be surprised or get upset, however, if your contact is no longer on your case; due to turnover and the fact that many lenders automatically rotate cases every 30 days or so, you may have to deal with someone new . . . which can sometimes be a good thing.

The tale of the lost hardship letter

Attention to detail often pays dividends, as demonstrated in this story about a hardship letter that the lender apparently had trouble keeping track of.

The central character in this tale is a borrower who did everything by the book. He obtained a loan modification packet from the lender and completed everything exactly as instructed. He faxed the application and all the required documents and took extra steps to label and document everything — extra steps that probably saved him from foreclosure:

- ✔ He labeled everything with his last name, loan number, date, and page number.

- ✔ He printed a copy of the fax report showing how many pages were sent and received.

When he called to follow up on the status of his application, the representative informed him that the servicer had not received his hardship letter and the modification was stalled or inactive until the borrower submitted that document.

He retrieved his copy of the package he submitted. Sure enough, marked as page 3 of 18 was his hardship letter. He also retrieved a copy of the fax report confirming that the lender's fax had indeed received it.

Picking his battles, the borrower resubmitted the hardship letter. He included a cover page with his name, loan number, and the date; a cover letter explaining the purpose of this transmission; and a copy of the fax report confirming receipt of the original packet. As before, he labeled every page with his last name, loan number, date, and page number, and he printed a copy of the fax report.

A couple of days later, he called to check the status of his modification and was told again that his file was missing a hardship letter. Keeping his cool, the borrower explained that he had sent it . . . twice. He offered to resend the hardship letter again, but he also explained that the first time he sent it, it was page 3 of 18, and the second time it was page 3 of 4.

Who knows whether the organized nature of the borrower or the weight of the evidence that the hardship letter was actually received caused the representative to mysteriously locate the document or process the modification without it. All the borrower cared about was that his loan modification request was received and approved, and it was.

Some people like to keep a separate phone list on a sheet of paper inside their document folders, but this approach usually buries the list in a stack of other documents. For quick access to contact numbers, consider jotting down the information on the outside or inside of the folder. If you have someone's business card, just tape it to the folder.

Sending or faxing a letter

To create a comprehensive paper trail of all communication you've had with the lender, consider following up every phone conversation with a fax or e-mail message that recounts the conversation. For example, if the loss mitigation representative instructs you to submit your financial statements and a copy of your credit report and an appraisal within 30 days so that she can complete your loss mitigation file, your letter should recap all those points, like this:

> Per your instructions to me in our phone conversation on February 26, 2012, I will be submitting to you within 30 days:
>
> - My completed financial statements
>
> - A copy of my latest credit report
>
> - A copy of the latest appraisal on my house
>
> As I understand it, this is the only information you still need to complete my file.

Always include your name and loan number on every piece of correspondence. If you hand-write the letter, make sure it's clear and legible. When you do finally submit the required documents, attach a cover letter that states you're fulfilling the request made on February 26, 2012, including a statement like this:

> Attached you will find: my completed financial statements, a copy of my credit report, and a copy of the appraisal on my house.

If you ever need to prove when an item was sent or what you were told to do, you have a nice neat paper trail to support your contact log from Figure 9-1.

Remaining in the loop via e-mail

E-mail messages enable you to create a sort of paper trail (albeit an electronic one), but be careful not to accidentally delete an e-mail message or overlook any messages requiring you to act quickly. To manage your e-mail correspondence with your lender most effectively, consider the following tips:

- ✔ Create a separate folder to store all your incoming e-mail messages from your lender.

- ✔ Set up an e-mail filter in your e-mail program to route incoming e-mail from your lender to the new folder you created.

✔ Print copies of important e-mails and file them chronologically in your loan modification folder with all your other records.

As soon as you receive and read a message instructing you to do something related to your loan modification, do it. It's too easy to read a message and then forget about it. If you're not able to perform the task right away, flag the e-mail or mark it as unread so you don't lose it in the sea of other e-mails that need answering.

Dealing with Lender Delays

While some lenders do a good job of expediting the loan modification process, others don't. Intentionally or unintentionally, they delay the process until the option falls through the cracks and the homeowners lose their home. We don't know precisely how often this happens, but for some lenders it's all too common.

In one case reported in the national media, a lender actually admitted in court that although it was running advertisements declaring its willingness to help struggling homeowners and despite its founder and CEO having testified in front of Congress that the company was making modifications a priority, it had no obligation or intention of modifying its customers' mortgages!

As a consumer, you have very little recourse other than hiring an attorney to add some pressure to your lender (see Chapter 4). If you're flying solo, the best you can do is keep in touch with the lender and try to keep the process moving forward. Here are some recommendations:

✔ **Track dates on which you were told you would hear something. If the date passes and you receive no word from the lender, call to find out what's going on.**

✔ **If your lender has a practice of rotating its customer service reps, submit a written request to have your case handled by one representative from start to finish.**

✔ **If the representative assigned to your case is unresponsive, ask to speak with the person's supervisor.** If service doesn't improve, speak with the supervisor again and request that your case be transferred to a different representative.

✔ **Make sure you're dealing with the right department.** The general customer service representative is probably not the person you need to speak with to get answers. You need to talk to a loss mitigation expert. Ask to speak with this person early on in the conversation or you'll find yourself having to repeat everything when you get transferred.

✔ **If you believe that your lender is delaying the process, contact your state attorney general and other consumer advocacy agencies listed in Appendix A.**

Negotiating an Extension or Adjournment

Don't be surprised if you continue to receive delinquency notices or late-payment phone calls during the modification process. Lenders rarely stop the foreclosure process until a workout solution is fully signed and in place. Ask your lender if your attempts to negotiate a solution will stop or at least postpone other collection actions.

If pursuing a repayment plan with your lender doesn't put a stop to collection activities or foreclosure actions, find out what that means for you. If the lender is able to foreclose in 30 days, but the proposed workout can take up to 90 days, you're obviously facing some serious timeline issues.

So, what can you do about it? Following are some suggestions for negotiating an extension or adjournment of the foreclosure process:

✔ **Push your lender to have all collection and foreclosure activities put on hold while your workout attempts are underway, and get any agreement in writing.** If your lender doesn't provide a written agreement, send a follow-up letter or e-mail confirming what you were told so you have *something* in writing.

✔ **If you've hired professional representation, ask your representative to explain what she's doing to postpone collections and foreclosure actions.**

✔ **Hire an attorney to contact your lender on your behalf to explain that you're currently in the process of negotiating a solution and to request that the lender put a hold on collections and foreclosure actions until you've had sufficient time to negotiate an agreement.** A foreclosure attorney who represents homeowners is usually the best person for the job. (For more about selecting and working with an attorney, check out Chapter 4.)

Get any agreement between you and the lender in writing. Also, be aware that postponing the foreclosure may cost the lender money. The lender is likely to add the cost of the stayed foreclosure to the principal balance when calculating the terms of your loan modification agreement. This price, even if you have to pay it, is likely to be less than the cost of you losing your house. Think about it, and pick your battles.

In the Meantime: Exploring Other Options

Applying for a loan modification doesn't mean you'll get one. Plenty of lenders reject requests for assorted reasons — usually because the applicant fails to submit complete and verifiable information, fails to meet the eligibility requirements, or has insufficient income to afford a reasonable lower monthly payment. In short, don't count on your lender to accept and approve your application, even if your chances are very good.

 Plan for the worst, and continue to explore other options. If the lender denies your request for a loan modification or is unwilling to negotiate an agreement you're willing to accept, what are you going to do? What's your plan B? If plan B fails, what's your plan C?

In addition, just because you applied for a loan modification doesn't mean it's the best option for you. Other options presented in Chapter 3 may be even better. Instead of letting your stomach get all tied up in knots waiting for your lender to decide your fate, take control of your own destiny. Consult a real estate broker about listing your home for sale. Talk to a mortgage broker or loan officer about refinancing. Speak with a bankruptcy attorney to find out whether filing bankruptcy would be a better choice.

 Spend some time getting your finances in order. Regardless of whether your loan modification goes through, having a solid cost-cutting budget in place is key in regaining your financial footing and improving the long-term success of any option you choose.

Part III

Hammering Out the Details with Your Lender

The 5th Wave   By Rich Tennant

"Sure, we can modify your loan. Now, did you want to go for the full procedure, or just a little outpatient nip and tuck?"

In this part . . .

*I*n our business, we examine plenty of loan modification offers that lenders pitch to their customers. These offers are usually good news — the lender approved the request for a loan modification! The bad news, however, is often hidden in the details — a monthly payment that's not truly affordable, step-rate increases that raise the interest rate too soon or too fast, legal sleight of hand that strips the homeowners of their legal rights, and other clever tricks to part borrowers from their money.

In this part, we focus on the devil in the details to lead you past the most common pitfalls. We show you how to evaluate different loan modification scenarios, closely examine your lender's initial offer, spot common red flags, and negotiate a better, more affordable loan modification.

Affordability is the word of the day. If your loan modification doesn't result in an affordable monthly payment, it's not good for you or your lender.

Chapter 10

Discussing Loan Modification Scenarios with Your Lender

*I*f you're like most people facing foreclosure, you're pretty bitter and angry right now, and you may be tempted to direct all that anger at your lender and the person who originated your loan. Although they may deserve the full force of your wrath, losing control won't get you any closer to negotiating a good deal. In fact, it could convince the lender to just hang up the phone. This chapter gives you a glimpse of the situation from the lender's point of view and provides suggestions on how to collaborate to reach a mutually beneficial solution.

Regardless of who owns your loan (a bank or investors), you will usually be negotiating through your servicer (the company that collects and processes your monthly mortgage payment).

Looking at the Situation through Your Lender's Eyes

You can optimize the outcome of your loan modification efforts by understanding your lender's perspective. This enables you to take a collaborative rather than confrontational approach to resolving issues. As you proceed, keep the following insights in mind:

✔ Your lender thinks that you obtained the loan and therefore you should honor the terms set forth in the original mortgage and promissory note. To overcome this expectation, you need to show that you experienced a hardship that has prevented you from honoring the original terms.

✔ Short of honoring the terms of the original agreement, your lender wants you to repay the amount you borrowed in full. Lenders tend to frown on requests for principal reductions.

✔ As a result of any loan modification, your lender is likely to collect less interest than under the original agreement, but it still wants to collect as much interest as possible.

✔ Before agreeing to a loan modification, your lender wants to know that you're willing and able to honor the terms of the new agreement — that you can afford the lower monthly payments.

✔ This is *loss mitigation*. Your lender stands to lose either way. If the lender stands to lose less from the loan modification than from foreclosure, you have a very good chance of qualifying.

✔ Your lender's loss mitigation department is probably overwhelmed with requests for loan modifications. They don't want problems or to deal with people they see as big headaches. By helping them solve the problem rather than adding to their problems, you significantly improve your chance to succeed.

Lenders are wary of borrowers bending the truth to qualify for loan modifications they don't really need or qualify for. Remember, lying on a loan or loan modification application is a crime. Don't try to bend the truth or fudge the numbers to qualify.

Practicing the Three C's of Working with a Loss Mitigator

Banks that own mortgage loans typically have *loss mitigators* to make sure the bank loses as little money as possible from bad mortgage loans. The loss mitigator can assist you in exploring options and implementing whichever option you agree on.

No matter how cold and calculating a loss mitigator may seem, he's a human being who appreciates being treated with respect and courtesy. If the loss mitigator has three bad loans to deal with and you're the only borrower acting civilly, you increase your chances of being the one person the loss mitigator assists.

To deal effectively with a loss mitigator, practice the three C's as discussed in the following sections:

- ✔ Communication
- ✔ Composure
- ✔ Credibility

If you doubt your ability to adhere to the three C's, hire professional representation, as described in Chapter 4.

The first C: Communication

"No" means "know," as in the person you're negotiating with doesn't yet "know" enough to say "yes." This is why communication is so important in achieving optimum results through a loan modification. Many loan modification applications are rejected outright because of the following:

- ✔ **The paperwork is unclear.** Rather than trying to decipher a cryptic application, a loss mitigator may simply delete the application or stack it in the "I'll get to this when I can" pile — the pile he never seems to get to.

- ✔ The loss mitigator fails to understand that foreclosure will cost significantly more than a loan modification.

- ✔ Based on the information you supply in your hardship letter or financial statement, over the phone, or through other communications, the loss mitigator believes you don't qualify for a loan modification or don't have sufficient income to afford a reasonable monthly payment.

- ✔ Based on your attitude, the loss mitigator believes you'll end up in default even with a loan modification, or he believes you're just too much trouble to deal with.

A loss mitigator's decision is based primarily on the information you provide. Make sure the information clearly communicates your situation and your commitment to keep your house.

Remember that in many cases the loss mitigator is rewarded for the number of loans he can get to perform, so working out a deal with you is in his best interest. Approach the mitigator as a teammate; you, your lender, and the mitigator should all be working together toward a resolution that benefits all of you.

Work with the loss mitigator as best you can, but remember that he doesn't work for *you* — he represents the lender. A solution is usually available that works for everyone involved, but don't let the loss mitigator dictate the solution. Gather your own information so you aren't at the mercy of what other people tell you.

The second C: Composure

The loss mitigator can pull the plug on negotiations at any time, which places you at a distinct disadvantage. If the loss mitigator begins to think that you're a pain in the shorts, he may decide that you're more trouble than you're worth and simply deny your request for a loan modification. After all, he has people lined up around the block waiting for loan modifications.

To achieve your goals, leave your anger and frustration at the door. They won't do you any good, and they increase the possibility of derailing your efforts. Prove that you're a rational human. Pretend you're Spock. Act calm, cool, and collected.

The third C: Credibility

This may sound callous, but a loss mitigator probably doesn't want to listen to your hard luck story. Sure, he requires a hardship letter and perhaps some proof that you've fallen on hard economic times, but beyond that, all you represent to him is a nonperforming asset. He's heard all the stories; all he wants now is the truth, and he'll be more willing to work with you if you're straight with him. Following are some tips on how to build your credibility:

- ✔ **Come clean.** The loss mitigator is likely to pull up records and may order a credit report to check your story. If it doesn't pan out, you instantly lose credibility. Remember that repeating the truth is easier than repeating lies. Stick with the true story — that's the one you'll never forget.

- ✔ **Act serious.** People are losing money here, so act as though you care and have a sincere interest in righting a wrong, even if you did no wrong to contribute to the current situation. Show up on time for meetings and treat everyone you meet with respect.

- ✔ **Honor your promises.** Promise only what you can reasonably do, and then do it. If you can only pay $1,000 per month, it's better to say that than to agree to pay $1,200 and default on it. Borrowers are often given only one chance to perform. If you default, you may not get a second chance.

People generally start out believing you until you do something that causes them not to believe you. Rebuilding trust is very difficult. If you don't do what you're supposed to, you may not get a next time.

Preventive loan modification? Forget about it

The goal of the loss mitigator is to lessen lender/investor losses, not to help you save money and build a nest egg. If you can afford your current payment, the lender is likely to deny your request for a loan modification. In the infancy of loan modifications, lenders were willing to modify without full documentation, which encouraged some unscrupulous homeowners to try to improve their financial positions at the expense of their lenders. As a result, most loss mitigation departments now require full documentation as a verification tool.

Long story short, if you've missed a couple of house payments and are current on everything else, including credit card payments, three car payments, and your boat payment, don't even think about applying for a loan modification. Any application is likely to get branded with a big rubber stamp — DENIED!

Making Your Case during the Homeowner Interview

Computers make it far too easy to misrepresent reality. In chat rooms, a 50-year-old guy can pass himself off as a 16-year-old girl. Anyone with a desktop publishing program and a $100 printer can forge "official" documents and even produce phony pay stubs and W-2s. As a result of all this opportunity for misrepresentation, most lenders want to speak with you directly prior to approving your loan modification. They want to hear you explain what happened and how committed you are to keeping your home. They want a homeowner interview.

In the following sections, we show you how to prepare for your homeowner interview and present your case during the interview in the best possible light.

If you hire someone to represent your case, your representative is likely to conduct a brief interview prior to agreeing to represent you. These interviews are typically short and sweet (30 minutes or less); they bring your representative up to speed on your situation and give the person an opportunity to see if your story matches the numbers. If your representative conducts this initial interview, you probably won't be interviewed by the lender.

Your lender may or may not require a homeowner interview. If your lender requests an interview, it simply wants to hear what went wrong, how you plan to fix it, and that you're committed to keeping your house. Credibility is key; if anything you say during the interview conflicts with information on your credit report or other documentation you submitted, you're likely to be dead in the water.

If you suspect your lender or loan originator of wrongdoing during the origination of your loan, don't tell your lender. Hire an attorney to present the facts rather than mere suspicions.

Prepping for your interview

The best way to prepare for your homeowner interview is to review your documents (see Chapter 8) and brush up on the facts of your case, including the financial hardship you experienced and the loan modification you need to regain your financial footing (see Chapter 8). You should be prepared to answer the following questions:

- ✔ What financial hardship have you experienced to make your house payment unaffordable?

- ✔ Have you missed any payments? If so, what is the total amount of the missed payments? How do you plan on catching up on missed payments?

- ✔ How do you propose to deal with your inability to make payments — loan modification, forbearance, sell the home, offer a deed in lieu of foreclosure, or something else? (See Chapters 3 and 7 for details about your options and what to ask for.)

- ✔ What, if anything, have you done so far to remedy the situation?

- ✔ How committed are you to keeping your home? How would you feel if you were to lose your home?

Do some research to determine what your lender stands to lose from foreclosure versus loan modification. Chapter 12 walks you through the process of calculating and comparing the two amounts.

Presenting your case

Assuming you prepared properly for your homeowner interview, the interview itself is anticlimactic. You simply lay the facts on the table, answer questions to the best of your ability, and express your sincere interest in doing what's necessary to keep your house.

Even though lenders often have much more to lose from foreclosure than from a modification, many would still prefer to end their relationships with borrowers who can't honor the terms of their original mortgages. We really can't comprehend the reasons for this, but it's obviously the case. Even though an affordable loan modification is usually so much better for the lender, the federal government practically had to twist the arms of major mortgage lenders to convince them to start modifying loans.

A pleasant twist

When negotiating the terms of a loan modification, the best approach is to be careful about what you ask for. The lender may surprise you with a better offer than you had ever imagined, which actually happened with one homeowner we knew — an investor who owned several investment properties out of state.

The investment properties were financed using adjustable-rate loans, and the adjustments were causing significant payment woes. The investor came to the conclusion that he would have to liquidate the investment properties or risk losing his primary residence, too. The value of the investment properties had dropped significantly as a result of the market downturn, so the investor contacted his lender about securing short sales on these properties. He gathered all the information about the lender's requirements and jumped through all the hoops, but the lender continued dragging its feet — it couldn't stomach the values it would have to accept to make the short sales happen.

The lender took a look at the numbers on all the properties and decided that short sales would be possible for some properties that had retained their value. No surprise there. On one of the properties that had lost a substantial amount of value, however, the lender proposed a jaw-dropping loan modification, reducing the payments on a $660,000 investment property to $600 per month, at least temporarily. To achieve this low monthly payment, the lender slashed the interest rate and accepted interest-only payments for several years. The lender simply decided it would be less costly and in its own best interest to keep the investor on the hook for the debt than to foreclose or accept a short sale. The investor hopes that the reduced payments will minimize the burden long enough to allow the market value of the property to recover.

This isn't a typical loan modification, but when the situation is right and lenders are staring huge potential losses in the face, they can become very creative, even to the point of being generous in their offerings.

Examining the MHA Initiative

As the foreclosure crisis deepened, servicers, lenders, and investors were all scrambling for solutions and developing their own workout plans and eligibility requirements. On March 4, 2009, all that changed when the United States Treasury adopted President Obama's Making Home Affordable (MHA) initiative. By adopting this plan, the Treasury hopes to standardize the guidelines, eligibility requirements, and workout solutions throughout the mortgage lending industry.

The MHA initiative provides a good model for how to structure a workout, so we include it here as an example. Keep in mind, however, that the guidelines and how lenders implement the plan are likely to change over time and vary among lenders. In addition, all lenders and investors may not be required to adopt the plan. In other words, your lender is likely to have a system in place similar to the one described here, but be prepared to deal with variations.

The MHA initiative provides two forms of relief for distressed homeowners: refinancing and loan modification. In the following sections, we describe the two components of the MHA initiative.

Not all homeowners automatically qualify for refinancing or loan modification under the MHA plan, and not all lenders and investors are required to abide by the plan (at least not at the time we were writing this book). Check with your lender and visit www.making homeaffordable.gov to find out more about eligibility requirements. If you don't qualify, you can explore other options with your lender, as described in Chapter 3.

Refinancing your loan

For "responsible homeowners" (those who have been making their payments on time), the MHA initiative offers a refinancing component to lower their monthly payments and convert any high-risk loans, such as interest-only loans or adjustable-rate mortgages (ARMs), into lower-risk, fixed-rate loans. Part of the idea here is to help homeowners *before* they find themselves in crisis.

The MHA initiative recognizes that many homeowners can't take advantage of low interest rates because their *loan-to-value* (LTV) ratios are too high for them to qualify for a refinance loan. (See Chapter 3 for more about LTV and refinancing.) Most lenders want to see an LTV of 80 percent or lower before they consider approving a refinance loan.

Given the fact that property values have dropped as much as 25 percent or more in some areas of the U.S., many homeowners have seen their LTVs rise above 80 percent (for example, they owe more than $80,000 on a home that's worth $100,000). In addition, many subprime loans started off with a loan balance above 80 percent LTV, which means refinancing for this class of borrower is difficult to impossible. The MHA initiative is designed to help more homeowners qualify for refinancing.

If you're current on your mortgage loan and don't qualify for a loan modification, refinancing can be an attractive option. By refinancing into a loan with a lower interest rate, you can save hundreds of dollars per month and thousands per year. For example, on a $200,000 30-year mortgage, an interest reduction from 8 percent to 6 percent drops the monthly payment by $268.43 — an annual savings of $3,221.16 and a whopping $96,634.80 over the life of the loan.

Modifying your loan

The loan modification component of the MHA initiative allocates $75 billion for at-risk homeowners, many of whom are stuck in adjustable-rate mortgages (ARMs) and have seen their house payments rise to 40 or even 50 percent of their monthly incomes.

The program offers cash incentives to lenders and borrowers for working out loan modifications that result in reasonable, affordable payments and enable the homeowners to keep their homes. Under the initiative, the lender and Treasury Department team up to reduce the monthly mortgage payment to an affordable level, defined as no greater than 31 percent of the household's gross monthly income. (See the following section "Structuring a Loan Modification" for details on these and other specifics of a loan modification.)

Structuring a Loan Modification

Even with a standard system in place, such as MHA, many variables are involved in structuring a loan modification. The two primary areas of focus deal with making the house payment affordable and catching up on deficiencies. You also need to attend to some details in structuring your loan modification. In the following sections, we provide guidelines to assist you in structuring a reasonable and affordable loan modification with your lender.

The process of structuring the loan modification can vary. In some cases, the lender or servicer gathers the details, reviews the application, and structures the deal without any additional input from you. In other cases, the borrower and the lender may work together to negotiate the details. Afterwards, in either case, the lender presents an offer in writing (as discussed in Chapter 11), which provides you with another opportunity to review the details and negotiate any outstanding issues.

Making the house payment affordable

Regardless of whether your lender adopts the MHA guidelines (voluntarily or involuntarily), the guidelines provide a very good model for achieving an affordable house payment.

The goal of the MHA plan is to establish an affordable payment, so the front-end DTI (debt-to-income) ratio is no higher than 31 percent. This means your monthly payment is no more than 31 percent of your gross monthly income (or household income if you and your partner are listed as co-borrowers on the note). If you earn $5,000 per month, your house payment (principal, interest, taxes, insurance, and association fees) can be no higher than $1,550:

$$\$5,000 \times 0.31 = \$1,550$$

We recommend a front-end DTI ratio no higher than 30 percent, but the MHA recommendation is pretty much on target. (For more about DTI ratios and how to calculate them, check out Chapter 2.)

The MHA plan also takes into consideration the back-end DTI ratio — the percentage of a household's gross monthly income that goes toward making all monthly debt payments, including minimum payments on credit card accounts and auto loans. If the back-end DTI exceeds 55 percent, homeowners are required to sign a statement pledging to obtain credit counseling as a prerequisite for obtaining the loan modification.

If you still have a back-end DTI ratio higher than 55 percent after the loan modification reduces your front-end DTI to 31 percent, you probably have a lot of unsecured debt, like credit card debt. In this case, we advise that you speak to a bankruptcy attorney before signing any agreements with your creditors (anyone to whom you owe money). Chapter 3 discusses the bankruptcy option in greater detail. To find out even more about bankruptcy, check out *Personal Bankruptcy Laws For Dummies,* 2nd Edition, by James P. Caher and John M. Caher (Wiley).

Catching up on deficiencies and penalties

If you have any late or missed payments, your loan modification must address how you'll catch up on these payments and any penalties or fees that the lender is charging you. (Under the MHA plan, lenders must drop any late fees and penalties.)

Push to have any penalties and fees dropped rather than capitalized. When you're already struggling to keep up, your lender shouldn't bury you deeper in debt with penalties and fees.

Following are common options you can discuss with your lender or the person representing you:

- ✓ **Capitalization:** Your lender can roll any missed payment amounts along with late fees and penalties (if applicable) into the balance and then re-amortize (recalculate) your payments.

- ✓ **One-time payment:** If you have some extra money lying around (yeah, right), you can pay off the amount in full.

- ✓ **Payment plan:** The lender may be able and willing to set up a separate payment plan to help you catch up. Of course, this arrangement is only practical if you have enough monthly income to absorb an additional monthly payment.

- ✓ **HSA loan:** Fannie Mae has a HomeSaver Advance (HSA) program that allows lenders to provide an advance to homeowners to enable them to catch up on past-due amounts. Penalties and fees are *not* included in the past-due amount, and the loan is up to 15 percent of the unpaid principal balance or $15,000, whichever is less. The loan isn't secured by the property, bears a 5-percent fixed rate of interest, requires no payments for the first six months, and matures in 15 years.

Addressing interest-rate issues

Until recently, homeowners often focused too much on the monthly payments the lenders were dangling in front of their noses. They should have been looking at the current and projected interest rates just as closely. When you're getting your loan modified, here's what you need to know and do regarding interest rates:

- ✓ **Check the current mortgage interest rates to make sure you're getting a fair deal.** You can look up interest rates at www.bankrate.com as well as many other Web sites.

- ✓ **A low introductory rate is good — the lower the better.**

✓ **It's normal for a lender to step up the rate later. Just make sure the steps are gradual and your monthly payment is still affordable at the cap (the upper limit).**

✓ **Beware of modifications that offer a *float rate* instead of a step rate.** If the rate floats with the margin plus index after a short low-interest introductory period, this fix could cause serious problems later, just like ARMs did.

✓ **Opt for a fixed-rate loan.** The lender may still step up the rate over the course of several years, but the steps are predictable (not tied to a fluctuating index), so you can plan for them.

✓ **Don't let the lender set you up in an interest-only modification.** These loans are interest-only for a limited time. The shell shock comes later when you have a balloon payment (a large chunk of change due all at once) or have to start paying down the principal along with interest.

Request Denied: Now What?

Your lender or servicer can deny your loan modification request for any number of reasons. If your request is denied and you're still committed to keeping your home, consider the following options:

✓ **Appeal.** Ask to speak with a loss mitigation supervisor, who may have greater authority to make an exception.

✓ **Explore your legal options, as explained in Part IV of this book.** If your lender or the person originating the loan violated certain consumer protection or lending laws, they may be required to rewrite your mortgage loan.

✓ **If your mortgage is investor-owned rather than bank-owned and you've experienced extenuating circumstances (such as contracting a serious medical condition), ask to have your case reviewed by the portfolio manager.** If you really want to push to have a portfolio manager review your file, you may need to hire an attorney or mortgage expert to put your case in front of the portfolio manager.

The MHA plan guidelines (see "Examining the MHA Initiative" earlier in this chapter for details) changed the rules for many of the big lenders and servicers, referred to in the industry as *Megas,* but it didn't (initially at least) force investors to comply, so if your mortgage is investor-owned rather than bank-owned, appealing any denial could be much more challenging. If the investor that owns your mortgage didn't accept TARP (Troubled Asset Relief Program) money from the federal government, it may not be required to follow MHA guidelines, and it certainly has greater power in denying any request for a loan modification.

Chapter 11

Evaluating Your Lender's Initial Offer

. . . .

In This Chapter

▶ Making sense of a loan modification agreement

▶ Gauging the affordability of an offer

▶ Watching out for interest rate hikes

▶ Tiptoeing around common legal land mines

. . . .

Lenders are odd creatures. They help put you in a loan you can't possibly afford, and then when you prove you couldn't afford it, many of them try to negotiate you into a modification you can't possibly afford. Understandably, their goal is to maximize their profit, but in the pursuit of this goal, they often lose money by negotiating terms that put homeowners back on the road to default and ultimately foreclosure.

Because your lender is unlikely to present an opening offer with the best possible terms the lender can afford, be prepared to evaluate the initial offer carefully. This chapter points out the pitfalls you need to watch out for. After you work through your evaluation, check out Chapter 12 for tips on negotiating a better offer.

Deciphering a Loan Modification Agreement

Attorneys have their own language. From a distance, it looks an awful lot like English, but upon closer inspection, it reads more like Egyptian hieroglyphics. Yes, we're well aware that the goal is to ensure that the language remains very precise, but it can befuddle even the most sophisticated consumers.

Fortunately, loan modification agreements are relatively short — shorter than the mortgages they modify. In *Foreclosure Self-Defense*

For Dummies (Wiley), we provide a primer on how to decipher a mortgage document, promissory note, and other closing and pre-closing documents. In the following sections, we highlight and explain key clauses in loan modification agreements.

Don't sign a legal agreement unless you've read it, fully understand it, and agree to adhere to everything it states. If you don't fully understand everything, ask your lender to explain it to you, and keep asking questions until you grasp the meaning. If you disagree with a provision in the agreement, do your best to have it removed or changed, or be sure you can live with it before you sign on the dotted line. If your lender is unable to clear up any confusion you may have, you may need to consult an attorney.

Checking the reference to your former mortgage

By definition, a loan modification *modifies* the terms of an existing legal agreement; that existing legal agreement is the mortgage or deed of trust that names the property as security for repayment of the debt (the note). Almost every loan modification agreement starts out by referencing that pre-existing loan agreement. The language may look something like this:

> This loan Modification Agreement ("Agreement"), made this 25th day of February, 2012, between Basil Floret and Sandy Floret (the "Borrower(s)") and Applewide Home Loans Servicing LP (the "Lender"), amends and supplements (1) the Mortgage. Deed of Trust, or Deed to Secure Debt (the "Security Instrument"), dated the 12th day of January, 2005, and recorded on the 12th day of January, 2005, in the Official Records of County, in the State of MI, and (2) the Note and Adjustable Rate Rider bearing the same date as, and secured by, the Security Instrument, and (3) any prior agreements or modifications in effect relative to the Note and Security Instrument which covers the real property described in the Security Instrument and defined therein as the 'Property', located at 20236 Cattle Drive, Boomtowne, MI 4882, collectively the prior documents shall be referred to herein as the "Note and Security Instrument".
>
> The real property described being set forth as follows:
>
> "SAME AS IN SAID SECURITY INSTRUMENT"

The key phrase in this clause is "amends and supplements," meaning the original security instrument (mortgage or deed of trust) and the note remain in place except for any changes stipulated in this new agreement.

Check your mortgage or deed of trust to ensure that your loan modification agreement is referencing the correct security instrument. If anything in the reference to your mortgage or deed of trust (such as the date, your name, or the property address) is wrong, have the information corrected prior to signing anything.

Analyzing the unpaid balance

The loan modification agreement always establishes the amount of the unpaid principal balance. This is the amount you still owe on the loan, which may represent any of the following:

- ✔ Only the unpaid principal

- ✔ The unpaid principal plus any missed payments and penalties that will be *capitalized* (added to the unpaid principal)

- ✔ An amount lower than the unpaid principal, if the lender agreed to a principal reduction or principal forbearance (see Chapter 3 for more info on this and other options)

If your loan modification is made available through the federal government's Making Home Affordable (MHA) plan, your lender or servicer is required to waive any late fees or penalties and is prohibited from charging a loan modification fee. (Chapter 10 gives you details on this plan.)

Following is a statement of the unpaid principal balance pulled from an actual loan modification document. When deciphering this clause, focus on the date and the amount of the unpaid principal balance. If the amount doesn't match your records, contact your lender and find out why.

Amount of Borrower's Unpaid Principal Balance

As of the 1st day of March, 2012, the amount payable under the Note and Security Instrument (the "Unpaid Principal Balance") is U.S. $230,000.00, consisting of the amount(s) owed by the Borrower to the Lender and which may include, but are not limited to, any past due principal payments, interest, escrow payments, fees and/or costs ("Unpaid Amounts") which the Borrower has agreed shall be capitalized (added to the amount the Borrower originally borrowed) as one of the terms of this agreement. Any late/delinquency fees associated with overdue loan payments remaining unpaid as of the date immediately before this modification have been waived and are not capitalized. The Borrower understands that capitalizing the Unpaid Amounts may result in the Borrower paying more interest over the life of the loan.

Closely examine any wording that addresses capitalization because this is an area that's open for negotiation. You may be able to convince the lender to drop any late fees and penalties and perhaps even forgive a portion of the missed payment total (part of the interest, anyway). You're not likely to get off the hook for past-due principal or escrow payments, however.

Acknowledging the promise to pay

When you purchased the property and closed on the deal, you signed a promissory note pledging to pay back the loan in full with interest on the date the loan matures (comes due).

Your loan modification agreement is likely to contain a borrower's promise to pay clause to reaffirm your commitment to pay back the loan. Just make sure the maturity date is correct. For example, if you're signing the agreement in 2010 for a loan modification with a 30-year term, the maturity date should be 2040, not 2035.

Make sure your lender isn't offering a loan modification in exchange for your agreement to pay off the note more quickly or as a balloon payment (a big lump sum that comes due on the maturity date). A balloon payment may be acceptable under two conditions:

- ✔ Your original mortgage called for a balloon payment.

- ✔ You and your lender have agreed to a principal forbearance, in which a portion of the principal is due on the maturity date (or earlier if you sell or refinance prior to the maturity date).

Ask your lender for a copy of the amortization table, showing how much of each payment is being applied to principal and interest. If your principal balance (including any capitalized delinquencies and penalties) is fully amortized, the final payment should show the balance being paid in full. It may be off by a few dollars and cents, but it should be close. Make sure that you don't have a large balance due at the end of the term, unless that's what you agreed to.

Inspecting the monthly payment details

Every loan modification agreement should state your projected monthly payment. Unfortunately, this information can become very complex depending on capitalization and interest rates. In many of these agreements, the lender doesn't simply drop the interest rate from 10 percent to 4 percent, for example. That would be too easy.

Lenders often prefer a more creative approach that provides a heavier dose of relief early on and then phases it out over time. For example, the lender may offer to drop the interest rate to 3.5 percent for the first year and then raise it each year until it hits 7.5 percent. As a result, your payment increases each year in what are known as *step-rate adjustments.* Here's a typical monthly payment clause that stipulates only the initial monthly payment that's subject to change:

Amount of Borrower's Initial Scheduled Monthly Payments

As of the 1st day of April, 2012, the scheduled monthly payment will be in the amount of U.S. $780.00. The scheduled monthly payment may change on that day of every twelfth month thereafter as described in Section 4 of this Loan Modification Agreement. The Lender will notify the Borrower prior to the date of change in the scheduled monthly payment. The amount of the monthly payment may change if the Borrower makes voluntary prepayments of principal.

(A) Monthly Payment Changes

Changes in the monthly payment will reflect changes in the unpaid principal and in the interest rate that the Borrower must pay. The Lender will determine the changed amount of the monthly payment in accordance with Section 5 of this Loan Modification Agreement.

Step increases in the interest rate are normal. Just make sure the step increases are delayed for enough time to catch your breath, the steps are gradual, the cap (maximum interest rate) is reasonable, and the modification ultimately results in a mortgage with an affordable fixed rate. You don't want a rate that steps up early and often. Your primary goal is to obtain a modification that keeps you in your home now and remains affordable for at least three to ten years, giving the market and the economy time to recover and providing you with sufficient time to improve your own financial situation.

When you're trying to determine whether the proposed house payment is affordable, account for any escrow payments to cover property taxes, insurance, and any homeowner association (HOA) fees. Under the MHA plan, all loans require escrow accounts, so house payments include principal, interest, taxes, insurance, and any association fees. If your lender doesn't require you to escrow these amounts, we strongly encourage you to ask your lender to do so.

Wading through any interest rate adjustments

As mentioned in the previous section, lenders can become very creative when offering interest rate reductions. We've seen offers from lenders that included annual hikes in the interest rate coupled with a ten-year interest-only payment option. In other words, a homeowner would pay only interest on the mortgage for the first ten years and wouldn't start paying down the principal until then.

We applaud the creativity of some lenders, but these sorts of offerings often confuse consumers. You really need to examine the net effect of any interest rate adjustments on your monthly payment and principal. If the details aren't presented clearly in the agreement, ask the following questions:

- **What is my interest rate going to be?**
- **Will my interest rate ever rise?**
- **On what dates is my interest rate scheduled to rise?** These are often referred to as the *change dates*.
- **How much will the interest rate rise on each date?**
- **How will the changes in my interest rate affect my payments?** Make sure you get concrete information showing *exactly* what your monthly payments will be with each adjustment.
- **What's the cap (the highest the interest rate can rise)?**
- **What's the absolute highest my monthly payment can be?**

- **Will I be notified in writing prior to the rate step? If so, how much time will I be given to prepare for the increase?**
- **If I have an interest-only period, how much will my payments be when I start paying principal?**
- **If I make my scheduled monthly payments as stipulated in the agreement, will I have paid the balance of the loan in full by the date on which the loan matures?**

Your lender is unlikely to tell you the total you'll be paying over the life of the loan, even if you ask. You can calculate this amount by using the formula in the following section. Use the same formula for your original loan for comparison purposes. If your new agreement has you paying tens of thousands of dollars more in interest, you may want to negotiate.

Inspecting any term extension

Loan modifications often use term extensions to lower the monthly payment. For example, a $200,000 30-year mortgage at 7 percent interest has a monthly payment of $1,330.60. Extend it to 40 years, and the payment drops about $90 per month. In and of itself, a term extension probably won't help save your home, but coupled with an interest rate reduction, it can make the monthly payment affordable.

Unfortunately, over the life of the loan you can pay a heavy price for a term extension — $117,772 in the previous example, assuming you make only the minimum payment each month and pay on the loan until its maturity date. That's a considerable amount of money for a $90 discount on your monthly payment. To determine the total cost of a loan over the life of the loan, multiply the monthly payment by the term (in years) by 12 months per year, as follows:

$$\text{Cost of Loan} = \text{Monthly Payment} \times \text{Term} \times 12$$

 Even though a term extension can cost more over the life of the loan, we still recommend that most homeowners extend the term as long as possible. Why? Because extending the term gives you flexibility. You can pay extra toward the principal whenever you can afford it, but when you can't afford it, you have the lower monthly payment to fall back on. Just make sure that when you pay extra, you specify that the extra amount be *applied to principal.* Then, check your statement to make sure it is.

 If your original mortgage stipulates a prepayment penalty, try to have it removed with the loan modification agreement. Otherwise, by making additional principal payments, you could be costing yourself thousands in the form of a prepayment penalty. If the lender refuses to remove the penalty, just make sure the prepayment penalty clause is reasonable in that it meets these criteria:

- ✔ The penalty is within the standard range of 1 to 3 percent of the total borrowed (the lower, the better). On a $200,000 loan, a "reasonable" prepayment penalty would be $2,000 to $6,000.

- ✔ The penalty phases out over 60 months or less.

- ✔ The penalty doesn't apply to prepayment due to sale of the home.

Capitalizing or waiving penalties and other fees

As mentioned earlier in this chapter in the section "Analyzing the unpaid balance," homeowners can typically catch up on late or missed payments in any of the following ways:

- ✔ Pay up in full.

- ✔ Catch up over the course of several months with an installment plan.

- ✔ Catch up over the life of the loan by having the late and missed payments *capitalized* (added to the principal balance).

If your loan modification is made available through the federal government's MHA plan, your lender or servicer can't charge you any additional fees or penalties. If your loan modification doesn't fall under this plan, request that all fees be itemized. A $1,500 "other advances" fee may include all sorts of hidden fees that you might question if you knew what they were for. Try your best to have all penalties and fees waived rather than capitalized.

Steering Clear of Common Traps

Contracts tend to be one-sided. They're almost always written in a way to protect the interests of the author of the contract while ignoring the interests of all other parties involved. This is one of the reasons you may want to hire an attorney or at least get the help of an independent loan modification expert or licensed consumer credit counselor (see Chapter 4).

Loan modification agreements are no different; they're legal contracts primarily designed to protect the interests of the lender or investor who holds the mortgage note. Sometimes, lenders even try to gain new rights under the agreement. In other words, you need to watch your back. In the following sections, we point out some of the most common traps hidden in the legalese.

Dismissing the take it or leave it threat

Almost all loan modification agreements include a cover letter with some sort of phrasing that suggests you have two choices: take it or leave it. Here's the way one lender likes to put it:

> In order to take advantage of the options above, you must agree to the enclosed modification agreement and return it to us as indicated below.

In other words, discussion time is over. Take it or leave it. The same letter contains another slightly more subtle take-it-or-leave-it threat:

> There are two ways you can resolve your past due amount of $9,000:
>
> **1. If you are able to pay the past due amount:**
> If you can pay back your past due amount and do not wish to add it to your loan balance, please contact us at [xxx] to make arrangements to pay this amount and receive new modification documents.

2. If you are NOT able to pay your past due amount:
Read and sign the enclosed modification. Accepting the
enclosed modification will resolve your past due amount and
authorize us to add the unpaid amount through February 2012
to the principal balance of your loan. If you agree to the terms
of this modification, your monthly principal and interest payment will be higher than it would have been had the past due
amount not been added to your balance.

In other words, unless you can come up with $9,000 in a hurry, the
deficiency will be capitalized into your unpaid principal balance.
(The unstated third option would be to forgive the deficiency or a
portion of it, but by the language used, that's not an option.)

An even more sinister and deceptive take it or leave it threat
comes in the form of what we like to refer to as the *ticktock provision.* The lender ships the loan modification agreement to you
with a cover letter dated February 5 that arrives at your house on
February 17, informing you that you have five days from the date
of the letter (the 5th) to return the signed documents to the lender.
This deadline gives you a whole 13 minutes to contemplate the
terms of the modification agreement, sign it, have it notarized, and
get it back in the mail to the lender. That's right, time is running
out on the opportunity for you to keep your home . . . tick . . . tock!

Even though the terms of just about every legal agreement are
negotiable, the lender wants you to think that this agreement is
nonnegotiable. Don't fall for these common traps. As long as your
lender has less to lose through a loan modification than through a
foreclosure, you can safely bet that the lender is willing to negotiate. (See Chapter 12 for negotiating strategies.)

Waving off legal waivers to your legal rights

Sometimes, lenders use loan modification as an opportunity to
strip homeowners of some rights afforded to them under the law
or through the original mortgage and note. Here's an example from
an actual loan modification agreement:

**Borrowers Agreement to Assist with Lost, Misplaced,
Misstated, Inaccurate or Missing Documents**

In consideration of this Modification, the Borrower agrees that
if any document related to the Note and Security Instrument
and/or Modification is lost, misplaced, misstated, inaccurately
reflects the true and correct terms and conditions of the loan
as modified, or is otherwise missing, the Borrower will comply

with the Lender's request to execute, acknowledge, initial and deliver to the Lender any documentation the Lender deems necessary. If the original promissory note is replaced, the Lender hereby indemnifies the Borrower(s) against any loss associated with a demand on the original note. The Borrower agrees to deliver the Documents within ten (10) days after receipt by the Borrower of a written request for such replacement.

In other words, if the *lender* loses documents, *you* have ten days to replace them or help the lender create new ones. The reason lenders often try to insert this language is because mortgage lending has become so complex that mortgages, promissory notes, and other documents are often lost in the shuffle. Consumers have gotten wise to this fact and are beginning to use it to their advantage, employing the *produce the note strategy* to delay foreclosure actions; see the sidebar of that name for the full story.

Warning! Shifting interest rates

Technically speaking, a loan modification that calls for steadily increasing interest rates (called *step-rate increases*) is not an adjustable-rate mortgage (ARM) because the adjustments aren't tied to any index over which you have no control. Instead, the lenders provide step-rate increases that start you off with a low interest rate (typically below the market rate). At scheduled intervals, the rate is stepped up by a predetermined percentage up to a maximum rate, which then typically remains fixed over the life of the loan.

A step-rate modification isn't all bad, especially if the percentage increase is low and the interval between adjustments is long, because the goal you set out to achieve is to make your payment affordable and keep your house.

Whenever the interest rate increases over time, you have a situation in which you need to modify your monthly budget with each rate increase. Make sure you know when an increase is coming so you can adjust your budget to accommodate your rising cost of living. See "Wading through any interest rate adjustments" earlier in this chapter for questions to ask your lender.

Ducking repeated defaults

More than half of all homeowners who receive a loan modification end up in the same situation within eight months of having their monthly payments lowered. The cause of *recidivism* (repeated defaults) can usually be traced back to one or a combination of the following:

Produce the note

One foreclosure self-defense move that seems to be growing in popularity is the *produce the note strategy,* which can be quite effective in stopping foreclosure in its tracks and buying a homeowner more time to pursue other options. Implementing the strategy differs depending on whether you live in a state that follows a judicial or nonjudicial foreclosure process:

✔ **In states that require judicial foreclosure,** the lender must file suit to obtain permission to proceed with the foreclosure sale. This initiates a legal process in which you can simply demand that the lender produce the note — the promissory note or IOU you signed when you took out the mortgage.

✔ **In states that allow nonjudicial foreclosure (more than half the states in the U.S.),** you receive a notice of intent from the lender prior to the foreclosure sale and the process occurs outside of the judicial system. You can bring your case inside the judicial system by filing your own lawsuit against the lender. In the course of the legal proceedings, you can demand that the lender produce the note.

Requesting that the lender produce the note challenges the lender to provide the document proving that you agreed to pay back the money, which isn't always as easy as it sounds. If the judge is sympathetic to your case, she may order the lender to produce the note. Although most lenders can track down the required documents, this strategy can delay the legal proceedings for several weeks, giving you more time to pursue alternatives to foreclosure, as described in Chapter 3. A lender's inability to locate the original note can create significant difficulties for the lender in proceeding with foreclosure.

✔ The loan modification failed to result in a truly affordable monthly mortgage payment.

✔ The homeowners failed to address the root cause of their financial hardship, essentially falling back into old habits.

✔ The homeowners experienced another financial hardship.

In Chapter 16, we provide tips to help you avoid becoming a recidivism statistic. When you're reviewing your lender's offer, you have an opportunity to short-circuit one of the major causes of recidivism — a loan modification that doesn't provide a truly affordable monthly payment.

Examine the terms of the agreement carefully in the light of your monthly income and expenses (see Chapter 2). If the proposed monthly house payment is unaffordable or makes your monthly budget so tight that you're just one large car repair bill or one major medical expense away from default, return to the negotiating table to push for a better deal.

I agreed to *what?!*

Selma obtained what she considered to be an affordable loan modification, and she did it all on her own. Unfortunately for Selma, lightning struck twice. Nine months later, she experienced another major financial setback, and her modified loan was no longer affordable. She needed another modification.

Unfortunately, when Selma signed that first loan modification agreement, she failed to read between the lines. She focused solely on the numbers — the lower fixed interest rate, the extended term, and the fact that she could catch up on the deficiencies over the life of the loan rather than having to pay them all at once. It looked like a great deal to her, and based solely on the numbers, it was a good deal. Unfortunately, this agreement included a clause stating that by accepting the modification, Selma was giving up the rights to any future loan modification. This isn't typical. Many lenders leave open the possibility for borrowers to obtain another loan modification if a change in circumstances justifies it. As soon as Selma signed and submitted that modification, she relinquished that right over the life of the loan. Foreclosure was imminent.

You can learn an important lesson from Selma's mistake: Don't judge a loan modification solely by the numbers. Read the agreement word for word and have your attorney review it, explain it, and highlight and explain any key issues before you sign the document. Those tiny clauses can have huge ramifications in the future.

Neither you nor the lender wants to go through this process again, so do it right the first time. We offer suggestions on how to negotiate a better deal in Chapter 12.

If you're committed to keeping your home, we're committed to arming you with the information and insight you need to make that happen through a loan modification or other solution. However, we encourage you to make an honest assessment of your situation. If you can't afford the house unless the lender essentially gives it to you for free, you need to make alternate arrangements for a graceful exit. (See Chapter 3 for alternatives to loan modification.) Don't obligate yourself to payments you can't maintain.

Chapter 12

Negotiating a Better Deal

. . . .

In This Chapter

▶ Reiterating your commitment to a win-win solution

▶ Reminding your lender to keep affordability in mind

▶ Remaining persistent

▶ Hinting at the possibility of legal action

. . . .

*Y*our lender's loan modification goal is to have you to pay as much as you can afford in monthly mortgage payments and eventually pay back the loan in full. Your goal is to pay as little as possible — a penny a month would be nice, yes?

Somewhere in between those two extremes is a reasonable solution that serves both your needs — keeping you in your home without making you feel like a servant to it, and enabling the lender to cut its losses and perhaps earn a reasonable profit.

In this chapter, we offer some guidelines to determine what's "reasonable" for homeowners and lenders, and we reveal various strategies for gaining more of what you want and need while still enabling the lender to mitigate its loss.

Recommitting to a Reasonable Solution

Each party involved in a loan modification has his own idea of what "fair" looks like. Homeowners may think the fair option is to reduce the balance to the current value of the property and then re-amortize the mortgage at 3 percent interest. The lender, on the other hand, may see a fair deal as one that capitalizes the deficiencies, penalties, and fees (meaning adds them to the unpaid balance) and drops the interest rate to 4 percent for three years, followed by incremental increases up to market rates. Usually, what's fair falls somewhere in between.

Fortunately, the United States Department of the Treasury provides some guidelines for determining what's fair and is likely to result in an affordable monthly mortgage payment. In the following sections, we cover the government guidelines in place during the writing of this book. These guidelines may change, but they still provide excellent parameters for determining what's fair for homeowners as well as for lenders or investors.

The federal government has rolled out a new Web site designed to help homeowners determine what an acceptable monthly payment looks like: www.makinghomeaffordable.gov. The calculator on this site is based on the premise that 31 percent of a household's gross monthly income is a "fair" and sustainable amount to pay on a mortgage loan. Visit the site and see what the federal government thinks is "fair" for your household. For more about the Making Home Affordable (MHA) program, check out Chapter 10.

The MHA program applies to all government-insured loans (including FHA and VA loans), loans owned by Fannie Mae and Freddie Mac, and loans owned by lenders who choose to participate in the program.

What's fair for homeowners

According to the MHA guidelines, a fair deal for homeowners means an affordable house payment, and the Treasury Department determines affordability based on *debt-to-income* (DTI) ratios. (See Chapter 2 for details on how to calculate your DTI ratios.) According to MHA guidelines, any loan modification should meet the following DTI ratio requirements:

- ✔ **Front-end DTI ratio must not exceed 31 percent.** The monthly mortgage payment resulting from the loan modification (including monthly principal, interest, taxes, insurance, and homeowner association fees) must be no greater than 31 percent of the monthly gross household income.

- ✔ **Back-end DTI ratio must not exceed 55 percent.** The total monthly debt payments (including mortgage, credit card, auto loan, alimony, and other such payments) shouldn't be greater than 55 percent of the monthly gross household income. If it is, debt counseling is required under the program.

MHA programs are available exclusively for owner-occupied residences — not rentals, second homes, or investment properties.

To achieve the targeted 31-percent DTI ratio, the MHA plan calls for lenders to first reduce the interest rate on qualifying mortgages to achieve a 38-percent or lower front-end DTI ratio. The

Treasury then matches further reductions in monthly payments dollar-for-dollar with the lender/investor, down to a 31-percent front-end DTI ratio.

To achieve the 31-percent DTI target, lenders/investors can lower the interest rate, extend the term, and reduce the principal balance, in that order. The plan advises lenders to first look at reducing the interest rate. If that doesn't do the trick (make the monthly payment affordable), lenders are encouraged to extend the term. If the rate reduction and term extension don't do the trick, then lenders can reduce the principal. The plan does allow lenders to go beyond the guidelines and offer more relief or even follow some other approach to achieving affordability.

Assuming homeowners and lenders can negotiate a mortgage modification that hits the 31-percent front-end DTI target, the next test is whether the back-end DTI ratio (taking the modified loan into consideration) is greater than 55 percent. If the back-end DTI ratio exceeds 55 percent, homeowners are required to sign a letter stating that they agree to work with a HUD-approved credit counselor. (HUD is the U.S. Department of Housing and Urban Development.) Any proposed modification doesn't take effect until the homeowners provide a signed statement indicating that they will obtain counseling.

MHA guidelines can change at any time and may not apply to all servicers, lenders, and investors. We provide these numbers only to give you some guidelines to judge whether a lender's offer is fair. As we suggest in Chapter 2, we prefer more conservative estimates of affordability based on *net* (after-tax) income rather than *gross* income. You need to determine for yourself what "affordable house payment" means to you based on your budget, debt level, and lifestyle.

What's fair for lenders and investors

To paraphrase a quote from Oliver Wendell Holmes, an individual's rights end where another's begin. When the Treasury Department drew up its MHA guidelines, it took this idea into consideration, acknowledging that the homeowner's right to an affordable house payment should not infringe on the lender's or investor's right to earn a reasonable profit (or at least not suffer too much of a loss) by modifying loans.

To determine what's fair and best for lenders, MHA requires that all participants in the program apply an NPV (net present value) test on every mortgage loan that's in "imminent default" or is at least 60 days delinquent under the MBA (Mortgage Bankers Association) delinquency calculation.

The NPV test consists of a collection of complex formulas that account for, among other things, cure rate, liquidation value, property value depreciation, REO (real estate owned) stigma discount (the fact that buyers typically offer significantly less for repossessed homes), selling costs, marketing time, and re-default rate. The Treasury provides an NPV tool that enables lenders to plug in information about a particular mortgage to determine whether the mortgage passes the test.

What it all boils down to is this: Lenders who participate in the MHA program are required to modify a mortgage only if the NPV test shows that the modification will cost them less than the estimated cost of foreclosure. Lenders still have the option to modify mortgages if the modification will cost more than the estimated cost of foreclosure, but they're *required* to modify only if the NPV test shows a net positive to the lender.

Again, at the time of writing, MHA guidelines and the NPV test don't apply to all lenders, servicers, and investors. However, most lenders have tools in place to compare the cost of a loan modification with that of foreclosure. Unfortunately, homeowners rarely, if ever, receive access to these same tools. Fortunately, we show you how to make some comparisons of your own in the upcoming section "Reminding Your Lender What It Stands to Lose."

Reminding Your Lender What You Can Afford to Pay

When you applied for your mortgage, the loan originator probably sat down with you, collected some financial data, plugged the numbers into a calculator, and then told you how much house you could afford. It probably sounded like more house than you thought you could afford, and it ended up being more house than you could afford, but back then, that was how many loan originators operated. The goal was to stretch a bit in order to earn a bigger return on your investment.

Unfortunately, when negotiating a loan modification, many lenders take the same approach. They crunch the numbers and tell homeowners how much they can afford to pay, often overlooking other expenses in the process.

Don't let anyone tell you how much you can afford to pay per month for housing. Your household budget should tell you all you need to know. In Chapter 2, we show you how to get a handle on your situation and estimate an affordable monthly payment. In Chapter 7, we show you how to crunch the numbers for yourself to achieve your goal. After working through those two chapters, you should have a clear idea of the monthly amount you can afford to pay for housing. Keep that bottom line in mind, and remind your lender as often as necessary how much you really can afford to pay.

What often occurs during negotiations is that homeowners become so frightened of losing their homes that they're willing to agree to just about anything to keep them. They end up agreeing to unaffordable house payments that put them back on the path to a future default. If you don't hire an expert to represent your interests, at least consult with a friend or relative who has a cool head and is less emotionally involved in the situation. Sometimes, you need someone on hand to remind *you* how much you can afford to pay.

 Approach the situation objectively. Some homeowners who have gotten themselves in trouble through their own carelessness often make the mistake of demanding that their lenders slash the mortgage payments so they won't have to adjust their budgets. This is rarely effective. Demonstrating to your lender that your budget is stretched as thin as possible and that you need a lower mortgage payment to make ends meet is a much better way to go — and more successful, too.

Reminding Your Lender What It Stands To Lose

Whenever you're in negotiations, you place yourself in a stronger position by knowing what the other party stands to gain or lose. In most cases in which a homeowner qualifies for a loan modification, the lender is looking at a lose-lose scenario in which the choices are

- ✔ A loan modification resulting in a lower interest rate and monthly payments, meaning the lender loses revenue, advances costs, and at times forgives principal.

- ✔ A foreclosure resulting in out-of-pocket costs for legal fees, rehabbing, and selling the property, possibly for less than the unpaid balance on the loan.

Lenders know what they stand to lose and gain by agreeing to loan modifications because they crunch numbers all day long, five to seven days per week. When negotiating with your lender, you need to know, too. If you know that the lender stands to lose $50,000 by foreclosing on your home and kicking you out, for example, and it's offering you a loan modification that's going to result in a net loss to the lender of only $7,000, you know that lender has a lot more room to negotiate. More importantly, you can use your knowledge to push for a better deal.

Estimating the lender's losses in foreclosure

To figure out what your lender has to lose by modifying your loan, do the math:

1. **Obtain a reliable home valuation (estimate of the property's current market value) from an appraiser or Realtor. (If you have one already that's less than 90 days old, it will do.)**

   In some states, only appraisers are allowed to provide official home valuations. If your state allows real estate agents to do it, some agents may provide a complimentary CMA (comparative market analysis) or BPO (broker's price opinion) or charge a reasonable fee that's usually considerably less than you'd pay an appraiser.

2. **Check your most recent mortgage statement or contact your lender and ask for your *principal balance* — the amount you currently owe on your home.**

   The easiest way to get an accurate amount is to request the pay-off balance. You may be able to simply dial the toll-free number on a recent mortgage statement and work through the automated menu system to obtain the pay-off balance.

3. **Subtract what you owe on the home (Step 2) from the current market value of your home (Step 1).**

If the result is a negative number, your lender stands to lose money if it forecloses. The bigger the negative number, the more it stands to lose. (This crude calculation assumes the lender will be able to sell the house at full market value, but lenders usually have to sell for even less than you could sell the home for, due to the stigma that surrounds bank-owned properties.) Still, this is only a portion of the potential loss. The lender also loses money before, during, and after the foreclosure in the form of the following expenses:

- ✔ Attorney fees for processing the foreclosure and eviction — at least a few hundred dollars

- ✔ Rehab costs for repairs required to make the property marketable — typically about 10 percent of your home's current market value)

- ✔ Real estate agent commissions for listing and selling the property (6 to 8 percent of the property's sales price) — multiply your home's market value by 6 percent for a rough estimate

✔ Holding costs, including property taxes, insurance, and utilities (for example, to keep the heat on so the pipes don't freeze in the winter) — estimate the holding costs for six months

✔ Internal costs governed by the agreement between the investor and the servicer, including the cost of pulling the loan out of a pool, if necessary, which you can't really predict (see the nearby sidebar "De-pooling a mortgage")

Add these costs to the loss the lender is likely to see from the actual sale of the property (Step 3), and you have a pretty good estimate of the lender's total loss.

Some experts estimate that a lender stands to lose between $50,000 and $80,000 on a single foreclosure. Lenders can usually modify a loan for a small fraction of that amount, enabling homeowners to keep their homes in the process.

Calculating the lender's losses from a loan modification

When evaluating your lender's loan modification offer, get out your calculator and figure out what your lender stands to lose in interest by modifying your loan. Before getting into the actual step-by-step calculations, consider the following example:

Five years ago, a couple took out a $200,000 30-year mortgage at 9.75 percent, making their monthly payment $1,718.31.

Under the current agreement, the lender would stand to earn $418,591.60: ($1,718.31 × 30 years × 12 months/year) – $200,000 = $418,591.60

After making payments for five years, the couple's balance is down to $192,821.91; they've paid $7,178.09 in principal and $95,920.51 in interest so far.

At the beginning of the sixth year, they can no longer afford to make payments.

The lender looks at the deal and proposes an interest rate reduction to 5.5 percent and extends the term to 30 years. These changes make the new payment $1,094.82, saving the couple $623.49 each month.

Under the new agreement, the lender stands to earn $201,313.29 plus the $95,920.51 it already collected in interest for a total of $297,233.80: ($1,094.82 × 30 years × 12 months/year) – $192,821.91 + $95,920.51 = $297,233.80.

This modification represents a "loss" to the lender of $121,357.80: $418,591.60 – $297,233.80 = $121,357.80.

De-pooling a mortgage

Lenders and government-sponsored enterprises, including Fannie Mae and Freddie Mac, often package mortgages that are similar and sell them as pooled mortgages to investors. When one of the loans in a pool goes bad or is modified, the lender usually must pull the loan out of the pool and pay a price for doing so.

The lender can recoup some of the cost by re-pooling mortgages it has successfully modified and selling them back to investors. Due to the complexities of de-pooling and re-pooling mortgage loans, estimating the average cost to the lender is nearly impossible. What's important to keep in mind, however, is that a lender stands to lose more from a bad loan than from a loan it can successfully modify and sell back to investors.

We use the word "loss" kind of loosely here. When the lender is still netting nearly $300,000 from a loan, the fact that it's earning $121,000 less than it would have gotten under the original agreement is a little tough to classify as a loss. In this example, the lender avoids a costly foreclosure (modest estimate of $50,000 to $80,000 loss) and earns about $200,000 more than it has already collected over the life of the loan by keeping a performing asset on its books.

Use these steps to figure out just how much your lender is losing by offering you a loan modification:

1. **Multiply your original term (in years) × 12 months/year × your monthly mortgage payment (principal and interest only) to determine the total amount you would pay over the life of the loan under the original agreement.**

   For example, if you have a $136,000 30-year mortgage at 8 percent interest, your monthly payment is about $1,000, so $30 \times 12 \times \$1,000 = \$360,000$.

2. **Calculate the total amount you already paid in principal and interest.**

   For example, if you already made 90 monthly payments, $90 \times \$1,000 = \$90,000$.

3. **Calculate the total amount you will pay under the new agreement.**

   For example, suppose the balance is now $125,000 on a $136,000 loan. If the lender lowers the interest rate to 5 percent and extends the term to 30 years, the new payment would be $671.03. Multiply 30 years by 12 months/year by $671.03 to get $241,571.

4. **Total the amounts calculated in Steps 2 and 3.**

   In this example, $90,000 + $242,000 = $332,000. This is the total amount you would pay the lender, as compared to the $360,000 you were scheduled to pay under the original agreement.

5. **Subtract the total calculated in Step 4 from the total calculated in Step 1 to determine the total interest the lender stands to lose with the new agreement.**

   In this example, $360,000 – $332,000 = $28,000.

In this example, the lender has the following choice: Foreclose and lose about $60,000, or modify and continue to collect more than $116,000 in interest over the life of the loan: $242,000 total – $125,000 remaining balance = $117,000. This difference leaves a lot more room for negotiation than your lender may be willing to admit. However, if the loan is FHA- or VA-secured, or if you carry private mortgage insurance (PMI), the calculations can change dramatically, as explained in the nearby sidebar "Accounting for mortgage insurance."

Gaining a strategic advantage with what you know

You don't want to play hardball with your lender by blurting out everything you know about what it stands to lose by foreclosing. Such a move may convince your lender to foreclose just because it can. Instead of being blunt about it, take a more subtle approach by trying one or more of these options:

- ✔ **If your home is worth significantly less than the unpaid principal balance, send a letter or fax to your lender indicating that you're upside-down in your mortgage and can't even qualify for refinancing.** If you have a recent appraisal, BPO, or CMA, include it with your letter and a copy of your latest mortgage statement with the unpaid principal balance highlighted.

- ✔ **Express your understanding that the lender has a great deal to lose from foreclosure.** You may even want to mention how many homes are for sale in your neighborhood and how long they've been on the market.

- ✔ **Let your lender know how committed you are to making this work.** Stress the fact that you've carefully examined your budget and are confident that the modified mortgage payment is truly affordable. Mention that by agreeing to the loan modification offer you're presenting, you appreciate the fact that the lender will be receiving less interest than under the original agreement.

Accounting for mortgage insurance

All things being equal, a loan modification is usually the best option for lenders because they avoid the high cost of foreclosure and continue to collect interest on loans — at a lower rate of return, but still enough to earn a profit.

In many cases, however, another factor comes into play — *mortgage insurance.* If a loan is FHA- or VA-secured, or if the homeowners are paying *private mortgage insurance* (PMI), the lender stands to lose much less from foreclosure because the insurance will make up a portion of the difference. In other words, the lender's motivation to work out a reasonable deal with the homeowner/borrower may be undermined by mortgage insurance — often mortgage insurance that the homeowner is paying for!

Fortunately, the party insuring the mortgage *is* motivated to work out a solution with homeowners to avoid having to pay a claim. Many mortgage insurance companies are contacting delinquent borrowers in an attempt to work out alternatives to foreclosure, even when the lender has been lax or unsuccessful in its attempts to work out a deal.

All these methods communicate what you know in a less threatening, less confrontational manner. Avoid the temptation to present your offer as though you're doing the lender a favor, even though, in a way, you are.

Not Taking "No" for an Answer

We live by the credo that "no" means "know." That is, if someone tells us "no," we assume they don't *know* enough to say "yes." In sales and in life, this approach has proven very effective for us. Persistence pays. Often, lenders and their representatives are in a hurry to clear cases off their desks. They take a tiny piece of information and draw huge conclusions, often to the detriment of both the homeowners and themselves, the lenders.

During negotiations, if the lender dismisses a request for compromise, assume that the lender doesn't *know* enough to say "yes." What are you communicating or not communicating to the lender, verbally or nonverbally, that's getting in the way of the lender saying "yes" to your request? You may be providing too little or too much information or are just not explaining your point of view in a clear and effective manner. Keep trying.

You have two ears and one mouth for a reason: You should listen twice as much as you talk. Your lender may be telling you exactly what it needs to hear in order to say "yes," so listen carefully and read between the lines. The clues may be very subtle. For example, your lender may reject your application on the grounds that you have insufficient income to afford a reasonable monthly payment, which could mean you failed to mention or your lender overlooked another source of income. By asking some follow-up questions, you can obtain more detailed information about what the lender is looking for.

Applying Some Subtle Legal Pressure

You may be able to gain a strategic advantage during negotiations by dropping some subtle hints about legal actions you can take to protect yourself or to at least throw a wrench in the foreclosure proceedings. You don't have to be ugly about it. Simply mentioning the fact that you may need to consult an attorney or see someone about how your mortgage loan got approved in the first place may be sufficient to bring reluctant lenders back to the negotiating table. The following sections include some suggestions.

Consider mentioning the B word: Bankruptcy

Filing for bankruptcy triggers an automatic stay against any collection activities, including foreclosure. If the date of the foreclosure sale is nearing and your lender is being uncooperative, a mere mention of consulting a bankruptcy attorney can give the lender reason to reconsider.

Be careful when playing the bankruptcy card. Lower-level employees may be trained to end discussions when they hear the word "bankruptcy" because lenders are afraid of violating the *automatic stay.* As soon as a homeowner declares bankruptcy, the automatic stay goes into effect, prohibiting them from moving forward with any collection activities, including loan modification.

Bring up concerns about predatory lending

Mention any concerns you have that you've been a victim of predatory lending. The definition of *predatory lending* can be very broad. One expert we spoke with defined it as "any loan that overextends the borrowers from day one, dooming them to failure." In other words, if you were placed in a mortgage with a low teaser rate that eventually rose to produce a monthly mortgage payment you could no longer afford, you're a victim of predatory lending. (See the nearby sidebar "What constitutes predatory lending?" for our take on the subject and some examples of predatory lending practices.)

When negotiating with your lender, you don't have to use the term "predatory lending," which could be taken as threatening. Instead, simply explain that you don't think you ever were really qualified for this loan and can't possibly afford it now, unless you can work out a reasonable payment. If you're unable to obtain an affordable payment, you'll be forced to explore your legal options.

Have an audit performed

If you really believe you were a victim of predatory lending or other lender violations, consider hiring an independent third party to audit your loan file. Armed with an audit that highlights the lender's bad acts, you may have some success obtaining a loan modification. Make sure you're submitting the audit through the lender's appropriate channels. For more about audits and the violations auditors usually look for, check out Chapters 13 and 14.

What constitutes predatory lending?

We define *predatory lending* as any unethical lending activity that harms borrowers to the benefit of lenders or loan originators. Common forms of predatory lending include the following:

✔ Charging excessive points, interest rate, or loan origination fees.

✔ *Equity stripping,* which means convincing homeowners to refinance again and again so the lender can pull equity out of the home to cover the loan origination fees and closing costs. The borrower may realize a temporary financial benefit, but it's far outweighed by the long-term detriment.

✔ Charging private mortgage insurance (PMI) premiums to homeowners who aren't required to carry PMI.

✔ Failing to fully disclose and explain the terms of a loan agreement.

✔ Using low teaser rates with adjustable-rate mortgages (ARMs) to convince homeowners to sign up for high-risk loans.

✔ Encouraging or facilitating the misrepresentation of facts and figures on a loan application to qualify unqualified applicants for a mortgage loan.

✔ Adding a single-premium life insurance policy (that pays off the balance if one of the borrowers dies) and charging the premiums as part of the loan.

✔ Representing to a borrower that he qualified for a higher rate when in reality he qualified for a lower one, and then placing him into a loan reflecting the higher rate or charging points to buy down the rate.

✔ Targeting of the poor, uneducated, elderly, or minority groups with oppressive or unfair loan products.

✔ Charging other unnecessary fees or costs.

Most predatory lending practices are prohibited under the Real Estate Settlement and Procedures Act (RESPA) and other legislation. For more about these and other legal protections for borrowers, check out Chapter 13.

Part IV
Dealing with an Uncooperative Lender

The 5th Wave   By Rich Tennant

"For us to consider your loan modification, we need you to fill out an application, accept a good faith estimate, and go 3 rounds with our Director of Finance."

In this part . . .

During the lending frenzy that set the stage for the mortgage meltdown and subsequent foreclosure epidemic, loan originators and even some lenders were bending and breaking the rules to qualify more borrowers and pad their profits with higher interest rates and unclear fees. As a result, many loans originated during this time show signs of lending law violations and predatory lending.

The good news is that if you or a professional loan auditor can prove that the loan originator or lender committed one or more violations, you may be able to leverage this proof to convince an unwilling lender to modify your loan. You may even have grounds to bring a civil suit against the lender to collect penalties for each violation.

In this part, we bring you up to speed on the legislation in place to protect borrowers, show you how to audit your loan to uncover possible violations, and provide tips on how to use proof of violations to convince your lender to modify your mortgage loan and think twice about taking advantage of consumers ever again.

Chapter 13

Brushing Up on Your Legal Rights

*W*hen a lender out refuses to cooperate with you in putting together a loan modification, you may be able to gain some leverage through laws designed to protect consumer/borrower rights. This chapter brings you up to speed on some of the rules and regulations that govern the mortgage industry. By knowing your rights, you can often encourage a reluctant lender to cooperate regardless of whether its representatives are willing to do so.

The mortgage lending laws presented in this chapter (TILA, HOEPA, and RESPA) allow for both public and private (civil) remedies. If a particular regulation doesn't allow a *private right of action,* only the attorney general or a regulatory agency can take legal action against the offender. If your lender or loan originator committed a TILA, HOEPA, or RESPA violation, you can file suit. Don't get your hopes up for a big payday, though. As we explain in Chapter 15, you're usually better off leveraging these laws to obtain a loan modification or workout solution. If you do file suit, a reasonable, quick settlement is almost always best.

Don't attempt to play the role of lawyer (unless, of course, you happen to be an attorney). We provide information about a few lending laws here only to equip you with the knowledge you need to understand and pursue your rights with an attorney's assistance.

Knowing Exactly What Your Lender Must Disclose

When most people buy a home, they borrow a lot of money to finance the purchase. Because so much money is at stake, disclosure laws have been put in place to ensure that borrowers know what they're getting into before they sign on the dotted line. If your lender fails to honor these disclosures, and you can prove it, your lender may be required by law to rewrite your mortgage and perhaps even pay damages.

If your lender is being uncooperative and you believe that your lender or the person originating your loan failed to provide the required disclosures, you may have legal recourse. Consult a reputable real estate attorney in your area to help you determine your legal options.

Even though a missed disclosure is technically a "bad act" by the lender, it's usually not sufficient grounds to win a lawsuit. Repeated offenses and a total disregard for the regulations in place may interest the state attorney general but won't help you personally. You may be able to use the lack of disclosure, however, to highlight the fact that you didn't understand the loan you were placed in. If you can demonstrate to the lender the lack of disclosure by its mortgage originator, you may gain just enough leverage to convince your lender to modify your loan. See Chapter 15 for details about applying legal pressure.

Disclosing loan terms and costs

Like any merchant, lenders sell a product; in the world of home financing, that product is a mortgage. By some counts, lenders offer more than 400 different products, including various types of adjustable- and fixed-rate mortgages, interest-only and negative amortization loans, and reverse mortgages. These products come and go to meet market demands and conditions in the lending industry.

Some of the riskier mortgage products that contributed to the mortgage meltdown disappeared as a result of the crisis, but history has a habit of repeating itself, so we can't say they're gone for good.

When presenting a product to you for consideration, the lender is required by law to label the product with a list of ingredients that you can understand. This breakdown enables you to comparison shop and more fully understand what you're buying. In the following sections, we describe the various disclosures lenders are required to make when selling a mortgage loan.

Terms

The terms of the loan (along with financing costs) are what ultimately determine the monthly payment and how much you pay over the life of the loan. Terms include the following:

- ✔ **Interest rate:** A percentage of the principal (loan amount). When advertising a loan, lenders are required to advertise the APR (annual percentage rate), as discussed in the nearby sidebar "Interest rate or APR?". This can be a fixed-percentage or adjustable rate (see "Adjustable-rate mortgages (ARMs)" later in this chapter).

- ✔ **Term:** Total time to pay back the loan in years, months, or number of payments, assuming you make all scheduled payments.

Fees

Fees include any amounts the loan originator or lender charges upfront to process the loan application. You can expect reasonable charges for the following items:

- ✔ Appraisal fee

- ✔ Closing or escrow fee

- ✔ Document preparation fee

- ✔ Credit report fee

- ✔ Flood certification fee

- ✔ Lender fee (negotiable)

- ✔ Processing fee (negotiable)

- ✔ Recording fees

- ✔ Reserves for paying taxes or insurance

- ✔ State or county tax/stamps

- ✔ Title insurance

- ✔ Underwriting fee (negotiable)

Some lenders or loan originators attempt to pad their profits by charging *junk fees* — inflated charges or fees for nonessential services or for services that few others in the industry charge. Here are some examples of junk fees:

- ✔ Administration fee

- ✔ Affiliate consulting fee

- ✔ Amortization fee

✔ Application fee

✔ Bank inspection fee

✔ Document review fee

✔ E-mail fee

✔ Express mail fee

✔ Funding fee

✔ Lender's attorney fee

✔ Lender's inspection fee

✔ Messenger fee

✔ Notary fee

✔ Photograph fee

✔ Pay-off request fee

✔ Settlement fee

✔ Sign-up fee

✔ Translation fee

Legally speaking, the lender can charge junk fees, but it must disclose fees in writing prior to formalizing the loan agreement by way of a Good Faith Estimate (GFE), upon your request prior to closing, and at closing on the HUD-1 form. See the section "Using the TILA and HOEPA to Your Advantage" later in this chapter for details about your protections with regard to a lender's fees.

The best way to determine whether a lender or loan originator is padding its profits with junk fees or charging too much for legitimate items is to compare fees that other companies were charging at the time. Unfortunately, you probably don't have copies of all the GFEs you received when you were shopping for your current mortgage. You may need to consult with a mortgage broker or real estate attorney who can more easily identify junk fees.

If you decide to refinance out of trouble (rather than seek a loan modification), don't spend a lot of money obtaining quotes. Ask the following questions:

✔ Do I have to pay an application fee or any other upfront fees to obtain a quote from you?

✔ What portion of any application or upfront fees is refundable in the event that I don't close on the loan?

Interest rate or APR?

You're likely to see interest rates presented in two ways: as an interest rate and as an annual percentage rate (APR), which tends to confuse consumers, especially given the fact that the APR is always higher than the interest rate.

So, what's the difference? *APR* is the percentage you pay on the money you borrow, including any loan origination fees and other prepaid costs. Congress created the APR in 1974 to give consumers a tool for quickly comparing the actual costs associated with loans. By law, lenders must advertise the APR as the rate they're charging, so consumers can compare apples to apples.

Adjustable-rate mortgages (ARMs)

Adjustable-rate mortgages (ARMs) have given many homeowners nightmares. Leading up to the mortgage meltdown, many lenders were pushing ARMs on unwary borrowers — often seducing them with low introductory (teaser) rates. Due to interest rate adjustments, some homeowners talked into ARMs have seen their monthly mortgage payments double in a very short period of time.

ARMs can adjust up or down. Ironically, during the worst of the mortgage meltdown, rates (and payment amounts) for many homeowners went down. Even so, the increase from a low teaser rate, such as 3.75 percent, up to a market rate of 6 to 7 percent was too much for some homeowners. In addition, you really can't count on rates staying low; if you have an ARM now, even if the rate seems stable, look toward moving into a fixed-rate mortgage.

Lenders should be required by law to show borrowers, in writing, the worst-case scenarios of the ARMs they're selling. This would probably be enough to convince most borrowers to steer clear of these products. Unfortunately, at the peak of the subprime lending boom, lenders were only required to disclose the following:

- ✔ **Interest rate:** The percentage you'll pay monthly until the interest rate is scheduled to adjust.

- ✔ **Adjustment period:** How often adjustments can be made — monthly, quarterly, semi-annually, or annually, for example.

- ✔ **Index:** The base interest rate set by market conditions and published by an unbiased third party. The fluctuation of the index is what makes an ARM adjustable.

- ✔ **Margin:** The lender's markup on the index. The interest you pay is determined by the index plus the margin. For example, if the index is 3 percent and the margin is 2.5 percent, you pay

5.5 percent interest. If the index rises to 5 percent, you pay 7.5 percent interest.

- **Cap:** The highest interest rate the lender can charge, regardless of how high the index goes. The lender often quotes a yearly cap and a lifetime cap, such as 2/6, meaning the interest rate can rise up to 2 percent per year but it can't increase more than 6 percent total over the life of the loan.

Lenders are supposed to give to borrowers who are contemplating ARM loan products a copy of the *CHARM (Consumer Handbook on Adjustable-Rate Mortgages)* booklet. You can access the latest version of the *CHARM* booklet online at `www.federalreserve.gov/pubs/arms/arms_english.htm`. (Failing to give borrowers *CHARM* booklets is a violation but not likely to be enough of an oversight to justify rewriting the loan or filing expensive litigation.)

Single premium life insurance

To protect their investments and earn a little extra money on the side, some lenders peddle single premium life insurance policies with their loans and pressure borrowers to buy them. (*Single premium* means you pay the entire premium upfront; the lender may roll the premium into the loan amount, but then you end up paying even more for it in interest.)

In a way, the life insurance policy protects the borrower's family from getting stuck with mortgage payments in the event of the borrower's death, but it also protects the lender. In other words, the borrower pays for a policy to protect the lender's interests. Several consumer advocacy groups have claimed that packaging this insurance with home loans borders on predatory lending.

We're not passing judgment against single premium life insurance or those who sell it, but lenders are required to disclose the fact that this insurance is optional and any decision not to buy it will not jeopardize the loan approval.

Disclosing other important information

In addition to disclosing the terms and costs of the loan, lenders are also required to disclose your legal rights as a consumer and other important details about the loan agreement, including the following:

- **Right of rescission:** The right of rescission granted by federal law gives you three days to back out of most types of major financial deals, including loan agreements. It's designed to protect consumers from high-pressure sales tactics. The right of rescission does have some limitations in that it applies only to

- Nonpurchase mortgages (such as refinance loans).

- Mortgages secured by the borrower's primary residence.

- Loan transactions that occurred within the last three years. In other words, a three-year statute of limitations applies to any claim that a right of rescission had been violated.

✔ **Auto pay:** If you've agreed to have your house payments automatically withdrawn from your bank account, the lender is required to disclose the details of how payments will be handled, including the day of the month payments will be withdrawn and the amount of the payments.

✔ **Escrow accounts and payments:** Many mortgage loans, particularly for first-time homebuyers, have escrow accounts attached to them. A portion of each monthly payment is set aside in escrow to pay property taxes, insurance, and any homeowner association fees. Lenders are required to disclose the following with regard to escrow:

- Whether property taxes, insurance, and homeowner association fees will be paid out of escrow or you will pay them separately.

- The amount of each payment to be deposited in escrow. The escrow amount changes over the life of the loan as the cost of property taxes, insurance, and homeowner association fees change. The lender must provide written notice whenever the escrow amount changes.

- How the escrow was spent for the year.

✔ **Force-placed insurance:** If you fail to buy insurance for your property or let the policy lapse, the lender has the right to buy insurance for you and charge you for it. However, several laws govern force-placed insurance, including:

- The mortgage should state the lender's right to force-place insurance if the homeowner fails to insure the property.

- The lender can't charge the homeowner more than it paid for the policy.

- In most states, the insurance policy and a disclosure letter must be provided to the state regulatory agency. (Regulations regarding force-placed insurance vary from state to state.)

✔ **Lender-affiliated business relationships:** If a lender has affiliated business relationships with any other parties involved in processing or approving your loan, it's required to disclose the nature of these relationships in writing. For example, if several real estate businesses partner to create a one-stop home shopping experience, the businesses need to disclose that they're all working together.

The disclosure is designed to prevent various businesses from collaborating to rip off consumers. For example, it discourages a real estate agent from recommending a mortgage broker who charges excessive fees and then kicks back a portion of the money to the agent as a so-called referral fee. Businesses can still create these informal partnerships, but they must disclose them to borrowers.

Using the TILA and HOEPA to Your Advantage

The Truth in Lending Act (TILA) and Home Ownership and Equity Protection Act (HOEPA, an amendment to TILA) are designed to give borrowers the information they need to make well-informed financing decisions, protect them from paying excessive fees and interest, and prevent them from falling victim to unethical lending practices. Here's a rundown of the basics:

- ✔ **TILA:** This legislation covers all residential loan transactions (one- to four-family units), whether they're owner-occupied or investment properties. TILA's purpose is to "promote the informed use of consumer credit by requiring disclosures about its terms and cost." TILA is responsible for all those lender disclosures described in the earlier section "Knowing Exactly What Your Lender Must Disclose."

- ✔ **HOEPA:** Also referred to as *Section 32* or *high-rate, high-fee loan disclosures,* HOEPA applies to residential owner-occupied dwellings for purchases and refinances. It covers one- to four-family owner-occupied properties in which at least one of the units is the owner's primary residence. HOEPA's purpose is to curtail predatory lending practices, particularly the practice of placing homeowners in high-interest loans.

In the following sections, we provide some suggestions on how you can use this legislation to your advantage.

Identifying noncompliance issues

Any failure on the part of the lender to fully disclose the terms of the mortgage or any other information that a borrower needs to make a well-informed choice of mortgage products constitutes a violation of TILA.

The easiest thing to check is whether your lender provided sufficient notice of your three-day right of rescission. This applies only to refinance and home equity loans. Review the loan documents you received in your closing packet. Sufficient notice of your right of rescission requires two copies of the Notice of Right to Cancel for each borrower on the note; the copies must be signed by all parties and must include the date of the transaction and the deadline for canceling.

Other TILA violations, such as a failure to fully disclose the terms of the loan agreement, force-placed insurance, and the lender's business affiliations, are tougher to spot and typically require the trained eye of an attorney who specializes in auditing mortgages. (For more about auditing a mortgage, check out Chapter 14.)

Suspect a HOEPA violation if you're paying a significantly higher interest rate on your loan than most homeowners you know. Under HOEPA, lenders must warn borrowers if the APR is more than 10 percent higher than the comparable Treasury yield (Treasury securities having a similar period of maturity, such as 30 years), or if the deal's total points and fees exceed 8 percent of the loan amount. To evaluate your APR in these terms, do the following:

✔ Total the points and fees your lender charged you, and divide that number by the total loan amount. If the result is higher than 0.08 and your lender didn't warn you about it, you've just spotted a HOEPA violation.

✔ Find an APR calculator on the Web (a search on your favorite search engine should turn up plenty of options) and plug in the numbers for your loan: loan amount, extra costs, interest rate, and term. The result is the APR your lender's charging you. Go to www.ustreas.gov, search for "30-year Treasury yield," click US Treasury – Daily Treasury Yield Curve, and then click Historical Data. Browse for the 30-year Treasury yield on the date on which you signed for your loan. If your APR is higher than the 30-year Treasury yield on the date you locked your rate plus 10 percent, your lender may be in violation of HOEPA.

Pushing for a resolution

If you suspect a TILA or HOEPA violation based on information in the previous section, contact a reputable real estate attorney who's experienced in auditing mortgage loans. The attorney can confirm your suspicions and assist you in pursuing your legal options or explain to you why the suspected violation isn't actually a violation. Don't try to play the role of an attorney unless you are one.

You can report suspected TILA or HOEPA violations to your state attorney general, certain regulatory agencies, or even law enforcement agencies. Chapter 15 has details on teaming up with state and federal regulators, and Appendix A has contact information for state attorneys general and regulatory agencies.

Loan originators who are out to fleece borrowers are usually pretty good at getting as close to the legal line as possible without crossing it. When dealing with these shades of gray, build your case to show a pattern of inappropriate activity. Your goal is to prove that your claims are more credible than those of the party that originated your loan so that your lender agrees to modify your loan.

Tapping the power of the law

Most homeowners try to refinance *out of* trouble. Bill refinanced *into* trouble. Fortunately for him, evidence of lending law violations convinced his lender to approve an affordable loan modification.

Bill's troubles began with health problems that eventually led to a period of unemployment. He was struggling to make his house payments and concerned that he would lose the home in which he had invested so much. He just needed to refinance into a lower interest, fixed-rate loan to avoid the payment increases he'd experienced with his adjustable loan.

The loan originator proposed a refinance loan with a reduced, fixed interest rate that made the monthly payment affordable without any significant increase in the unpaid balance. When Bill showed up to close on the loan, however, the loan was nothing like the one his loan originator had proposed. The fixed rate he expected was now an adjustable rate that reset almost immediately. The principal balance had increased by more than $23,000. The value assigned to the house was significantly higher than Bill thought the house was worth.

Bill called his loan originator, who conveniently wasn't in attendance at the closing, and complained. His loan originator assured Bill that the loan could easily be converted at a later date to the loan Bill was expecting. With medical expenses and other bills piling up and being out of time and options, Bill reluctantly signed for the loan.

To no surprise, Bill was unable to convert the loan to what he had expected. He struggled to make the payments and fell behind. Fortunately, he sought expert advice and discovered that several violations were evident in his loan origination, including misstated income and an inflated appraisal.

When confronted with the violations, the lender offered to reset the interest rate to a low fixed rate and extend the term to help reduce the payments. Negotiations weren't easy, but with professional assistance, Bill was able to contact the lender's loss mitigator and obtain an affordable loan modification.

Leveraging the Power of RESPA

The Real Estate Settlement Procedures Act (RESPA) standardizes closings for residential real estate transactions to prevent unethical or confusing lending practices. According to the act, all closings must use a HUD-1 form to disclose loan costs and show where all the disbursed funds are going.

RESPA also controls certain actions of settlement providers (such as the closing agent) and service providers (including the title insurance provider, credit company, and appraiser) to prevent them from working together against the best interests of the consumer (as in the case of price-gouging or kickbacks). Section 8 of RESPA has two important components:

- ✔ It prevents a lender from overcharging for settlement services and keeping the difference or charging for services that weren't provided. For example, if the appraisal costs $400, the lender can't charge you $600 and pocket the extra $200.

- ✔ It prevents lenders and service providers from accepting or offering kickbacks for referral business. For example, a lender can't refer a specific appraiser and then accept part of the appraiser's fee.

RESPA provisions cover all aspects of services, companies, and individuals, including title companies, attorneys, and real estate agents.

 One of the best ways to protect yourself against RESPA violations at closing is to compare the closing costs listed on the HUD-1 statement with the costs quoted on the Good Faith Estimate (GFE). This step also helps identify violations after the fact, assuming you kept a copy of the lender's GFE — and you should. (See the next section for details on spotting RESPA violations.)

Identifying RESPA violations

Before you can seek restitution for a RESPA violation, you need to be able to prove that your lender committed a violation. Unfortunately, spotting a RESPA violation simply by inspecting the loan documents you received at closing can be nearly impossible. How can you tell whether the lender overcharged you for a service and pocketed the surplus? How can you spot undisclosed business relationships if they weren't disclosed?

The only reliable way for a consumer to check for RESPA violations is to have an expert review the documents. A reputable lender or mortgage broker could certainly provide such a service, but many of them are reluctant to take action against experts in their own industry. We recommend you turn to a qualified real estate attorney who has experience in auditing mortgage loans. The attorney can quickly identify charges that seem out of the ordinary and can investigate and identify any business relationships that parties involved in the transaction failed to disclose or tried to obscure.

Recognizing potential penalties for violations

RESPA violations can carry some steep penalties. Any individual who violates a RESPA provision may be fined up to $10,000, imprisoned for up to one year, or both. Even better for you, the violator is liable for paying damages of up to three times the amount paid for the settlement services, and you may pursue a private lawsuit for additional damages.

An attorney can confirm your suspicions and assist you in pursuing your legal options or explain to you why the suspected violation isn't an actual violation. Don't try to play the role of an attorney unless you are one.

As a consumer, you can report suspected RESPA violations to your state attorney general, certain regulatory agencies, or even law enforcement agencies. Turn to Chapter 15 for details on contacting your attorney general and working with state and federal regulators, and check out Appendix A for guidance in contacting your state attorney general as well as regulatory agencies.

Getting Special Treatment: Military Servicemembers Only

While members of the military are defending American interests overseas, many of their families are fighting foreclosure at home. Fortunately, the federal government has provided active servicemembers (including reservists called to active duty) and their families with an arsenal of legal tools to protect them from foreclosure and other financial and legal hardships via the Servicemembers Civil Relief Act (SCRA) of 2003.

Several of the legal and financial protections under the SCRA have little or nothing to do with homeownership, at least at first glance. But some of these provisions may have a related effect in the long run. And several, such as the following, do pertain to homeownership:

✔ **Automatic stay on courtroom and administrative proceedings:** Upon written request from the servicemember, the judge, magistrate, or hearing officer must grant a minimum 90-day delay in proceedings related to civil (not criminal) cases.

✔ **Overturning of default judgments:** Upon written request during the servicemember's active duty or within 60 days after the release from active duty, the court may overturn any default judgment issued against the servicemember, assuming the servicemember can prove that active service materially affected his or her ability to defend against the action.

✔ **Reduced interest rates during active duty:** For any debt incurred prior to entering active duty (such as a mortgage, credit card, or personal loan), servicemembers can have the interest rate reduced to no higher than 6 percent upon written request, assuming they can prove that active duty materially affected their ability to repay the financial obligation.

✔ **Lifting of the acceleration clause:** An acceleration clause gives the lender the power to demand full payment of the balance of the loan if the borrower fails to make payments as stipulated in the mortgage. The SCRA prohibits the lender from accelerating the payback for the duration of the active service and up to 90 days after the period of active service expires.

✔ **Stay for evictions:** Under the SCRA, landlords in *all* states are required to obtain court orders to evict servicemembers in active duty or their dependents.

✔ **Stay for foreclosures or repossessions:** During the period of active service and up to 90 days after the period of active service expires, lenders must obtain court orders to proceed with foreclosure or repossession of servicemembers' property, and servicemembers may request a stay of the proceedings.

For additional details about SCRA, check out the U.S. Armed Forces Legal Assistance SCRA Fact Sheet at `legalassistance.law.af.mil/content/legal_assistance/cp/scra_fact_sheet_dec04.pdf`.

The 6 percent loan cap provision applies to both conventional and government-insured mortgages. However, to take advantage of this provision you must submit a written request to your lender no later than 180 days after the date of your release from active military duty. We recommend submitting your written request as soon as possible. When contacting your lender, provide the following:

✔ A letter indicating that you've been called to active duty and that active duty will materially affect your ability to continue making payments at the current interest rate.

✔ A copy of the military orders you received, calling you to active duty.

✔ Your FHA case number, if applicable; your lender should be able to supply you with your FHA case number, assigned when you applied for the loan.

✔ Evidence that you took on the mortgage debt before being called up to active duty.

What makes you eligible for an interest rate cap during the period of your active military service? You must be on active duty, have had your mortgage before being ordered to active duty, and be unable to afford your mortgage payments due to being on active duty. You also have to belong to one of the following groups:

✔ Army, Navy, Marine Corps, Air Force, or Coast Guard

✔ Commissioned officers of the Public Health Service or the National Oceanic and Atmospheric Administration engaged in active service

✔ Reservists ordered to report for military service

✔ People ordered to report for induction (training) under the Military Service Act

✔ Guardsmen called to active service for more than 30 consecutive days

The relief and protections granted within the SCRA extend to other persons that hold secondary liability. For example, if your spouse signed on the house note and you're called up to active duty, your spouse is protected from collection actions on the obligation as well.

If you're in the military, you've been called to active service, and you're having trouble making payments on your mortgage, credit cards, and other loans, contact the U.S. Armed Forces Legal Assistance immediately by visiting legalassistance.law. af.mil for a searchable directory of offices by state. You're putting your life on the line for your country, so don't hesitate to call on your country to defend your rights at home. One more thing: Thanks for your service and your family's sacrifice.

Chapter 14

Auditing Your Mortgage Loan

. . . .

In This Chapter

▶ Spotting common signs of unethical lending practices

▶ Searching your memory for clues

▶ Inspecting your loan documents for signs of fraud

▶ Hiring a qualified professional to audit your mortgage loan

. . . .

During the borrowing binge leading up to the mortgage melt-down, many lenders became guilty of *predatory lending* char-acterized by bending and breaking laws to boost their bottom lines at the borrowers' expense. If proof exists that the lender or loan originator acted inappropriately in selling you a high-cost mort-gage, "helping" you complete your loan application, or approving a bad loan, you may have legal grounds to compel them to modify your mortgage.

Remember, the secret to having your loan modification request approved is to prove to your lender that it's the most cost-effective option. With a legitimate claim of predatory lending, you do just that. Your lender must then decide whether to spend money defending the indefensible, losing big, and paying even more in fines; or to modify your loan and settle for a fraction of the cost. It's all about greenbacks: If a modification makes sense financially, you're speaking the lender's language.

The information we provide in this chapter is intended only to inform you of possible problems with loan originations that could provide a legal basis for having a mortgage loan rescinded and rewritten. Regardless of what you read in this chapter, if you sus-pect your lender or loan originator of acting unethically in selling you your mortgage or processing your loan application, consult a reputable real estate attorney, preferably one who specializes in auditing mortgage loans. Every case is unique, and many borrow-ers who are victims of predatory lending never suspect it. Some experts estimate that violations can be found in a majority of the subprime mortgages originated during the mortgage frenzy.

This chapter helps you identify common signs of predatory lending and other lending law violations. In Chapter 15, we show you what to do with the information you gather to convince your lender to modify your loan to affordability. We encourage you to try to resolve the dispute with your lender first; if that fails, you can enlist the assistance of government regulatory and consumer-protection agencies and perhaps even law enforcement authorities to compel your lender to do the right thing, as we explain in Chapter 15.

Recognizing Common Signs of Predatory Lending

Just before the housing bubble burst, the United States was engaged in what can only be described as a borrowing frenzy. Wall Street investors ramped up demand for mortgage-backed securities (MBSs), lenders and investors rolled out new products to qualify more borrowers, loan originators pushed these products, and consumers lined up to borrow more than they could ever repay.

Caught up in the frenzy (or simply out of greed), some loan originators bent and broke the rules, and lenders relaxed their underwriting standards to approve more loans. These unethical practices are commonly categorized as *predatory lending*. In the following sections, we describe the most common of these unethical and illegal practices so you can more effectively determine whether you may have legal grounds for seeking justice.

Inflated interest rate

If you had a credit score above 700 at the time you signed for the loan and the loan originator placed you in a loan with an interest rate significantly higher than the going rate, the originator acted unethically. A high credit score earns you the right to a competitive interest rate and low or no closing costs.

You can search the Web for historical interest rates. Freddie Mac has a market rate that's published and tracked historically. So is Prime Rate and just about everything else in between, even index rates on ARMs. ERATE has a mortgage rates history that goes back to 1980 at www.erate.com/mortgage_rates_history.htm. Head to research.stlouisfed.org/fred2/data/PRIME.txt for a history of prime rates that reaches back to 1929.

Lenders have been known to reward loan originators with kickbacks for placing borrowers in loans with inflated interest rates — higher than the borrower would normally qualify for with a particular lender. The kickbacks are packaged as *yield-spread premiums* (YSPs) to make them sound more socially acceptable. Check your HUD-1 statement to determine whether your broker received a YSP at closing. Charging a YSP isn't illegal, but it can indicate a pattern of abuse.

One practice that made this rate game even more distasteful is that some brokers specifically targeted low-income, elderly, or minority borrowers, which constitutes discriminatory lending (see the section "Discriminatory interest rate" later in this chapter for details).

Inflated appraisal

Long before President Obama rolled out his Making Home Affordable (MHA) plan, which we cover in Chapter 10, some loan originators were busy pushing their own home affordability plans. Unfortunately, their plans included the use of *inflated appraisals,* a key tool in many forms of real estate and mortgage fraud. These fraudulent appraisals can take the form of phony documents, forgeries, or real appraisals performed by so-called cooperative, unethical appraisers.

Inflated appraisals provide consumers with inflated credit in the following ways:

- ✔ **Cash back at closing:** You borrow more than the purchase price and pocket the surplus. Some people mistakenly believe that this is perfectly okay. It's not. It's illegal.

- ✔ **Cash-out refinancing:** An inflated appraisal inflates the equity in the home, enabling you to borrow against more equity than you actually have. See the nearby sidebar "The cash-out refinancing scam" for details.

- ✔ **Facilitating loan approval:** Lenders approve loans only if the appraisal justifies the property value, so loan originators find cooperative appraisers who make sure the appraisal is sufficient to justify the amount of money you need or want.

To check whether your lender used an inflated appraisal to get your loan approved, do one of the following:

- ✔ **Compare the appraised value of your home to what comparable homes were selling for at the time.** You may need to consult a real estate broker or attorney to check historical property values in your neighborhood or search for this information on the Web.

✔ **Examine the percentage appreciation of your home over time.** If the appraisal shows that your property appreciated more than 10 percent a year, the appraisal is likely to be inflated.

✔ **If you have a copy of the appraisal, check out the comparable properties used to value your house.** Are the comparable properties really similar to yours in location, size, and features? Many inflated appraisals use properties that are better than the subject property to inch the value up, or they use comparables that are farther from the subject property than need be. Generally, the closer a similar house is to the subject property, the more comparable it is. Some sly appraisers select which comparable homes to use to justify the value, sometimes even when other, more comparable sales are on the same street or just around the corner.

Doctored loan application

Whenever you apply for a mortgage loan, you're required to complete and sign a copy of the Uniform Residential Loan Application, or 1003 (ten-oh-three). Right above the space for your signature is a statement saying that the information on the 1003 form is accurate and complete, to the best of your knowledge. It also states that misrepresenting any information is a crime.

The cash-out refinancing scam

Loan originators often encourage homeowners to cash out equity in their homes in order to catch up on their bills or pay off high-interest credit balances (debt consolidation). This isn't necessarily bad advice, but some loan originators cross the line by using inflated appraisals to create equity that isn't truly there.

The borrowers are usually excited to hear that their house appraised for a larger amount because it means they've made a good investment. They have no reason to question the appraiser's findings and are happy to receive approval for their refinance loan.

It's not until the homeowners are having trouble making payments and discover they can't refinance because their house is really worth much less than they were led to believe that they begin to suspect foul play. Rectifying the situation can be difficult if the lender/broker is adept at deflecting responsibility or, even worse, if the broker and the appraiser are out of business.

Loan originators have been known to fudge the numbers on loan applications and even submit phony supporting documents (like fake pay stubs and W-2 forms) to qualify unqualified borrowers. In some cases, a loan originator has even instructed the applicant to sign an incomplete mortgage application that the loan originator would later fill in with numbers as soon as he identified the best loan program the applicant would likely qualify for.

Understandably, borrowers trust the professionals they consult. After all, you don't go to see a doctor and then question her judgment when she prescribes a medication, or doubt that your car really needs new brake pads when your mechanic recommends replacing them. Likewise, when a loan originator offers advice or assistance, borrowers rarely question what they're being told, and even when they do pose questions, they have no way of knowing whether the answers they receive are accurate. As a result, loan originators often deceived borrowers into providing inaccurate information on their loan applications.

 If you feel that the professionals who "helped" you obtain your current mortgage provided false or misleading information and advice, you may be a victim of predatory lending practices, even if you benefited in the short term. Ignorance of the law may be an excuse, at least for you, the consumer, but the professionals who are paid to help consumers navigate the complex procedures and documents are obligated to provide clear and accurate information and guidance — not to steer you into a dark alley to get mugged by the system.

As for you, the borrower, if you were complicit in falsifying information and signing a document that you knew contained false information, you could (technically speaking) be liable for criminal prosecution, too. This is highly unlikely, however, particularly if you're seeking a loan modification for the mortgage on your primary residence. As long as you and your lender can work out a payment plan, law enforcement agencies won't be in any hurry to bust you for mortgage fraud.

Approving an unaffordable loan

If you can't afford your house payment due to financial hardship, that's one thing, but if you're earning about the same as you were earning when you signed for the mortgage and your house payment is way more than 30 percent of your gross monthly income, it's likely that your lender approved you for a loan you should never have been approved for. And that's a form of predatory lending.

Placing blind trust in professionals

Time and time again we hear stories of borrowers who trusted their brokers or loan officers to do the right thing. After all, you don't have to look over your doctor's shoulder to make sure she prescribes the right medicine or look under the hood of your car to make sure your mechanic did his job. Even if you did, you may not have the knowledge and experience to determine whether your doctor or mechanic did the right thing.

Unfortunately, some greedy loan originators (mortgage brokers and loan officers) intentionally misled clients during the height of the mortgage frenzy. Linda has a textbook case. When she first sought our help, she was several months behind on her mortgage and was completely at a loss concerning her options. As we always do, we asked her to start from the beginning and explain to us what happened during the loan process. What we discovered was not uncommon but pretty shocking given the degree of abuse.

Linda was a first-time homebuyer who obtained a referral to what she thought was a reputable mortgage broker. She looked to the broker as a trusted expert and advisor, so when her broker instructed her to add her name to her father's bank account, that's exactly what she did. The broker explained that this was a common practice in the industry and tantamount to her father co-signing on the loan for her.

When Linda began struggling with the payments, the same "trusted" loan officer refinanced her loan. Again, he played fast and loose with the numbers, tweaked the property value enough to garner an approval, and placed Linda into an aggressive adjustable-rate mortgage she didn't qualify for without escrows to pay taxes and insurance. She was set up to fail from the start, and fail she did.

Fortunately for Linda, an attorney agreed to take on the case pro bono. After identifying the various violations committed in selling Linda her mortgage and pushing her application through the approval process, the attorney was able to convince the lender to modify Linda's mortgage into a lower-interest fixed-rate loan with escrows to cover taxes and insurance. Linda is now living the more affordable American Dream of homeownership.

Lenders don't have the right to set you up for failure. Unfortunately, it was common practice leading up to the mortgage meltdown to dangle low teaser-rate loans in front of unwary borrowers to suck them into signing up for high-cost, high-risk mortgages. When the teaser rates on these loans adjusted up, many homeowners found themselves paying 40 or even 50 percent or more of their incomes on their house payments.

If your house payment is more than 38 percent of your gross monthly income, and that's not due to an income reduction, you may be a candidate for a Making Home Affordable (MHA) modification under President Obama's plan (see Chapter 10). You may also be a victim of predatory lending, so if your lender won't modify to affordability, consult an attorney to explore other (legal) options.

Equity stripping (loan flipping)

When property values were soaring, some unethical lenders took undue advantage of homeowners by refinancing their loans over and over again without providing any net tangible benefit to the homeowners. The lender would profit by collecting loan origination fees and closing costs with every refinance, and the borrower would have less and less equity in the home with nothing to show for it. This practice is referred to as *equity stripping* or *loan flipping*.

If you refinanced your mortgage several times over the course of only a few years and saw your equity gobbled up in refinance charges, you may be a victim of predatory lending.

Equity stripping can be tough to prove. If you used your home as an ATM to cash out equity, your lender will try to show that you realized a financial benefit, and you may be out of luck. If, however, the evidence shows that the loan originator manipulated the information (perhaps even by obtaining an inflated appraisal) or the lender relaxed its underwriting standards to enable you to qualify for a loan you otherwise wouldn't qualify for, you may have a case, especially if you were unaware of the game being played.

High-risk loans

Just about everybody who bought a home prior to the 1990s used a 30-year fixed-rate mortgage to finance the purchase. In the '90s, lenders began to get more creative to qualify more borrowers and feed Wall Street's growing appetite for mortgage-backed securities. As a result, lenders rolled out mortgage loan products that carried a much higher potential risk. These products typically feature one or more of the following:

✔ **Subprime or ARM (adjustable-rate mortgage) interest rate:** The interest rate is variable. We refer to these as *always-rising mortgages* because the rates tend to rise more frequently than they fall. (*Subprime* is an interest rate that's 3 or more points higher than the going rate for borrowers with good credit.)

- ✔ **Interest-only arrangement:** Interest-only loans can reduce monthly payments and allow consumers to buy more house. As long as property values continue to rise, you can build equity in the home, but if property values flat line or head south, you begin losing equity, which places your home in peril. With little, no, or negative equity, you can't refinance out of trouble or cash out equity to get through the lean times.

- ✔ **Balloon payments:** Interest-only mortgages often include balloon payments that require you to come up with a good chunk of cash on the predetermined due dates.

According to Fannie Mae, up to half of homeowners placed in adjustable-rate mortgages could have qualified for fixed-rate mortgages with better terms. Unfortunately, they were sold risky loans with variable interest rates.

Discriminatory interest rate

Lenders are prohibited by law from discriminating among borrowers based on race, color, gender, religion, national origin, marital status, age, or where the borrower happens to live. They're not allowed, for example, to charge a larger down payment or set a higher interest rate for applicants who are single as opposed to those who are married.

If your lender required a higher than average down payment or is charging you higher than average interest based on something other than your income and credit history, you may be a victim of discriminatory lending. To determine what constitutes "higher than average" at the time you signed for your loan, consult a mortgage broker or an attorney who's well-versed in these matters.

Excessive or unwarranted fees

According the Real Estate Settlement and Procedures Act (RESPA), loan originators and lenders are prohibited from charging fees for services not performed or overcharging for services performed by third-party suppliers and then pocketing the surplus as a referral fee.

One of the most common ways lenders inflate closing costs is by charging excessive points without providing a corresponding reduction in the interest rate.

The HUD-1 form you received as part of your closing packet should contain a complete list of fees. If any of the fees seem exorbitant or are for services that sound phony, bring them to your attorney's attention. See Chapter 13 for lists of common legitimate and questionable fees.

ARMs not all bad

Guns don't kill people, but guns in the wrong hands do tend to have that effect. The same is true with certain mortgage loan products. Interest-only loans and ARMs aren't necessarily bad and can be very useful in certain situations. An investor, for example, can use an interest-only loan to improve cash flow so he has more money available to invest in other properties.

What's bad is when loan originators and lenders place homeowners into certain mortgages that the homeowners don't fully understand or know how to manage. These products aren't "one size fits all" solutions, but that's exactly how some lenders and loan originators were marketing these products leading up to the mortgage meltdown. Many homeowners failed to fully understand the possible ramifications of these riskier loans.

With more than 400 different loan types available at any given time, we can't expect loan officers and lenders to educate borrowers on all their options, but they should have educated borrowers on any packages they were considering or ended up signing for.

 Reasonable fees are usually about 1 percent of the total loan amount, meaning $1,000 for every $100,000 you borrow. If the fees are 3 percent or higher, take a closer look at what you've received for those fees. (As explained in Chapter 13, your lender is required to warn you if the fees exceed 8 percent of the total loan amount.) Figuring out what's "reasonable" at the time you closed on the loan can be difficult for anyone who's unfamiliar with the industry, so you may need to consult a mortgage broker or real estate attorney.

Stiff prepayment penalties

According to the Center for Responsible Lending, "up to 80 percent of all subprime mortgages carry a prepayment penalty — a fee for paying off the loan early." For comparison purposes, about 2 percent of the loans in the prime market carry prepayment penalties of any serious length.

Attaching a prepayment penalty to a mortgage loan is understandable. Lenders don't want to go through the trouble of processing a loan if they're likely to collect interest for less than a couple years, especially when the interest on that two-year period was a very low teaser rate. However, the prepayment penalty should be reasonable so you can refinance into a lower fixed-rate mortgage without being slapped with a huge fine.

Although it's hard to state exactly what a *reasonable* prepayment penalty is, it should be sufficient to compensate the lender without making refinancing cost prohibitive for you. Suppose a loan originator placed you in a $100,000 adjustable-rate mortgage with a low teaser rate of 1.75 percent and a three-year prepayment penalty of six months' interest. Now, suppose the interest rate jumps to 9.75 percent in the second month, and your payment jumps from $357 to $841. You now have the option of making those payments or refinancing, which will cost more than $4,000 in a prepayment penalty plus the cost of refinancing. Such a prepayment penalty would make refinancing cost prohibitive. The dilemma is that the more than $400 per month increase in your payment may be income prohibitive, leaving you with a no-win decision to make.

One of the benefits of a loan modification over refinancing is that you don't get hit with a prepayment penalty. During negotiations for a loan modification, try to have any prepayment penalty eliminated so you can freely refinance in the future if you can get a better deal.

Requiring mandatory arbitration

To protect themselves from lawsuits, some lenders attempt to discourage or prohibit borrowers from taking legal action. Instead, their contracts call for mandatory arbitration for any disagreements between the lender and the borrower.

Limiting your legal rights in a mortgage contract may not be illegal, but it's unethical. Your attorney may be able to convince the courts that this practice, along with other questionable activities, constitutes predatory lending.

High-pressure sales tactics

At the height of the mortgage lending frenzy, many loan originators engaged in activities best described as "pump and dump." They would pump up the benefits of their mortgage loan products and then dump the borrowers into high-cost, high-risk loans. If anyone employed any of the following high-pressure sales tactics to sell you financing secured by your home, you may be a victim of predatory lending:

- The loan originator quoted you much more attractive terms and lower fees on the Good Faith Estimate than the actual terms and fees presented on the HUD-1 at closing.

- The loan originator tried to convince you that it was your only chance of financing or refinancing your home, or discouraged you from comparison shopping for the best financing.

✔ The loan originator informed you that the Federal Housing Administration (FHA) insures your loan, protecting you from foreclosure. It does not. FHA insurance only protects the lender.

✔ Your loan originator told you that refinancing would solve your credit or financial problems.

✔ A contractor presented you with a good deal on a home or home improvement only if you financed through the contractor or through its recommended lender.

Recalling and Documenting the Experience

Buying a home is a significant event — not quite on par with a high school graduation, wedding day, or birth of a child, but sort of in the same league. Homeowners usually have some memory of the processes they went through to finance or refinance their homes, even if the details are a little fuzzy. (Sometimes, all borrowers remember is that it happened so fast.)

To pick some of the fuzz off the details and identify signs of predatory lending, take some time to think back and document your experience with the loan originator and lender as you remember it. If a co-borrower was involved (your spouse or partner, for instance), team up to piece together the details of your experience.

 Pull out any documents you kept related to the purchase, financing, or refinancing of any loans you've taken out against your home. You should have received a closing packet with each loan. These documents often contain details that can trigger the recollection of other key details. For more about analyzing your loan documents, see the next section "Combing Through Your Loan Documents for Fraud Flags."

As you piece together the details of your experience, try to answer the following questions:

✔ Do you feel as though your loan originator sold you a bad loan? If so, why?

✔ Did you feel pressured or rushed during the application process? If so, what made you feel that way?

✔ Did you apply over the phone without ever meeting your loan originator in person and without receiving a copy of the completed loan application?

✔ Did the loan originator encourage you to fudge the numbers on your loan application or otherwise direct you in how to make your numbers appear more flattering than they actually were?

✔ Did the loan originator have you sign an application that contained blanks he or she filled in later?

✔ Looking back, do you feel that the nature of the loan was misrepresented to you at the time? In other words, do you feel as though you were set up?

✔ Were you encouraged to refinance your mortgage loan multiple times over a short period?

✔ Do you feel as though the loan originator overcharged you in closing costs and other fees? Were the costs not disclosed or not explained to you?

If you answer "yes" to any of these questions, consider consulting an attorney for assistance in digging a little deeper for evidence. These questions are intended only to assist you in identifying potentially unethical lending practices. You still need to confirm any suspicions with evidence.

Combing Through Your Loan Documents for Fraud Flags

The best evidence that a lender violated a borrower's rights is usually sitting in the borrower's filing cabinet in the form of the Good Faith Estimate (GFE) and closing documents. We encourage you to pull out these documents, dust them off, and examine them for signs of predatory lending along with any RESPA, TILA, or HOEPA violations. (See Chapter 6 for more about gathering essential documents.) In the following sections, we provide some guidance on what to look for in these documents.

The well-trained eye of an experienced attorney is better suited to identifying potential violations. We strongly encourage you to enlist the assistance of a qualified attorney, as explained in the section "Hiring a Pro to Do It All for You" later in this chapter.

Comparing the GFE to the HUD-1

Perhaps the easiest violation to spot is the ol' bait and switch. The loan originator quotes you loan terms and fees upfront on the Good Faith Estimate (GFE), but the HUD-1 presented at closing quotes a loan with a higher interest rate and closing costs or some other loan product entirely, such as an adjustable-rate mortgage when you were led to believe it would have a fixed rate.

Pull out the GFE and HUD-1 and compare them line by line. Highlight any discrepancies between the two, regardless of how minor they may seem.

In addition to seeing whether the details on the GFE and HUD-1 match up, you should also consider whether the costs outlined on the HUD-1 were in line with the rest of the market when you closed on the loan. This is usually difficult for the typical homeowner who's understandably no expert in the mortgage lending industry. If you're unsure of whether a particular fee you paid was excessive, ask a mortgage broker (preferably *not* the one who originated your loan) or a real estate attorney in your area.

Inspecting the Universal Residential Loan Application (1003)

The Universal Residential Loan Application, or 1003, can be a tremendous source of evidence for homeowners that the loan originator or lender acted unethically. Inspect your 1003 closely for the following signs that the lender committed a violation:

- ✔ **Information that wasn't on the form when you signed it:** Someone filled in missing information or changed what had been written down.

- ✔ **Co-borrowers you don't know:** Some unscrupulous loan originator added co-borrowers to approve a loan when you didn't qualify on your own.

- ✔ **Inflated income:** Facts and figures about employment and income that were incorrect based on your situation at the time should raise suspicion, especially if you supplied verification documents to the loan officer showing the correct information.

- ✔ **An inflated estimate of the value of assets you owned at the time.**

- ✔ **Double-booking the home's value to present a positive net worth:** To boost a borrower's net worth (assets minus liabilities), the loan officer listed the home twice as an asset but only once as a liability. For example, if you owned a $200,000 home and still owed $180,000 on it, double-booking would make it look as though you had $40,000 equity in the home rather than the true amount of $20,000.

- ✓ **Bank accounts or liquid asset accounts that aren't yours or that have strange numbers associated with them.**

- ✓ **Failure to include installment accounts or debts you know you told the loan officer you were obligated to make payments on each month:** The loan originator kept some debts off the books to lower the debt-to-income ratio to an acceptable level. For more about debt-to-income ratios, see Chapter 2.

- ✓ **Failure to include other real estate you owned and had outstanding mortgages on.**

Before crying foul, try to recall your conversations with your loan originator concerning the loan application. If the loan originator clearly explained the form and answered all your questions, and if you knew what you were getting yourself into, perhaps your loan originator committed no foul. Even if your lender is at fault, it's likely to claim that you were complicit in any misrepresentations. If you were complicit, you may not have a case. If you weren't complicit, be prepared to counter any accusations with the evidence you're collecting.

Examining your mortgage and promissory note

The mortgage and the note are the final written memorial of the agreement between lender and borrower. Unfortunately, the mortgage usually provides little or no evidence of illegal or unethical lending practices; it merely consummates the lender/borrower relationship.

If you have an adjustable-rate mortgage, check your mortgage for a rider that contains the details of how the loan can adjust — including the base interest rate, when the rate will adjust and how often, and the maximum interest rate. If the terms specified seem too burdensome, they may be a sign of predatory lending. Look closely for the following:

- ✓ Convoluted or complicated interest rate calculations

- ✓ A very volatile index for an adjustable-rate mortgage

- ✓ Very short periods of time between adjustment periods

- ✓ A large margin percentage (for example, index plus 9.75 percent)

- ✓ A high minimum interest rate, especially if it's immediately above what the current index plus margin would be, meaning you have no chance of receiving the benefit of a low index at the time of rate adjustment

The promissory note typically contains more evidence of foul play if it occurred, but even strong evidence can be tough for the average borrower to pick out. Following are a few items you may want to look at closely:

✔ A huge prepayment penalty that extends for a long period

✔ A very short introductory period, so any benefit from the teaser rate is quickly swallowed up by the increase in the interest rate at the first adjustment

✔ A loan amount completely out of line for comparable homes in the area (usually supported by an inflated appraisal)

✔ Loan payments that represent the lion's share of your income each month

✔ 100 percent or higher loan-to-value (LTV) with interest-only payments and a relatively short timeline before a balloon payment is due, meaning refinancing is only possible if property values rise suddenly and significantly or if you take out another 100-percent-plus LTV loan

✔ A balloon payment that triggers a prepayment penalty, meaning you're required to pay back the loan, but by doing so you incur a stiff prepayment penalty

✔ A very low introductory interest rate on an ARM used to help you qualify for a loan — for example, your loan originator knew you didn't qualify for a 6 percent fixed-rate loan, so he put you into an adjustable-rate mortgage with an introductory rate of 1.5 percent, and now that your interest rate is at 9 percent, you can't afford the payments

The provisions in the note may not constitute predatory lending, but if you read through them and conclude that nobody in their right mind would agree to such terms if they understood them, you have a pretty clear indication that you're a victim of predatory lending. This is especially true if you had a credit score at the time that would have qualified you for a more stable loan product, such as a 30-year fixed-rate loan.

Hiring a Pro to Do It All for You

By following the advice in this chapter, you may be able to identify several symptoms of unethical lending practices related to your mortgage loan. Many of the most common signs, however, are identifiable only in the context of the marketplace. For example, determining whether the interest rate your lender charged is excessive or certain fees are unwarranted depends a great deal on what other lenders in the same market were charging at the time and your status as a credit-worthy borrower. This is why we recommend hiring a professional to perform a forensic audit of your mortgage loan.

A professional who's well trained in legal issues and the accounting practices surrounding mortgage loans can often spot questionable practices that seem perfectly normal to the average consumer. In addition, a forensic mortgage audit can provide you with leverage in negotiating an affordable loan modification, stopping any foreclosure actions, and perhaps even pursuing legal action against the lender or the company that brokered your loan.

Don't hire the first forensic mortgage auditor you find on the Web. Perform your due diligence and select a reputable expert who has plenty of experience auditing mortgage loans. Follow the same guidelines for choosing a forensic mortgage auditor as you would for choosing a loan modification expert (see Chapter 4). You may even want to choose an attorney who serves a dual role — one who can perform the forensic audit and oversee the loan modification for you.

Anticipating the Lender's Response to Any Legal Claims

Just because you have a loaded gun doesn't mean you should aim and fire every time you feel threatened. In the same way, having proof that a lender violated certain state or federal laws doesn't necessarily mean you should file a lawsuit. Sometimes a rational presentation of the evidence is enough to get you what you need without a long and messy legal battle.

Lending law violations rarely result in huge monetary judgments, but they can help get you favorable terms in a loan modification.

When you kick down the door and scream "Mortgage fraud!" and "Predatory lending!" lenders understandably get a little defensive. Tempering your findings with tact can result in the most beneficial outcome for you. Many lenders are willing to correct broker wrongs but for obvious reasons would prefer to do so out of court and beyond the media spotlight. The lender may even be more willing to offer more favorable terms than you could get by trying to force its hand in court. Look into, or have your attorney look into, the best options and processes to pursue to get you what you want. It does no good to claim victory only to have the cost of the war outweigh the spoils. (In Chapter 15, we show you how to use the information you gathered in the most effective way.)

Chapter 15

Applying Some Legal Pressure

· ·

In This Chapter

▶ Reminding the lender of your legal options

▶ Filing a complaint with state, federal, or professional agencies

▶ Suing your lender for damages

▶ Notifying local and federal law enforcement agencies

· ·

If your lender fails to listen to your request to modify your loan, or if you've fallen victim to predatory lending practices, you may need or want to play a heavier hand. Government regulatory and law enforcement agencies are in place at least partially to protect consumer rights. By knowing which agencies can assist you and how to spur them into action, you can often make progress. In this chapter, we show you how to rally the troops in a pursuit of consumer justice.

Keep detailed records of everything you do, every document you send and receive, and every phone call you make, whether you're speaking with your lender, your attorney, state or federal regulators, or law enforcement personnel. Jotting down dates, times, and names of all parties involved is particularly important. For more about keeping accurate, detailed records, check out Chapter 9.

Appendix A has a list of state attorneys general, government agencies, and advocacy groups that may be able and willing to support your efforts to secure justice.

Filing a Formal Complaint with Your Lender

You don't always need to file a lawsuit to secure your legal rights. Sometimes, reminding your lender of your rights as a consumer and what's at stake is sufficient to encourage it to do the right thing. We recommend starting with a gentle nudge and ramping up the pressure until you begin to see results.

Filing a lawsuit sounds easy enough, but it can be very costly, time-consuming, and aggravating (refer to the later section "Filing a Lawsuit" for the complete story). If you can accomplish the same or nearly the same goals without suing your lender, you're usually better off handling matters outside the legal system.

Start by writing a brief letter to your lender explaining your rights and how you think the lender violated those rights. See Figure 15-1 for a sample letter. Specify the date on which you expect a response, giving the lender sufficient time to respond (10 to 20 days should be enough), and explain what your next step will be if you don't receive a satisfactory response by that date.

Send your letter in a separate envelope, not with your mortgage payment. When waiting to hear from your lender, continue to make your payments as you're able. Always lodge your complaint with the lender's consumer complaint department or the department designed to handle these special investigations. Lenders are required by law to keep a record of complaints for auditing. Having your complaints on file can also strengthen your case.

If you don't receive a satisfactory response to your letter on the specified date, send a follow-up letter. Be sure to carbon copy your state attorney general or the regulatory agency of your choice (see the following section "Filing a Complaint") on this letter. In your follow-up letter, do each of the following:

- ✔ Reference your previous letter and summarize its main points

- ✔ Mention that you expected to hear from the lender on the specified date and did not

- ✔ Explain what you're now doing in response to the lender's failure to reply

- ✔ Describe what you want the lender to do and by what date

- ✔ Explain what you will do if the lender fails to comply with your request

You can also choose to file a complaint with federal regulatory agencies (see "Filing with federal regulators" later in this chapter).

Sam Spade
Loan #: 56980857
Phone: (555) 123-4567

2220 North Simpson Drive
Chicago, Illinois 60629
January 13, 2013

Second First National Bank
2211 West 59th Street
Chicago, Illinois 60629

Dear Sir or Madam:

I understand that Section 6 of the Real Estate Settlement Procedures Act (RESPA) provides me with certain rights. I am submitting this <u>qualified written request</u> in an effort to resolve an issue that occurred during the origination of my loan. I believe my income and credit score at the time I signed for my current mortgage loan qualified me for a loan with a more favorable rate and terms. I believe I was inappropriately placed into a subprime adjustable-rate loan that was not explained to me or understood by me at that time. My credit score, income, and payment history should have qualified me for a fixed-rate mortgage at a rate around 6.25 percent.

I have already submitted an application requesting a loan modification and have received a letter of denial, dated January 10, 2013, claiming that I could afford to make the payments on the loan I had signed for. However, I believe that the loan officer who sold me the loan committed a RESPA violation, and I am requesting a loan modification in an effort to settle this matter.

I have enclosed the following items to show that at the time I obtained my existing mortgage, I was well qualified for a low-interest fixed-rate mortgage:

- Pay stubs dated just prior to obtaining the mortgage
- Copies of my W-2s for the two years leading up to the mortgage origination date
- Copies of my federal income tax returns leading up to the mortgage origination date
- Copy of my credit report at the time of my mortgage origination

I understand that under Section 6 of RESPA you are required to acknowledge my request within 20 business days and must try to resolve the issue within 60 business days.

Sincerely,

Sam Spade

Figure 15-1: Sample letter of complaint.

If you suspect that your lender or loan originator committed a violation in placing you in your current loan, request that the lender perform an internal audit of your loan file. (Hiring an expert to perform an audit may be necessary later.) Write a letter, as suggested earlier in this section, pointing out the suspected violations. This can be part of your "complaint" letter or a separate letter addressed to the department in charge of handing legal matters. (In most cases, the complaints department can route the letter to the proper department, if necessary.)

Considering legal options

Sometimes sizing up your situation means looking for possible legal options in the application process that placed you in your current mortgage. I (Ralph) was involved in a case that resulted in the homeowner discovering an option she hadn't realized was available.

Like many homeowners, she refinanced during the refinance boom of the mid-2000s. Unfortunately, her lender placed her in an adjustable-rate mortgage that was scheduled to adjust up significantly very soon after we had met. As she'd done in the past, this homeowner wanted to refinance out of trouble, but this time, she couldn't; property values had dropped significantly, so she could no longer qualify for refinancing. She figured she had one option: foreclosure. She would live in the house rent-free during the redemption period, save some money, and then move to an apartment.

During our initial conversation, I suspected that the mortgage broker was guilty of some unethical lending practices in obtaining approval for this loan. Answers to my follow-up questions confirmed my suspicions. This homeowner was likely a victim of mortgage broker greed. The lure of loan origination fees apparently clouded this broker's judgment.

With the homeowner's assistance, I gathered some additional evidence, including the documentation used to obtain loan approval. After examining the documentation, I concluded that this homeowner probably wasn't qualified for the loan she was in. And I discovered that the property certainly hadn't been worth as much as the appraised value used to secure funding for the loan; the appraisal was inflated. The appraiser initially arrived at one value, which likely didn't meet an acceptable value for loan approval, so he reissued the appraisal for a higher value. To justify the new, higher value, the appraiser listed comparable properties that weren't really comparable. I'd seen this trick before.

I advised my client to seek legal counsel, and she did. With the assistance of a competent attorney, she was able to convince her lender to provide her with a loan modification that allowed her to keep her home and lower her monthly mortgage payments to an affordable level.

Filing a Complaint

Regardless of whether you file your own lawsuit against a lender, you can file a complaint with state and federal regulatory agencies to encourage them to investigate. The more credible complaints the agency receives, the more likely it is to launch an investigation into the lender's practices. Agencies often ask whether any litigation is pending regarding the matter stated in the complaint; if so, they may suspend investigations until that suit is resolved.

If you're working with an attorney, don't do *anything* without your attorney's permission. If your attorney is negotiating with your lender and your lender gets word that you're filing separate grievances, you could completely undermine your attorney's efforts.

Taking action at the state level

Each state has agencies to protect consumer rights, including a state attorney general; real estate commission; banking authority; and other regulatory, certification, and licensing boards. These agencies don't function as free private attorneys, filing lawsuits on behalf of citizens. Instead, they primarily take disciplinary action against professionals they determine have acted inappropriately. The good news is that the threat of disciplinary action may be enough to convince your lender to cooperate with you.

In the following sections, we tell you how to get in touch with your state attorney general and track down state regulatory bodies in order to find out more about filing a complaint.

Contacting your attorney general

Each state's attorney general has a host of responsibilities for protecting the state's citizens' rights, freedoms, and safety. These responsibilities can generally be grouped into two categories:

- ✔ **Consumer services,** such as no-call lists, privacy rights, oversight of various industries (including healthcare), Medicaid fraud, and unclaimed assets
- ✔ **Legal services** related to litigation, appeals, victim assistance, and complaints filed against attorneys or judges

When you contact your state attorney general, you want the consumer services division.

Appendix A provides Web site and contact information for the state attorneys general. Most of the Web sites have a complaint form you can download, print, complete, and then mail. Read and follow the instructions carefully. If you don't have access to the Internet, try your local library, or call your attorney general and request that a complaint form be sent to you in the mail.

Your state attorney general's office may not be able to address your complaint itself, but it can refer the matter to whichever state agency is best equipped to follow up on it.

Filing with state regulatory agencies

State regulatory agencies specialize in different areas, so they may be very responsive to your requests and yield a great deal of influence over the business or individual you feel acted inappropriately. This is especially true if the agency or its commissioner is responsible for approving or renewing the license of the business or individual. The challenge is in tracking down the best agency for the job.

Head to your favorite Internet search engine, and search for your state by name followed by the word "state" — for example, "California state." This usually calls up a link for your state's central Web site, where you can find links to state services.

Upon arriving at your state's Web site, you're pretty much on your own and have to browse for consumer-related assistance. Some sites offer links for filing a complaint. Others provide a list of links to the different regulatory agencies that accept consumer complaints. Look for the agency or office that's most likely to regulate the type of business you're filing a complaint against, as follows:

- ✔ **Mortgage broker:** Your state may have a licensing or certification board for mortgage brokers. In many states, the secretary of state provides oversight.

- ✔ **Real estate agent:** Almost all states have a real estate commission that provides oversight for the real estate industry, including certification for real estate agents.

- ✔ **Lender:** Every state has a regulator in charge of banking. The federal government also has several regulatory bodies that provide oversight for the lending industry, as explained in the following section "Filing with federal regulators."

If you can't figure out which office to contact, call an office that sounds close to what you want. State offices are usually pretty good about transferring callers to the right departments.

Call in the muscle

Sometimes having some well-placed friends with muscle can help you convince your lender to sit down with you at the negotiating table. This is exactly what happened for some homeowners in Arizona, California, Connecticut, Florida, Illinois, Iowa, Michigan, North Carolina, Ohio, Texas, and Washington who had fallen victim to one lender's particularly notorious lending practices. They called in the muscle, and the attorneys general of these states joined forces and decided to do something about it. As a result, the lender entered into a settlement whereby it agreed to modify loans on a grand scale.

The resulting settlement, although not an admission of wrongdoing, means that thousands of homeowners in danger of losing their homes are now eligible for a streamlined modification and/or rate reduction. (Of course, homeowners must meet certain eligibility requirements to qualify, but this shows at least one case in which someone was looking out for the little guy.)

As an individual homeowner, you may not have the power to pressure your lender into approving an affordable loan modification, but with the help of other homeowners in similar situations, you may be able to spur a giant, like a state attorney general, into action to take up the cause on your behalf and help the lender see that loan modification is clearly in everyone's best interest.

Filing with federal regulators

The federal government knows the critical role that the housing industry plays in the health of the national economy. As a result, it has several agencies (often referred to as *administrations, commissions,* or *boards*) in place to make sure the system operates in accordance with the rules and regulations already in place. We provide contact information for the most popular and powerful of these agencies in Appendix A.

For a searchable directory of federally regulated lending institutions, visit www.ffiec.gov, the Web site of the Federal Financial Institutions Examination Council (FFIEC). Click the Consumer Help Center link and then the Bank Complaints or Questions link. Enter the name of your lending institution, and the site displays the name of the regulatory agency you should contact.

Upon contacting a regulatory agency, you need to file a formal complaint, usually in writing, although some agencies may be willing to take your information over the phone. Be prepared to supply the agency with the following information:

- ✔ Your personal information, including name, address, phone number, and e-mail address

- ✔ Your lender's or servicer's name and contact information

- ✔ Your loan number(s)

- ✔ A brief description of the problem you're having

- ✔ A list of what you've already done to remedy the situation

- ✔ A brief statement of what you think the lender needs to do to make this right with you

Contacting professional associations

Many industries attempt to police themselves to set and maintain standards, enforce rules, and boost consumer confidence. If you have a credible grievance with a certain real estate or lending professional, consider filing a complaint with any professional association the business or individual belongs to.

If an individual holds any type of state-issued license, he or she is subject to disciplinary procedures. Although most agencies (public and private) clearly state that they won't serve as private attorneys, they can put the lender on notice, help move your case to the front of the line, and perhaps even encourage the lender to agree to a favorable settlement. If and when the time comes to negotiate a settlement, having an attorney on hand is always a good idea.

If the association compiles a disciplinary report or a findings report, request a copy of it. If the professional association finds the conduct of the professional unethical or in violation of regulatory rules, you should have that report for your records. (If you need an attorney for your case, he or she should have a copy of the report as well.)

One of the best ways to track down state associations is to hop on the Internet and search your state followed by the industry — real estate, mortgage bankers, mortgage brokers, appraisers, title companies, home inspectors, and so on. Following are the Web sites of some national professional associations that may also be helpful:

- ✔ National Association of REALTORS: www.realtor.org

- ✔ Mortgage Bankers Association of America: www.mbaa.org

✔ National Association of Mortgage Brokers: www.namb.org

✔ Appraisal Institute: www.appraisalinstitute.org

Following through on your complaint

Regardless of which regulatory agency you contact, always follow up a few days after filing your complaint to make sure it reached the agency and is in the system. Typically, the agency assigns the complaint to a case representative. Try to find out the person's name, identification number, and phone number, so you know whom to contact for follow-ups. Then follow up by asking these questions:

✔ When will your lender (or individual in question) be notified of your complaint?

✔ How many days does your lender (or individual) have to respond to your complaint?

✔ What happens if your lender (or individual) fails to respond by the specified date?

✔ Have any other complaints been filed against the lender (or individual)? If so, how many? The more complaints, the better for you; when it comes to regulatory agencies, the squeakiest wheel gets the most attention.

If the lender or individual that you file a complaint against responds to your complaint (and they usually do), expect them to deny your allegations and explain away the issues. If you're not satisfied and have hard evidence that your lender (or individual) has broken the rules, submit a rebuttal letter to the regulatory agency so it doesn't close the case. If you don't respond, the regulatory agency typically assumes "case closed."

Don't let slow-moving wheels of justice crush your determination. Remain persistent and remind the agency case representative that you're going to keep checking in until all issues are resolved to *your* satisfaction.

Filing a Lawsuit

When all else fails, take 'em to court . . . assuming, of course, you're willing to invest the time, effort, and perhaps even cash to prove your claim. This section outlines the lawsuit process, so you know how to get started and what to expect.

If you live in a state that doesn't practice judicial foreclosure, filing a lawsuit against the lender may delay the foreclosure sale, giving you time to pursue other options, as covered in Chapter 3. By filing a suit against the lender, you can bring a nonjudicial foreclosure into the court system to provide yourself with additional legal rights and perhaps a more favorable timeline.

Ordering a mortgage audit

Whether you decide to represent yourself or hire an attorney, hire an experienced professional to audit your mortgage. It may cost over $1,000, but a mortgage audit arms you or your attorney with the firepower you need to fight the good fight . . . and win. A comprehensive audit

- ✔ Assesses the strengths and weaknesses of your case.

- ✔ Ensures that you or your attorney includes all viable allegations in the complaint.

- ✔ Provides leverage for settling the case out of court, which is almost always in the borrower's best interest.

An audit report can serve as valuable evidence in court, especially if it identifies blatant violations. If the facts speak for themselves, your lender's position becomes very tenuous, and your lender is likely to push for a settlement. With strong evidence in hand, you have the leverage you need to negotiate a very attractive settlement.

Getting up to speed on the procedure

Filing a lawsuit is a complicated endeavor best handled by an experienced attorney. However, as the plaintiff, you should have a clear idea of the steps involved in filing a lawsuit:

1. You or your attorney draft the complaint.

2. You or your attorney file the complaint with the court clerk who then issues summons to appear. You have the whole package served on the parties involved and provide the court with proof of service.

3. The defendant (the lender in this case) is given time to file its answer to the complaint. The answer may include counterclaims and may be accompanied by a motion to dismiss the complaint altogether or at least to dismiss certain claims.

4. You file a response (called a *reply*) to the answer and/or any motions filed, which may include a brief of the issue and/or amendment to your complaint.

5. The defendant will already have filed or will file a brief in support of the motion to dismiss.

6. A judge schedules a hearing on the motion to dismiss (if one was filed).

7. If your complaint survives a motion to dismiss, the judge schedules the case for trial and establishes a timeline for discovery, pretrial or settlement conferences, and so on.

8. At trial, each side presents its proofs before a judge or a jury who then issues a decision, preferably in your favor.

Eight steps, short and sweet, right? Well, not exactly and certainly not in most cases. The process can be very long, drawn out, and time-consuming, and this timeline doesn't account for appeals if any are filed after the decision.

State court and federal court procedures can vary. Check the state or federal court rules for where to file your complaint and what to include. Court Web sites generally provide you with an explanation of the civil process, the local or special rules for that court, and other very useful information such as fees, court costs, and docket information. If you're representing yourself, check your court's Web site; it can be an invaluable resource.

Securing professional representation

By reading this book, you've proven that you're no fool, but as the old saying goes, "A person who chooses to represent himself in court has a fool for a client." If you choose to file a lawsuit against your lender or an individual involved in your mortgage origination, we advise hiring an attorney who's skilled and experienced in real estate and mortgage banking — someone who understands the rules and regulations that lenders and loan originators were supposed to follow when they sold and approved your loan.

One of the best ways to dig up a qualified attorney is to network with real estate professionals you already know and trust (that rules out the professional who sold you the bad loan). You can also ask friends, relatives, neighbors, and colleagues for referrals, but that means disclosing your situation. If you have no leads, consider searching the American Bar Association online directory for an attorney at www.abanet.org. Click Public Resources and then

Lawyer Locator; you can search by town, city, county, or state and then by area of specialization (we recommend choosing Debtor And Creditor or Real Estate).

Another option is to run an Internet search on the issue that's applicable in your case and see which attorneys pop up as having written articles on that issue. However, be sure to validate the person's credentials with the state bar association to which he or she belongs . . . or claims to belong.

Perform your due diligence in selecting an attorney, as you would in selecting a professional to provide any service. (For details on vetting your options, check out Chapter 4.) It doesn't hurt to find an attorney or law firm that has represented plaintiffs successfully against your specific lender in the past. If your lender sees you've engaged an attorney who knows the issues and has held the lender's feet to the fire before, settlement is more likely.

Calling the Cops

Although you rarely hear about it in the news, real estate and mortgage fraud is rampant. We believe that massive fraud is one of the primary contributing factors to the mortgage meltdown and resulting foreclosure epidemic. Unfortunately, much of this fraud was committed under the radar in a gray zone that law enforcement and regulatory agencies prefer to steer clear of. However, if you believe that the actions of one or more parties involved in your mortgage loan rise to the level of criminal activity, turn the matter over to law enforcement.

Pressing criminal charges is only warranted if you feel you've been conned out of some money. It's not something you do just because your lender is being uncooperative.

Don't bother calling your local police department or county sheriff. Chances are pretty good that they'll just refer you to the state police or Federal Bureau of Investigation (FBI), so start there. Your state may have a mortgage fraud task force that works alongside the FBI to investigate real estate and mortgage fraud and bring the perpetrators to justice.

When you contact law enforcement, provide them with the same information that federal regulators would need. Refer to the section "Filing with federal regulators" earlier in this chapter for details.

Part V
The Part of Tens

The 5th Wave · By Rich Tennant

'Tell Her Highness we're almost out of time. If she's going to negotiate a loan modification, she better do it now.

In this part . . .

Welcome to the Part of Tens . . . the mainstay of any *For Dummies* book, including this one. In this Part of Tens, we provide ten tips and strategies to achieve long-term success and avoid becoming another recidivism statistic. We even let you in on what *recidivism* is.

We also reveal the top ten myths about loan modifications — the types of misinformation you're likely to hear from well-intentioned friends and relatives. We then proceed to bust each myth wide open so you know the real truth about loan modification.

Chapter 16

Ten Tips for Long-Term Success

*B*y some estimates, the *recidivism* (a $5 word for "relapse") rate for homeowners who receive a loan modification is upward of 60 percent in the first eight months. The cause usually can be traced back to the fact that the initial loan modification didn't result in a truly affordable monthly mortgage payment or that the homeowners failed to address the root cause of their initial default — insufficient income or excess expenditures. In this chapter, we provide ten tips for staying out of financial trouble in the long-term.

Get the Best Deal You Can

One of the problems with negotiating a lower mortgage payment is that the lender's goal is to shake as much money out of you as possible. As a result, lenders often push for and homeowners often agree to a lower monthly payment that's not really affordable. Or the new monthly payment makes the homeowner's budget so tight that he's one unexpected car repair or medical bill away from falling into default again.

One of the keys to long-term success is to negotiate the absolute best deal you can get the first time around — a deal that leaves you with a financial buffer to handle unexpected expenses.

If your lender refuses to budge and you really can't afford the payment being offered, don't agree to the deal unless the loan modification provides you with sufficient temporary relief to implement a long-term solution, such as selling your home.

Get Credit Counseling

In Chapter 2, we encourage you to rough out a budget so you know where all your money is coming from and where it's going. If you're really not into budgeting, you're going to do either a lousy job writing up your budget or an even lousier job sticking to it, and you'll benefit from working with a credit counselor. A credit counselor can assist you in the following ways:

- ✔ Analyze your current financial situation and set reasonable goals to trim spending

- ✔ Itemize your current spending and group expenses by category

- ✔ Prioritize credit accounts to pay off high-interest credit first

- ✔ Negotiate workout solutions with your other creditors

- ✔ Keep the bill collectors at bay

- ✔ Hold you accountable, so you stick with the plan

Work with a reliable and reputable credit counselor or agency. The United States Trustee Program provides a searchable directory of reputable counseling agencies at www.usdoj.gov/ust/eo/ bapcpa/ccde/cc_approved.htm. The Federal Trade Commission (FTC) offers an informative online article on how to choose a reputable credit counseling agency at www.ftc.gov/bcp/edu/pubs/ consumer/credit/cre26.shtm, or you can check out *Credit Repair Kit For Dummies* by Steve Bucci (Wiley). If your state requires credit counseling agencies to be licensed or registered, contact the agency that regulates the industry, make sure the agency is licensed and certified, and check for licensing complaints or disciplinary actions.

Try Modifying Other Loans, Too

When the economy suffers, everyone hurts, including banks, credit card companies, and new car dealerships. They all face the very real possibility that many of their customers will stop making payments or be forced into bankruptcy. Like your mortgage lender, many of these institutions would rather you pay less than pay nothing. Creditors who hold unsecured debt (that's debt not secured by a valuable asset, such as your home) are particularly at risk of losing out if you declare bankruptcy.

A new car loan may be one of the best places to start. By some estimates, a new car loses up to $8,000 in value as soon as you drive it off the lot. If the finance company repos the car and tries to resell it, the company stands to lose $8,000. This fact coupled with a previously good payment history may be all you need to convince the finance company to work out a solution with you.

Try cutting a deal with your credit card company, too. They can be tough negotiators, but it's worth a try. You may be able to convince them to lower your interest rate or drop a late payment penalty. You won't know unless you ask. The worst they can do is say "no."

If you have student loans, contact the servicer and ask about solutions to provide relief. Many government-backed student loans offer "out of work" forbearance so you can put off making payments until you find a job. If you lost your job and go back to school to advance your skills, most student loans cease to require payments. Call or go online to explore your options.

Get all loan modification agreements, even those with smaller companies, in writing.

Prioritize Your Debt Payments

Most credit counselors are going to tell you to pay more than the minimum monthly payments on your credit card bills and other high-interest accounts. However, paying more than the minimum due on *all* your accounts isn't the savviest strategy. Prioritize your accounts first.

Find your most recent credit card statements and inspect them carefully to see which one is charging the highest interest. This is the credit card balance you want to pay off first. You may be able to transfer the balance to a credit card account that's charging a lower interest rate, but find out how much it'll cost you (if anything) before making the transfer.

Slash Discretionary Spending

Discretionary spending consists of unnecessary expenses, such as going out for dinner and a movie or buying fried chicken when you could bake one yourself for less. These are the expenses that sink most budgets, so here are a few suggestions on how to cut back:

- ✔ **Team up with your partner, if you have a partner.** When both of you have a say in how much each of you spends and for what, you can hold one another accountable.

- ✔ **Grocery shop once a week.** The more times you pop into the grocery store, the more likely you are to make an impulse purchase . . . or two or three.

- ✔ **Buy only what's on the grocery list.** The person in the family with the strongest shopping self-control — the one who's best at buying only what's on the list and at finding bargains — should do all the shopping. And don't be too proud to clip coupons; they can make a significant impact on your bottom line.

- ✔ **Eat in.** You spend a lot more for food when someone else prepares it. That goes for fountain drinks, too. And don't cheat by purchasing prepared foods at the grocery store; those fried chicken strips from the deli and TV dinners can be very expensive, too.

- ✔ **Trim your phone bill.** One phone for the family should be sufficient. Also, call your phone company and look into more affordable plans.

- ✔ **Trim your cable TV bill.** You can live without the premium channels.

- ✔ **Cut back on vacations.** If you and your partner take separate vacations, those should be the first expenses that get the ax. Look at ways to pare back on your other vacations, too.

- ✔ **Dress fashionably poor.** You don't need to change your wardrobe every year. In addition, you may be able to find great deals on gently used clothing at Goodwill, the Salvation Army, garage sales, flea markets, and consignment shops.

- ✔ **Lose the car, if possible.** If you can get by with public transportation or car-pooling, you can save a lot on auto expenses — fuel, maintenance and repairs, and auto insurance.

Pay Yourself an Allowance

Parents often put their kids on allowances to teach them responsibility and to keep the kids from nickel and diming their parents into the poor house with constant requests for money. Few adults, however, consider the possibility that perhaps they're nickel and diming themselves into the poor house by stopping at the ATM every time they need some cash.

This week, go to the ATM only once and pull out a reasonable amount of cash (within your budget) to cover your personal expenses — haircut, coffee, soft drinks, green fees, whatever. When that money's gone, it's gone . . . at least until next week when you visit the ATM again.

Haggle Over Every Purchase

In foreign countries, particularly third-world countries where consumers are time rich but cash poor, haggling is a way of life. In the U.S., this practice has fallen out of favor, but over the past ten years or so, *neo-hagglers* have begun to popularize this type of negotiation again. In bad economic times, haggling becomes even more popular because consumers need to get prices down and businesses need to make sales.

Granted, this strategy isn't very realistic when you're dealing with your gas or electric company or shopping at a major grocery chain, but it does work for a surprising number of businesses. Here are some ideas to get you started:

- Start haggling with online purchases. It's easier to negotiate when you don't have to look the other person in the eye.

- Haggle with your phone company to get the services you want for less. (What they charge for text messaging is outrageous!) When other offers come your way for services you already have (like phone and cable), make your current provider aware and use those other offers to try to leverage a better deal or even get the same deal that the other company is offering.

- Negotiate a lower room rate the next time you book a room in a hotel or motel. If you're a member of AAA, AARP, or some other such group, ask about discounts.

- If you get lousy food or service at a restaurant, ask to speak with the manager about getting a discount or having the entire meal or your next meal *comp'ed* (that's restaurant lingo for "complimentary").

- Look for minor blemishes on clothing or shoes and ask the sales clerk to discount the damaged item for you.

- Ask sales clerks whether you can get a discount for buying other items you really need.

- If the quote for a car repair seems steep, talk to the manager to see if you can get a discount. He may be so afraid of losing your business that he's willing to drop the price. The best time to haggle over this price is before the work is done because the manager won't want to lose your business and you'll be able to negotiate from a position of greater strength than if he's already done the work.

Save your receipts and watch prices even after you've made your purchases. Many stores issue price adjustments within 30 days of the purchase date to keep you from just returning the item if you see it for sale somewhere else or even at the same store.

Moonlight to Earn Extra Income

Unless you have a contract with your employer that prohibits moonlighting, you may be able to earn some extra money on the side. Auto mechanics, plumbers, electricians, hair stylists, and others who have marketable skills have been doing it for years.

Don't moonlight if it compromises your ability to perform your day job or violates any agreement you have with your current employer. You don't want to lose a steady paycheck in the process of trying to earn some extra cash.

Put Everyone to Work

Short of selling your entire family into indentured servitude on eBay, consider asking everyone in the family who's capable of working to at least cover the cost of their personal expenses — whatever electronic gadgets and services they feel they need, movie tickets, shoes and clothing, cosmetics, snacks, and so forth.

In a real pinch, your partner or your kids can even toss a little money your way to cover the household expenses, at least temporarily until conditions improve. In many cases, the kids want to help — they just don't know how. By having everyone pitch in and celebrating your financial success together, you may even find that your family becomes much closer.

Check Your Progress

Budgeting isn't a one-time deal. You need to set your budget and then revisit it at least every month (more frequently when you're getting started) to make sure you're on track or to get back on track. It's like a diet or trying to quit smoking: Even if you cheat, you have to get back on the wagon.

If you're teaming up with family members, get them all involved in the budget review process, so everyone involved knows where the money is going and is aware of any problems as soon as they arise. You have a much better chance of success when you work together.

Don't forget to celebrate your success. Come up with an affordable way to celebrate — maybe a special home-cooked meal and a movie rental. It doesn't have to be expensive to be fun!

Chapter 17

Ten Common Loan Modification Myths

In This Chapter

▶ Getting over the fear that your bank wants your home

▶ Overcoming the notion that you can't qualify until you're in default

▶ Appreciating just how much time you really have

▶ Realizing the benefits of paying for legal representation

*L*oan modification offers real help to homeowners who can't afford their monthly payments. For homeowners who qualify, lenders are able and often willing to adjust the terms of the loan. In some cases, the lender may even reduce the principal balance due in order to make the monthly payments more affordable.

Unfortunately, homeowners often mistakenly believe they can't possibly qualify for a loan modification, or some other psychological barrier stands between them and the help they need. To overcome any barriers that may be standing in your way, this chapter busts ten common myths about loan modification.

My Bank Wants To Take My Home

Many homeowners believe that as soon as they miss a single payment, the bank is standing ready to kick them out of their homes and seize their land. The truth is that banks don't profit from foreclosure, even if the home is worth way more than what you owe the bank. Here's how it works: Suppose the bank sells your home at the foreclosure auction for $50,000 more than you owe on it. The bank is entitled to receive only what it's owed, which includes the principal, past due interest, and any penalties and fees you owe — late-payment fees, attorney fees, and so on. The rest of the money goes to any junior lien holders to pay off their claims to the property. If any money remains after paying off all the liens, it goes to you. Getting your share is usually as easy as asking for it and signing a receipt.

According to a report from the Joint Economic Committee of Congress, an average foreclosure costs the lender $50,000 to $60,000 in lost interest, attorney fees, expenses for rehabbing the home, commissions for listing and selling it, and sometimes having to sell at a loss.

My Credit Score Is Too Low

Many homeowners try to refinance their way out of foreclosure by taking out a new loan with a lower interest rate. Unfortunately, they often can't qualify for the new, low-interest loan because their credit history has been damaged by several late or missed payments or because lenders have tightened their requirements.

As a result, these folks often walk away with the mistaken belief that they're out of luck. If they couldn't qualify for refinancing, how could they possibly qualify for a loan modification?

Unlike the option of refinancing your way out of trouble, which requires you to apply for a new loan, loan modification simply adjusts the terms and perhaps reduces the balance of a loan you already have. Because you're not applying for a new loan, your credit score is much less of a factor in determining whether you qualify for a loan modification.

A successful loan modification focuses more on affordability than on good credit. Obtaining and adhering to the terms of a loan modification can actually improve your credit score over time, especially if it prevents foreclosure or bankruptcy.

I Can't Qualify until My Loan Is in Default

When lenders and government agencies first identified loan modification as a potential cure for the foreclosure epidemic, they slapped all sorts of restrictions on it to prevent people who didn't really need a loan modification from qualifying for one. Some early eligibility requirements stated that you had to be 61 days delinquent (that's two full payments behind) in order to qualify.

The truth is that the eligibility requirements are constantly changing and differ among lenders. During the height of the foreclosure epidemic, many lenders began negotiating loan modifications with borrowers who were up to date on their payments. Conditions dictated that they needed to take a more proactive approach.

You can't determine whether you qualify for a loan modification simply by reading about "standard" requirements in this book or on the Internet. You really need to discuss your situation with your lender or, better yet, with an attorney who's knowledgeable and experienced in loan modifications and who can work with your lender to determine whether you qualify.

I'm Better Off Declaring Bankruptcy or Walking Away

Unless you have a huge amount of *unsecured debt* (typically credit card debt), bankruptcy is probably not the best option. It's likely to cost more and blemish your credit history without delivering any better results than you can expect from a loan modification.

In some cases, declaring bankruptcy *is* the best option, so we don't want you to rule it out entirely. It's particularly attractive if you're buried in unsecured debt or if the bank is pursuing a deficiency judgment against you. Bankruptcy can erase the deficiency or unsecured debt (or a significant portion of it) or can allow you to restructure your secured debt (such as your mortgage) depending on the bankruptcy chapter. It also can buy you some valuable time.

We discuss the bankruptcy option in *Foreclosure Self-Defense For Dummies* (Wiley). For a more detailed presentation, check out *Personal Bankruptcy Laws For Dummies*, 2nd Edition, by James P. Caher and John M. Caher (Wiley).

Walking away and abandoning the home is a risky option. If you're lucky, the bank takes your home, sells it at foreclosure, and writes off the loss. The only thing you have to deal with is a negative mark on your credit history. In some jurisdictions, however, the bank may have the legal right to pursue a *deficiency judgment,* in which case you may be obligated to pay the difference between what you owed and what the bank realized from the sale of the home. A successful loan modification is always a more prudent choice. (For more about alternatives to loan modification, refer to Chapter 3.)

I Can Negotiate Myself for Free

This myth has some truth to it. You certainly may be able to negotiate a loan modification with your lender on your own. However, an attorney who has experience in the field is more capable than most people at negotiating the best deal possible.

Experienced attorneys know what the lenders are willing to negotiate and how far they can be pushed. Attorneys also carry more legal weight than consumers. With the threat of a possible lawsuit sitting on the negotiating table, the lender is usually more open to considering a reasonable deal.

In addition, an attorney is likely to be less emotional and more rational in dealing with your lender. If you call and begin to argue with the lender's representative, you may get accidentally disconnected or your application may mysteriously disappear. Lenders are often more willing to negotiate with calm, cool, and collected attorneys.

For more information on making the decision to work with an attorney (and how to go about the collaboration) or go it alone, turn to Chapter 4.

It's Too Late to Modify My Loan

When homeowners receive a foreclosure notice, many assume they have only two options remaining: pay up or move out. The fact is that the foreclosure notice signals only the beginning of the end. The lender can stop the foreclosure as easily as it started the process — assuming you can convince the lender of your willingness and ability to make reasonable monthly payments.

As long as you still reside in the home — that is, you didn't voluntarily abandon it and the sheriff hasn't shown up to evict you — you may still have time to save your home. By contacting the lender (prior to the foreclosure sale) or, better yet, having your attorney contact the lender on your behalf, you demonstrate a good faith effort to work out a solution and can often buy yourself extra time to negotiate a loan modification. You may even have time to save your home after a foreclosure sale if you live in a state that allows redemption; contact your county register of deeds or a local consumer-focused foreclosure attorney for more information.

The Lender Doesn't Have to Negotiate

Lenders often feel compelled to negotiate solutions with borrowers for the simple reason that they don't want the expense of foreclosure, bad loans on their books, or a huge inventory of properties they can't sell. If a lender has too many bad loans, its reputation in the industry suffers, and it may have trouble borrowing money to make future loans available. A lender/originator with a reputation for high default ratios can find itself on the secondary market blacklist, which prevents it from replenishing the cash reserves necessary to originate new loans. From this point, it's a slow painful death.

Lenders may also be required to refinance or offer loan modifications if they participate in government-sponsored home retention plans, such as the Making Home Affordable initiative.

In addition, many loans in default contain evidence that the lender or someone else involved in originating or approving the loan acted inappropriately. In cases such as these, the lender is legally obligated to either renegotiate the loan agreement with the borrower or repurchase the loan. A knowledgeable attorney can perform a forensic audit that often identifies regulatory violations or fraudulent activities that most consumers would never notice on their own. (For more about leveraging the law to pressure your lender to cooperate, see Part IV.)

Upfront Fees Are a Scam

Almost all consumer advocates warn against paying upfront fees for loan modification, credit counseling, and similar services. In most situations, this is excellent advice. In fact, some states have passed laws barring upfront fees unless certain requirements are met. When you're obtaining legal services from bona fide attorneys, however, the rules change.

Attorneys almost always charge upfront fees in the form of *retainers*. The key is to work with a reputable loan modification company that offers legal representation and has a reasonable refund policy if it can't help you.

Make sure the company has a mailing address (not just a P.O. box number or Web site address) and a phone number, and do some checking to make sure the company is legitimate and has successfully negotiated loan modifications for its clients. For more about choosing reputable experts to help you with your situation, see Chapter 4.

I'll Lose My Home If I Don't Qualify for a Loan Modification

Not everyone qualifies for a loan modification, but other options and exit strategies are available. In fact, most homeowners have about a dozen options they can pursue to either keep their homes or get out from under them gracefully. Options include placing the home on the market, refinancing, borrowing money from a friend or relative to reinstate the loan, and working out a payment plan with the bank to catch up on deficiencies, to name a few.

If you live in a jurisdiction that offers a redemption period, you even have the option of buying back the property from whoever happens to purchase it at the auction. An attorney can help you analyze the various options and offer guidance on which one is best for your situation. For more about alternatives to loan modification, refer to Chapter 3.

I Can Modify Only the Loan on My Primary Residence

Loan modification is designed for homeowners, not investors, so you have a better chance of qualifying for a modification of a mortgage on a primary or secondary residence — that is, for a home you actually live in — than an investment property. However, when the mortgage lending industry is in dire straits it can't afford to have any loans go into default, and so lenders become more willing to work with investors.

If you hold mortgages on more than one home, you may not be fully aware of the options you have until you do your research. The mortgage lending landscape is constantly changing, and only by consulting with someone knowledgeable in the field of loan modifications can you truly become educated enough to make the best decision. A good call to make (or have made for you) is to the lender/servicer. Ask if it modifies loans on secondary or investment properties; if the answer is "yes," follow the steps to find out what you need to do to qualify.

Part VI
Appendixes

"I was looking for a loan that came with a rate that was fixed, not neutered."

In this part . . .

Tacked on to the end of this book are two valuable appendixes (or appendices, depending on which side of the tracks you live on). The first is a collection of additional resources that can come in quite handy. It includes Web site and contact information for the major lenders, a list of federal agencies and consumer advocacy groups you can contact for assistance, and contact information for the attorney general in each of the 50 states (plus the District of Columbia and U.S. territories).

The second appendix is a glossary of typically unfamiliar terminology and acronyms we use throughout the book, such as *loan-to-value (LTV) ratio, debt-to-income (DTI) ratio,* and *deficiency judgment.* With this glossary in hand, you not only have a better understanding of what the experts are telling you, but you can also confidently weave these terms into your next dinner conversation. (It's a good idea to become familiar with these terms so you don't have to look them up while on the phone with your lender, but you can still use this glossary as a crutch, just in case.)

Appendix A

Resources

● ●

*T*he mortgage meltdown and foreclosure epidemic are national crises that have generated a huge amount of negative press, but every cloud does have a silver lining. In this case, the silver lining is in the form of unprecedented assistance for homeowners facing foreclosure and lenders who stand to lose big time from the rash of defaults on mortgage loans.

In this appendix, we highlight various resources, both online and off, where you can go for information and assistance for saving your home from foreclosure. We cover everything from major lenders to government agencies, including your state attorney general, and consumer advocacy groups to private organizations.

Major Lender Web Sites and Customer Service Numbers

If you have a mortgage in the United States, chances are pretty good that your mortgage is with one of the top ten mortgage lending institutions. They appear in the following list along with more than 50 other mortgage lending institutions. We provide both customer service phone numbers and Web site addresses so you can use whatever method of contact you're most comfortable with.

 Some of the information provided in this list may have changed between the time this book was published and the time you're reading it due to acquisitions, mergers, or some lenders simply going out of business. In addition, although we attempted to locate phone numbers that connect directly to each lender's loss mitigation or loan modification department, some of the numbers may connect you to the lender's switchboard operator or loan origination department; you'll need to work your way past the gatekeepers to the right person, as explained in Chapter 5.

ABN AMRO Mortgage
See Citi

Accredited Home Lenders
(877) 683-4466
www.accredhome.com

Acqura Loan Services
(866) 660-5804
www.acqura.net

American Home Mortgage Servicing, Inc.
(877) 304-3100
ahmsi3.com

AmTrust Bank
(800) 860-2025 ext. 2897
www.amtrust.com

Aurora Loan Services
(866) 521-3828
www.myauroraloan.com

Avelo Mortgage
See Litton Loan Servicing

Bank of America
(800) 846-2222
www.bankofamerica.com

BankersWest Funding Corporation
(800) 518-1172
www.bankerswest.com

Bear Stearns
(866) 339-8355 or (800) 634-1428
www.bearstearns.com

Carrington Mortgage Services
(800) 790-9502
myloan.carringtonms.com

Cendant Mortgage Corporation/Reology
(800) 257-0460
www.cendant.com or www.realogy.com

Central Pacific
(800) 342-8422 option 3
www.centralpacificbank.com

Charter One Mortgage
(800) 234-6002
www.charterone.com

Chase
(866) 550-5705
www.chase.com

Chevy Chase Bank
(800) 933-9100 or (301) 939-4087 (loss mitigation)
www.chevychasebank.com

Citi
(866) 915-9417
www.mortgagehelp.citi.com

CMG Mortgage & CMG Mortgage Servicing
(800) 501-2001
www.cmgmortgageservices.com

Colonial National Mortgage
(800) 937-6002
www.cnmcs.com

Countrywide Home Loans
(800) 669-6607
my.countrywide.com/media/FinancialAssistance.html

Ditech
See GMAC/Homecomings

Downey Financial
(800) 824-6902 ext. 6696
www.downeysavings.com

EMC Mortgage Corporation
(866) 550-5705
www.emcmortgagecorp.com/hasp/

EverHome Mortgage Company
(800) 669-7724
www.everhomemortgage.com

First California Mortgage Company
(877) 885-3262
www.firstcal.net

First Franklin Loan Services
(800) 346-6437
www.viewmyloan.com

First Guaranty Bank
(904) 301-2000
www.firstguarantybank.com

First Horizon
(800) 364-7662
www.firsthorizon.com

FirstMerit Bank
(800) 562-6694
www.firstmerit.com

Flagstar Bank
(800) 945-7700 ext. 9780
www.flagstar.com

Freemont Investment and Loan
See Litton Loan Servicing

GMAC/Homecomings
(866) 899-5308
www.gmacmortgage.com or
www.homecomings.com

GreenPoint Mortgage
(800) 784-5566
www.greenpointmortgage.
com

Guild Mortgage Company
(800) 365-4884
www.guildmortgage.com

Home Loan Services, Inc.
See First Franklin Loan Services

HomEq Servicing
(877) 867-7378
www.homeq.com

HSBC Consumer Lending
(800) 958-2540
www.beneficial.com or
www.hfc.com

HSBC Mortgage Corporation
(800) 338-6441
www.us.hsbc.com

HSBC Mortgage Services
(800) 395-3489 or (800) 365-6730
hsbcmortgageservices.com

Huntington National
(800) 562-6871
(current on payments)
(877) 477-6855 (more than 30
days behind on payments)
www.huntington.com/hasp

IndyMac Federal Bank
(866) 355-7273 or
(877) 908-HELP (4957)
www.imb.com

JPMorgan Chase
(866) 550-5705
www.chase.com

KeyBank
(800) 422-2442
www.key.com

LaSalle National Bank
See Bank of America

Litton Loan Servicing
(800) 999-8501
www.littonloan.com

LoanCare Servicing Center
(800) 909-9525
www.myloancare.com

Midland Mortgage
(800) 552-3000
www.mymidlandmortgage.com

National City Mortgage Company
(800) 523-8654
www.nationalcity
mortgage.com

Nationstar Mortgage
(888) 480-2432 (ext. 7203 if ARM
will adjust in next 90 days)
www.nationstarmtg.com

Nationwide
(866) 350-8884
www.nationwide.com/
avoid-foreclosure.jsp

New Century (Carrington)
See Carrington Mortgage Services

Ocwen
(877) 596-8580
www.ocwencustomers.com

Option One
*See American Home Mortgage
Servicing, Inc.*

PHH Mortgage
(800) 210-8849
www.phhmortgage.com

PNC Mortgage
(888) 762-2265
www.pncmortgage.com

Prodovis Mortgage, LLC
(888) 878-0522
www.prodovis.com

Provident Funding
(800) 696-8199 option 4
providentfunding.com

Regions Bank
(800) 748-9498 (mortgage)
www.regions.com

ResMAE Mortgage
(866) 804-5604
www.resmaemortgage.com

Saxon Mortgage
(888) 325-3502
www.saxononline.com

Select Portfolio Servicing, Inc.
(888) 818-6032
www.spservicing.com

Sky Bank
See Huntington National

SunTrust Mortgage
(800) 443-1032 option 3
www.suntrustmortgage.com

Taylor, Bean & Whitaker
(800) 530-2602
www.taylorbean.com

Third Federal Savings
(888) 844-7333
www.thirdfederal.com

U.S. Bank
(866) 932-0462
www.usbank.com

Wachovia Bank
(800) 922-4684
www.wachovia.com

Washington Mutual
(877) 551-2736
(current on payments)
(866) 926-8937
(late on payments)
www.wamu.com

Wells Fargo Financial
(877) 898-4227
financial.wellsfargo.com

Wilshire Credit Corp./ Merrill Lynch
(888) 502-0100
www.wcc.ml.com

Consumer Support and Federal Agencies

Although the United States government has been criticized for doing too little too late for homeowners, the fact is that several consumer groups and federal agencies are in place to help homeowners, but you need to take the initiative and contact them. In the following sections, we list consumer groups and federal agencies that can assist you in pursuing a loan modification, some other foreclosure solution, or a claim against a lender or someone else involved in originating your loan who may have committed fraud.

Start with your lender or one of the consumer groups listed here. If that doesn't work to your satisfaction, one or more federal agencies may be able to crank up the heat enough to convince your lender to work with you.

Consumer support

Several consumer groups have staff and volunteers on hand who can offer assistance in sizing up your situation, contacting your lender, and getting your financial house in order. Here, we provide a list of the top resources to reach out to:

- **Don't Borrow Trouble:** This is Freddie Mac's anti-predatory lending initiative dedicated to helping consumers identify the common signs of predatory lending and avoid taking out loans designed to fleece consumers. Before you take out a loan to finance your way out of your current situation, visit this site to learn how to protect yourself.

    - Phone: (888) 995-HOPE (995-4673)

    - Web site: www.dontborrowtrouble.com

- **Home Loan Learning Center:** The Mortgage Bankers Association created and maintains the Home Loan Learning Center to provide consumers with step-by-step information on how to become financially literate. The Web site includes a Foreclosure Prevention Resource Center that can bring you up to speed on the foreclosure process and your options.

    - Phone: (800) 348-8653

    - Web site: www.homeloanlearningcenter.com

- **Homeownership Preservation Foundation:** This organization is dedicated to developing innovative solutions for preserving and expanding homeownership by partnering with consumers, policymakers, and the mortgage lending industry. The Homeownership Preservation Foundation spearheaded the HOPE NOW alliance.

- Phone: (888) 995-HOPE (995-4673)
- Web site: www.995hope.org

✔ **HOPE NOW:** This alliance between HUD-approved counseling agents, servicers, investors, and other mortgage market participants provides free foreclosure prevention assistance. The HOPE hotline is staffed by HUD-approved credit counselors who can help you sort out your financial situation and explore your options. Hope Now also maintains a list of lenders on its Web site. Because lenders and servicers are constantly changing as companies fail and mega-lenders gobble up the little guys, a quick check at the HOPE NOW site may give you the contact information you need if the information provided earlier in this appendix becomes outdated.

- Phone: (888) 995-HOPE (995-4673)
- Web site: www.hopenow.com

✔ **Making Home Affordable (MHA):** This is the federal government's primary home retention plan, commonly referred to as *the Obama Plan*. It offers qualifying homeowners two options: refinancing for homeowners who pay their mortgages on time but are unable to refinance to take advantage of a lower interest rate; and loan modification for homeowners who are struggling to make their monthly house payments. Visit the plan's Web site for details and to determine whether you're likely to qualify.

- Web site: makinghomeaffordable.gov

✔ **MyMoneyManagement.net:** This collaborative effort by the financial services industry aims to provide consumers with access to financial education and tools to help inform their personal finance decision process. The Web site is sponsored by the Council on Consumer Finance, a working group of the Financial Services Roundtable.

- Web site: www.mymoneymanagement.net

✔ **The National Foundation for Credit Counseling (NFCC):** Founded in 1951, the NFCC is the nation's largest and longest-serving national nonprofit credit counseling organization. The NFCC's mission is to promote the national agenda for financially responsible behavior and help its members deliver the highest quality financial education and counseling services. NFCC members annually help more than two million consumers through nearly 1,000 community-based offices nationwide.

- Phone: (866) 845-2227
- Web site: www.housinghelpnow.org

✔ **NeighborWorks America:** Congress formed this national nonprofit organization to "create opportunities for people to live in affordable homes, improve their lives, and strengthen their communities." This is a great place for foreclosure prevention professionals and community organizations to obtain information about how to help distressed homeowners in their communities. Consumers may also find some useful links on the Web site for finding help in their communities.

- Phone: (202) 220-2300
- Web site: www.nw.org/network

Federal agencies

Federal agencies are unlikely to provide you with the personal attention you need to resolve your issue, but they may be able to get the attention of your lender and help move your case to the front of the line. In addition, the more complaints an agency receives, the more likely it is to launch a full investigation, which could be a good thing for other homeowners who are facing issues similar to yours.

✔ **Fannie Mae:** This government-sponsored enterprise (GSE) is chartered by Congress with a mission to provide liquidity and stability to the U.S. housing and mortgage markets. At the Fannie Mae Web site, you can find out more about programs designed to help distressed homeowners avoid foreclosure, including foreclosure prevention workshops. This site also provides links to other online resources and organizations that can help.

- Phone: (800) 732-6643
- Web site: www.fanniemae.com

✔ **Federal Bureau of Investigation (FBI):** The FBI investigates suspected federal crimes, including real estate and mortgage fraud. If you suspect someone of committing real estate or mortgage fraud against you or someone you know, contact the FBI to report the incident.

- Phone: Refer to Web site or phone book for local number
- Web site: www.fbi.gov

✔ **Federal Deposit Insurance Corporation (FDIC):** The FDIC is "an independent agency created by the Congress that maintains the stability and public confidence in the nation's financial system by insuring deposits, examining and supervising financial institutions, and managing receiverships." Its Consumer Response Center handles complaints about state banks that aren't members of the Federal Reserve System. Filing a complaint online is best. Go to the FDIC Web site, click the Consumer Protection tab, and then click Consumer Assistance Online Form to get started.

- Phone: (800) 378-9581 or (800) 925-4818

- Web site: www.fdic.gov

✔ **Federal Housing Administration (FHA):** Part of HUD, the FHA is the largest government insurer of mortgages in the world, insuring over 35 million mortgages since its inception in 1934. Like HUD, the FHA is a great place to go to find out about the latest programs available to help homeowners. The FHA Web site also provides a Lender Locator and mortgage calculator.

- Phone: (800) CALL-FHA (225-5342)

- Web site: www.fha.gov

✔ **Federal Reserve Board:** This regulatory agency primarily oversees state-chartered banks but also investigates complaints related to federal consumer protection laws, such as the Equal Credit Opportunity Act, Fair Credit Reporting Act, and the Truth in Lending Act. The best way to file a complaint with the Federal Reserve Board is to file online. The Web site also provides information about what the Federal Reserve Board will and won't do, what you can expect after filing a complaint, and additional contact information.

- Web site: www.federalreserveconsumerhelp.gov

✔ **Federal Trade Commission (FTC):** The FTC is "the nation's consumer protection agency." It collects complaints about companies, business practices, and identity theft, and it detects patterns of wrongdoing that lead to investigations and prosecutions. The FTC is responsible for enforcing financial privacy statutes, including the Fair Credit Reporting Act (FCRA); laws targeting deceptive, unfair, and abusive practices in the subprime market; and many of the nation's other consumer-credit statutes, including the Truth in Lending Act.

The FTC Web site also contains a link to the Military Sentinel for information on consumer protection issues that affect members of the U.S. Armed Forces and their families and a link for filing a complaint about a business that's located in a foreign country. The FTC doesn't resolve individual consumer disputes; rather, it gathers information, enters it into a database, and then investigates and prosecutes violators whom it suspects of violating a law.

- Phone: (877) FTC-HELP (382-4357)

- Web site: www.ftccomplaintassistant.gov

✔ **Freddie Mac:** Like Fannie Mae, Freddie Mac is a government-sponsored enterprise (GSE) chartered by Congress with a mission to provide liquidity and stability to the U.S. housing and mortgage markets. Freddie Mac, along with Fannie Mae, the Federal Housing Finance Agency, and the Hope Now Alliance, has launched a streamlined loan modification program for distressed homeowners. You can learn more about this and other programs at Freddie Mac's Web site.

- Phone: Refer to Web site or phone book for local number

- Web site: www.freddiemac.com

✔ **National Credit Union Association (NCUA):** Although credit unions aren't immune to the mortgage lending problems that many of the mega-lending institutions have experienced, they're less likely to be involved in a mortgage lending dispute. However, if you have a dispute with a credit union that you've tried and failed to resolve, the National Credit Union Association may be able to help.

- Phone: (800) 755-1030

- Web site: www.ncua.gov

✔ **Office of the Comptroller of the Currency (OCC):** If a bank holds your mortgage; has "National," "N.A." (National Association), or "NT&SA" (National Trust & Savings Association) in its name; and can't resolve your dispute to your satisfaction, call on the Office of the Comptroller of the Currency (OCC) for assistance. Its Consumer Assistance Group (CAG) specializes in consumer complaints. The OCC Web site also provides additional information and a searchable directory of national banks so you can confirm that your bank is a national bank before filing your complaint.

- Phone: (800) 613-6743

- Web site: www.occ.treas.gov, www.helpwith mybank.gov

✔ **Office of Thrift Supervision:** This government office oversees the operation of savings associations insured by the federal Savings Association Insurance Fund (SAIF) as well as Federal

Savings Banks (FSBs). As such, it's dedicated to ensuring that thrift institutions comply with consumer protection laws and regulations.

If you tried and failed to resolve your dispute with your lender, you can file a complaint with the OTS. Visit its Web site and click the Active OTS Institution Directory link to find out whether your lender is regulated by the OTS before filing your complaint. If your lender is on the list, under Information for Consumers, click File a Complaint. During the writing of this book, the OTS has no online form and doesn't recommend sending sensitive information via e-mail. However, the File a Complaint page provides a link to download a printable complaint form along with additional information on how to resolve disputes.

- Phone: (800) 842-6929 or (800) 877-8339

- Web site: www.ots.treas.gov

✔ **Security and Exchange Commission (SEC):** The SEC is dedicated to protecting investors; maintaining fair, orderly, and efficient markets; and facilitating capital formation. As such, it does very little to directly help distressed home- owners, but you can file a complaint with the SEC if you think that a lender violated an SEC regulation in dealing with your loan.

The SEC is becoming more involved in consumer affairs as the mortgage meltdown turns its attention to mortgage- backed securities (MBSs) as the root of the problem. Multiple class-action lawsuits are likely to arise involving failure to adequately disclose the risk involved with the MBS pools of loans.

If you feel you were set up with a loan you really couldn't afford and you find out that your mortgage is owned by investors, help from the SEC is worth looking into. The SEC investigates issues of fraud in mortgages that were securitized.

- Phone: (888) 732-6585

- Web site: www.sec.gov

✔ **U.S. Department of Housing and Urban Development (HUD):** This is the federal agency of choice for solutions that enable you to avoid foreclosure and keep your home. You can find out about the latest programs available as well as access con- tact information for local HUD offices. In the mortgage arena, HUD plays a key role in enforcing Real Estate Settlement Procedures Act (RESPA) statutes. On the Web site under Homes, click the Foreclosure link.

- Phone: (202) 708-1112

- Web site: www.hud.gov

If you think someone involved in the origination or processing of your loan application violated a RESPA statute (see Chapter 13), you can file a complaint with the HUD director in charge of RESPA and Interstate Land Sales. Unfortunately, at the time of writing this book, HUD doesn't provide an online complaint form, so you have to send your complaint via snail mail:

> Director, Office of RESPA and Interstate Land Sales
> U.S. Department of Housing and Urban Development
> Room 9154
> 451 7th Street, SW
> Washington, DC 20410

Identify the suspected violation(s) and the alleged violators by name, address, and phone number. You should also provide your own name and phone number for follow-up questions from HUD. If you prefer not to have your identity shared with the accused party, be sure to specify that in your letter.

✓ **U.S. Department of Veteran Affairs (VA):** This department is dedicated to providing excellence in patient care, benefits, and customer satisfaction to veterans of the armed forces. If you're a veteran, you may have even more resources for saving your home from foreclosure than nonveterans, so contact the VA to find out what's available.

- Phone: (800) 827-1000

- Web site: www.homeloans.va.gov

State Attorneys General

Your state attorney general can't save you from foreclosure, but if you believe that you're a victim of fraud, your attorney general is one of the first people you should contact. Whether the fraud was perpetrated prior to your current troubles (for example, by a predatory lender) or after (by a con artist pretending to help you), your attorney general wants to know about it.

The following list contains the Web site addresses and phone numbers for the attorneys general in each of the 50 states, the District of Columbia, and U.S. territories. (You can pull up an updated list of state attorneys general, complete with names, addresses, and phone numbers, at the National Association of Attorneys General Web site at www.naag.org.)

Ask your state attorney general for information on other state agencies or licensing boards that may monitor and regulate lenders in your state. All states have designated consumer protection divisions in their AG offices and forms to download off the states' official Web sites.

Alabama
(334) 242-7300
www.ago.state.al.us

Alaska
(907) 465-2133
www.law.state.ak.us

American Samoa
(684) 633-4163
www.samoanet.com/asg/
asgdla97.html

Arizona
(602) 542-5025 or (800) 352-8431
www.azag.gov

Arkansas
(501) 682-2007 or (800) 482-8982
www.ag.arkansas.gov

California
(916) 322-3360 or (800) 952-5225
ag.ca.gov

Colorado
(303) 866-4500
www.ago.state.co.us/
index.cfm

Connecticut
(860) 808-5318
www.ct.gov/ag

Delaware
(302) 577-8600 or (800) 220-5424
attorneygeneral.
delaware.gov

District of Columbia
(202) 727-3400
oag.dc.gov

Florida
(850) 414-3300 or (866) 966-7226
myfloridalegal.com

Georgia
(404) 656-3300
www.ago.georgia.gov

Guam
(671) 475-3324
www.guamattorney
general.com

Hawaii
(808) 586-1500
www.hawaii.gov/ag

Idaho
(208) 334-2400
www2.state.id.us/ag

Illinois
(800) 386-5438 (Chicago); (800)
243-0618 (Springfield); (800)
243-0607 (Carbondale)
www.illinoisattorney
general.gov

Indiana
(317) 232-6201 or (800) 382-5516
www.in.gov/attorney
general

Iowa
(515) 281-5926 or (888) 777-4590
www.iowaattorney
general.org

Kansas
(785) 296-3751 or (800) 432-2310
www.ksag.org/home

Kentucky
(502) 696-5300 or (888) 432-9257
ag.ky.gov

Louisiana
(225) 326-6465 or (800) 351-4889
www.ag.state.la.us

Maine
(207) 626-8800
www.state.me.us/ag

Maryland
(410) 576-6300 or (888) 743-0023
www.oag.state.md.us

Massachusetts
(617) 727-8400
www.mass.gov/ago

Michigan
(517) 373-1140 or (877) 765-8388
www.michigan.gov/ag

Minnesota
(651) 296-3353 or (800) 657-3787
www.ag.state.mn.us

Mississippi
(601) 359-4230 or (800) 281-4418
www.ago.state.ms.us

Missouri
(573) 751-3321 or (800) 392-8222
ago.mo.gov

Montana
(406) 444-2026 or (800) 481-6896
www.doj.mt.gov

Nebraska
(402) 471-2682 or (800) 727-6432
www.ago.state.ne.us

Nevada
(775) 684-1100 or (800) 266-8688
ag.state.nv.us

New Hampshire
(603) 271-3658 or (888) 468-4454
www.state.nh.us/nhdoj

New Jersey
(973) 504-6200 or (800) 242-5846
www.state.nj.us/lps

New Mexico
(505) 827-6000 or (800) 678-1508
www.nmag.gov

New York
(518) 474-7330 or (800) 771-7755
www.oag.state.ny.us

North Carolina
(919) 716-6400 or (877) 566-7226
www.ncdoj.gov

North Dakota
(701) 328-2210 or (800) 472-2600
www.ag.state.nd.us

Ohio
(614) 466-4320 or (877) 244-6446
www.ag.state.oh.us

Oklahoma
(405) 521-3921 or (918) 581-2885
www.oag.state.ok.us

Oregon
(503) 378-4400 or (877) 877-9392
www.doj.state.or.us

Pennsylvania
(717) 787-3391 or (800) 441-2555
www.attorneygeneral.gov

Puerto Rico
(787) 729-2516; (787) 729-2106;
(787) 729-2185
www.justicia.gobierno.pr

Rhode Island
(401) 274-4400
www.riag.state.ri.us

South Carolina
(803) 734-3970
www.scattorney
general.org

South Dakota
(605) 773-3215 or (800) 300-1986
www.state.sd.us/attorney

Tennessee
(615) 741-5860 or (615) 741-1671
www.attorneygeneral.
state.tn.us

Texas
(800) 252-8011 or (800) 621-0508
www.oag.state.tx.us

Utah
(801) 366-0260 or (800) 244-4636
attorneygeneral.utah.gov

Vermont
(802) 828-3171
www.atg.state.vt.us

Virgin Islands
(340) 774-0001

Virginia
(804) 786-2071
www.oag.state.va.us

Washington
(360) 753-6200 or (800) 551-4636
www.atg.wa.gov

West Virginia
(304) 558-2021 or (800) 368-8808
www.wvago.us

Wisconsin
(608) 266-1221 or (800) 422-7128
www.doj.state.wi.us

Wyoming
(307) 777-7841 or (800) 438-5799
attorneygeneral.state.
wy.us

Appendix B

Glossary

adjustable-rate mortgage (ARM): A home loan whose interest rate can rise and fall. ARMs may contribute to triggering "rate shock" and default when the interest rate jumps, making the monthly payments less affordable.

automatic stay: A freeze imposed on lenders as soon as you file for bankruptcy that prevents lenders from moving forward on debt collection activities. Lenders can ask the bankruptcy court to lift the stay.

back-end ratio: Your debt ratio for your house and all other loans (such as a car loan). According to the Federal Housing Authority (FHA), your back-end debt payments shouldn't exceed 41 percent of your gross monthly income. See also *debt-to-income (DTI) ratio* and *front-end ratio*.

bankruptcy: A legal process allowing the debtor to discharge certain debts or personal obligations. The two most common forms of bankruptcy for homeowners are Chapter 7 and Chapter 13. See also *Chapter 7 bankruptcy* and *Chapter 13 bankruptcy*.

broker's price opinion (BPO): See *comparative market analysis (CMA)*.

Chapter 7 bankruptcy: Liquidation of all nonexempt assets to repay as much debt as possible and discharge all remaining debt. See also *bankruptcy*.

Chapter 13 bankruptcy: Reorganization of finances to pay off all or some debts over time. See also *bankruptcy*.

comparative market analysis (CMA): An estimate of a property's anticipated sales price based on recent sales prices of similar properties. Also referred to as a home valuation or broker's price opinion (BPO). CMA values are for arm's length transactions and aren't calculated based on fire-sale pricing.

debt payment: The monthly amount required on a mortgage, loan, or credit card account.

debt-to-income (DTI) ratio: The mathematical relationship between how much you pay out in monthly bills and your gross monthly income. Banks use your DTI to determine your credit worthiness and often examine both front-end ratio and back-end ratio. Also referred to as a debt ratio. See also *front-end ratio* and *back-end ratio*.

deed: A legal document that identifies an official ownership interest in real property, such as a home and the land on which it sits. Several types of deeds exist. See also *quit-claim deed*, *sheriff's deed*, and *warranty deed*.

deed in lieu of foreclosure (DIL): An arrangement in which the lender agrees not to foreclose in exchange for the deed to your home. If you offer a DIL, make sure you also receive a document stating, "This deed given in satisfaction of a mortgage dated [XX]." This protects you from the lender pursuing a deficiency judgment against you. See also *deficiency judgment*.

default: The failure to honor an agreement. In foreclosure, the most common default is failure to make monthly payments on the agreed-upon dates.

deferred payment: Any payment the lender has agreed to postpone as part of the workout.

deficiency judgment: A court document stating that a borrower owes and must pay the balance that remains on a loan after the foreclosure sale. The judgment gives the bank or lender the right to take additional legal process to collect on the deficiency if the borrower refuses to pay.

discounted payoff: A reduction in the unpaid principal balance (UPB) that the lender agrees to accept as payment in full for the loan.

durable power of attorney: Assigns the grantee power to make decisions and take action on the grantor's behalf. The grantee can execute deeds, mortgages, bills of sale, and so on. The grantee holds this power and will continue to hold it even in the event that the grantor becomes incapacitated (that's the "durable" part). See also *power of attorney (POA)*.

equity: The amount of cash you have in your house. If you sold the house today and paid off all liens against it, equity is the money left to stuff in your pockets or purse.

escrow: A separate account into which a portion of each monthly payment is deposited to cover annual property taxes and assessments, insurance, and (in some cases) homeowner association (HOA) fees.

exempt assets: Stuff you own that can't be taken and sold to repay debts to creditors. See also *Chapter 7 bankruptcy*.

Fannie Mae: A government-sponsored enterprise (GSE) responsible for making investor money available to the mortgage lending industry.

Federal Housing Authority (FHA): A division of the U.S. Department of Housing and Urban Development (HUD) that administers loan programs and issues loan guarantees to make housing more affordable and accessible. See also *Housing and Urban Development (HUD)*.

financial statement: A detailed account of a borrower's assets, liabilities, monthly income, and expenses used for determining the borrower's ability to make monthly payments on a loan.

forbearance: The lender's promise not to foreclose or proceed with other collection activity for a specific period, giving the borrower time to regroup. The borrower may be required to make a reduced payment during this time or no payment at all.

foreclosure: The legal process by which a creditor can enforce the terms of the mortgage or deed of trust to recover all or a portion of the money loaned and secured by the property. Money is recovered by selling the property at a public auction.

front-end ratio: Your debt ratio for only your home. According to the Making Home Affordable program, the monthly payment on your first mortgage (including principal, interest, taxes, insurance, and association fees) shouldn't exceed 31 percent of your total gross monthly income. See also *debt-to-income (DTI) ratio* and *back-end ratio*.

Ginnie Mae (Government National Mortgage Association, or GNMA): A government-owned corporation within HUD that guarantees investors the timely payment of principal and interest on mortgage-backed securities backed by federally insured or guaranteed loans — mainly FHA- and VA-insured loans.

home equity line of credit: A mortgage loan that lets you borrow as much or as little money as you need against the equity in your home and pay interest on only the amount you borrow. See also *equity* and *home equity loan*.

home equity loan: A mortgage loan that enables you to cash out some or all of the equity in your home in a lump sum. See also *equity* and *home equity line of credit*.

Housing and Urban Development (HUD): Department of the U.S. government that funds free or very low-cost housing counseling nationwide. Housing counselors can help you understand the law and your options, organize your finances, and represent you in negotiations with your lender if you need this assistance.

index: A starting point from which the interest rate on an adjustable-rate mortgage (ARM) is calculated. More than 80 percent of all ARMs use the CMT, COFI, and LIBOR indexes.

junior lien: A legal encumbrance on a home's title that's subordinate to the senior lien. A junior lien could be a second mortgage, a home equity loan or line of credit, or a loan taken out against the home for improvements. See also *home equity line of credit*, *home equity loan*, *senior lien*, and *tax lien*.

lease-option agreement: A rent-to-own agreement between a seller and a buyer. The buyer typically agrees to make a down payment on the property and pay rent for a specified number of months, after which time the buyer has the right (the option), but not the obligation, to purchase the property.

limited (or specific) power of attorney: Typically restricts a person's power to a specific transaction. This allows the grantee to handle the transaction as if the grantor were doing it herself, but it doesn't give the grantee the power to do anything else except what's specifically listed. See also *power of attorney (POA)*.

loan modification: An alteration of a mortgage agreement typically to make the monthly payments more affordable. A lender can modify the mortgage in any number of ways, including adding time to the end of the mortgage or reducing the interest rate. See also *mortgage*.

loan workout: An alternative to foreclosure that typically benefits the borrower and lender. Workout examples include loan modification, forbearance, reinstatement, and deed in lieu of foreclosure.

loan-to-value (LTV) ratio: The mathematical relationship between how much you owe or will owe on your home and its appraised value. If you owe $80,000 on a home that appraises for $100,000, it has an LTV ratio of 80 percent.

loss mitigation: Any effort by the lender to limit the financial loss resulting from a nonperforming asset because of the borrower's failure to make payments on a loan.

margin: A fixed percentage added to an index on an adjustable-rate mortgage (ARM). The margin and index combined determine the interest rate.

means test: A provision in the bankruptcy code that determines whether you qualify for Chapter 7 bankruptcy or must file for Chapter 13 bankruptcy. If your income falls below a certain level, you may qualify for Chapter 7 bankruptcy. The means test is intended as a way to curb Chapter 7 bankruptcy abuse. See also *bankruptcy*, *Chapter 7 bankruptcy*, and *Chapter 13 bankruptcy*.

mortgage: A security instrument that pledges real property as security (or collateral) for a loan. The note (promissory note) is your promise to pay. See also *mortgagee* and *mortgagor*.

mortgage satisfaction (discharge): A document filed with the register of deeds stating that the mortgage on a property has been paid in full (or settled in some other manner) and released as a lien.

mortgage-backed security (MBS): A bond or other investment instrument secured by a pool of mortgages. MBSs are sold to investors on Wall Street to provide banks with funds for additional mortgage loans.

mortgagee: The lender in a lender-borrower agreement. See also *mortgage* and *mortgagor*.

mortgagor: The borrower in a lender-borrower agreement. See also *mortgage* and *mortgagee*.

net worth: The amount of money that would remain if you were to sell all your stuff and pay all your debts. In other words, what you own minus what you owe.

note (promissory note): A written promise to pay, like an IOU. When you take out a loan to finance the purchase of property, you usually sign a mortgage and a note. See also *mortgage*.

notice of default: A written announcement that a borrower has failed to honor the terms of payment stated in the mortgage. In most states, delivering or recording the notice of default is the first step in the foreclosure process.

power of attorney (POA): A legal document that gives someone else the right to make decisions, sign legal documents, or act on your behalf. POAs can be limited or durable (remaining in effect if the principal party becomes incapacitated). See also *limited (or specific) power of attorney* and *durable power of attorney*.

principal forbearance: An agreement between a borrower and a lender to defer a portion of the unpaid principal balance until the home is sold or the loan is refinanced. Payments are recalculated on the unpaid principal balance minus the deferred amount, resulting in a lower house payment.

pro se: Acting as your own attorney.

quit-claim deed: A deed that makes no warranties or guarantees but conveys to the grantee ownership interest the grantor has in the property (if any). See also *deed*.

reaffirm debt: To re-obligate yourself to a debt that was discharged in bankruptcy. A homeowner may reaffirm a mortgage debt in bankruptcy to keep the home by bringing it out of bankruptcy in order to work out a repayment plan with, or resume payments to, the lender.

Real Estate Settlement and Procedures Act (RESPA): A federal consumer-protection statute requiring lenders to fully disclose closing costs and prohibiting practices that artificially increase closing costs.

recidivism: Fancy word for "relapse"; instance in which a homeowner negotiates a solution with the lenders and then defaults again later.

redemption: The process of buying back a property after a foreclosure auction. Some states have a redemption period in which a homeowner has the right, but not the obligation, to buy back a property plus interest from the lender or investor who entered the winning bid.

register of deeds: The county office that records legal documents related to the transfer of real property. Your county's register of deeds should be a great resource for foreclosure information and ideas of where to look for additional assistance. It may be called something different in your county, such as the deeds office, the recorder's office, or the county clerk's office.

reinstatement: Curing the default of a mortgage by catching up on past payments and paying any fees (including legal) or penalties that resulted from the default prior to the foreclosure sale.

repayment plan: An agreement with your lender that cures the default and addresses missed payments through an installment plan. In most cases, you're required to make your normal monthly payment plus a portion of any past-due payments and penalties that have accrued as a result of the default.

reset: An agreement in some mortgages that allows the initial interest rate to change at some time in the future, usually two to three years into the mortgage term. If the initial rate was set very low (as in a teaser rate), the reset rate can jump dramatically. Dramatic rate increases can result in "rate shock" and affordability issues.

secured loan: A loan that has some sort of collateral attached to it that the lender can take and sell if you don't repay the debt. Home mortgages and car loans are two examples of secured loans. See also *unsecured loan*.

securitization: A process of bundling loans into pools and then selling certificates or securities (like stocks or bonds) to investors based on those loan pools. *See also **mortgage-backed security (MBS)**.*

senior lien: A legal claim to a home that takes precedence over all other liens, except a tax lien. See also *junior lien* and *tax lien*.

Servicemember's Civil Relief Act: An act passed by Congress to afford certain financial protection and legal protections for individuals serving in the military.

servicer: A company that works on behalf of your lender, for a fee, to collect and process your monthly mortgage payments.

sheriff's deed: Issued by the sheriff's office to the purchaser of a property at a foreclosure sale, indicating that the purchaser is the new owner of the property subject to certain conditions, such as a redemption period, where applicable. See also *deed* and *redemption*.

sheriff's sale: A public foreclosure auction typically conducted by the county sheriff. See also *foreclosure*.

short re-fi: A refinance loan allowing the homeowner to remain as owner but which is based on a discounted principal that allows a homeowner to refinance when the property is worth less than what's owed on it. See also *short sale*.

short sale: An arrangement between a lender and borrower in which the lender agrees to accept, as full payment, less than the total amount due but which doesn't allow the homeowner to retain ownership. By negotiating a short sale, a homeowner may be able to sell the home without having to take a loss on it. Rarely does a lender agree to a short sale if it means that the distressed homeowner profits from the sale.

tax lien: A claim against the property to ensure payment of property taxes. Tax liens or tax deeds can be sold at auction, providing the winning bidder with the rights to the property (in the case of a tax deed) or the right to foreclose on the property (in the case of a tax lien). Tax liens are priority liens even if their position on title suggests that they're in a junior position. See also *junior lien* and *senior lien*.

term: The duration of a loan. For example, a 30-year mortgage has a term of 30 years.

Truth in Lending Act (TILA): Federal regulation requiring lenders to fully and clearly disclose the terms and costs related to a loan and giving consumers the right to cancel certain types of loans within a set period. TILA has given rise to the annual percentage rate (APR), which helps consumers compare the actual costs of different loans.

unpaid principal balance (UPB): The amount of money you still owe on a loan after having paid back a portion of it.

unsecured loan: A loan that's not backed up by collateral. Credit card debt and medical expenses are usually considered unsecured loans. See also *secured loan*.

U.S. Department of Veterans Affairs (VA): A department of the federal government dedicated to serving military veterans. As one of its benefits, the VA secures low-cost financing at competitive interest rates for veterans to purchase homes.

warranty deed: A document that transfers legal ownership and contains warranties of title and other legal interests from the grantor to the grantee. In contrast, quit-claim deeds contain no such warranties. See also *quit-claim deed*.

Index